MIKE SAVAGE, NIA
FIONA DEVINE, SA
DANIEL LAURISON
ANDREW MILES, HELENE SNEE
AND PAUL WAKELING

# Social Class in the 21ˢᵗ Century

## A PELICAN INTRODUCTION

PELICAN
*an imprint of*
PENGUIN BOOKS

## PELICAN BOOKS

UK | USA | Canada | Ireland | Australia
India | New Zealand | South Africa

Penguin Books is part of the Penguin Random House
group of companies whose addresses can be found at
global.penguinrandomhouse.com.

Penguin
Random House
UK

First published in 2015
002

Text copyright © Mike Savage, Niall Cunningham, Fiona Devine,
Sam Friedman, Daniel Laurison, Lisa Mckenzie, Andrew Miles,
Helene Snee and Paul Wakeling, 2015

Book design by Matthew Young
Set in 10/14.664 pt FreightText Pro
Typeset by Jouve (UK), Milton Keynes
Printed in Great Britain by Clays Ltd, St Ives plc

A CIP catalogue record for this book is
available from the British Library

ISBN: 978-0-241-00422-7

MIX
Paper from
responsible sources
FSC® C018179

Penguin Random House is committed to a
sustainable future for our business, our readers
and our planet. This book is made from Forest
Stewardship Council® certified paper.

www.greenpenguin.co.uk

# Contents

# List of Tables

# List of Figures

# ACKNOWLEDGEMENTS

This book has been a massive, wonderful, sprawling, collaborative effort. Mike Savage (Professor of Sociology at the London School of Economics) and Fiona Devine (Professor of Sociology at the University of Manchester) were the directors of the Great British Class Survey (GBCS), key points of liaison with the BBC, and led the project throughout. Mike took responsibility for the overall analytical strategy of the project as a whole, took the lead on analyses of our relationship to other studies of class (chapters 1 and 5), cultural capital (Chapter 3) and the analysis of elites (Chapter 9). Fiona made a significant contribution to the analytical strategy, took the lead in the media presentation of the results in 2013, and was responsible for the analysis of economic capital in Chapter 2, along with Niall Cunningham (Lecturer in Geography at the University of Durham), Helene Snee (Lecturer in Sociology at Manchester Metropolitan University) and Andrew Miles (Reader in Sociology at the University of Manchester). Niall took responsibility for the initial organization and analysis of the GBCS data when it was delivered from the BBC, and has used his Geographical Information System (GIS) skills to lead our research on space and class (Chapter 8). Sam Friedman (Assistant Professor of Sociology at the London School of

Economics) played the key role in organizing the fifty qualitative interviews which we report from in this book, in drafting our arguments about social mobility (Chapter 6), and snobbery and class identity (Chapter 11), as well as contributing to the chapters on cultural capital and the elite. Daniel Laurison (post-doctoral Research Fellow, London School of Economics) has taken the lead in preparing the GBCS for archiving and in conducting much of the GBCS analysis, especially of social capital (Chapter 4) and of social mobility (Chapter 6). Lisa Mckenzie (Fellow at London School of Economics) conducted the research on the precariat reported in Chapter 10. Andrew Miles assisted with data organization and analysis throughout. Helene Snee assisted with the organization of qualitative interviews in the north of England and helped to draft the chapters on economic capital (Chapter 2) and snobbery and class identity (Chapter 11). Paul Wakeling (Senior Lecturer in Education, University of York) took the lead in our analysis of universities and social mobility reported in Chapter 7.

Mike was responsible for the drafting of the different chapters of the book into an integrated narrative and wrote the conclusion. He is ultimately responsible for all the book's failings!

We would like to thank numerous others who have not contributed to this book, but have assisted invaluably to the underpinning research along the way. These include Johannes Hjellbrekke (University of Bergen, Norway), Yaojun Li (University of Manchester), Mark Taylor (University of Sheffield) and Brigitte Le Roux (Université Paris Descartes – Sorbonne Paris Cité), who have all carried out data analysis on the GBCS (which has informed our work). At the Department of Sociology at the London School of Economics there has been a wonderful team of outstanding graduate students – Nell Beecham, Katharina Hecht and Georgia Nichols – who have provided supplementary research, critical reflections and moral support. Wilf Horsfall has provided excellent graphic visualizations of some of our work. We would also like to thank Mel Nichols for his astute insights on an earlier draft, which only an experienced journalist could bring, and which helped enormously in redrafting the final version of this book. Georgia did a remarkable job correcting the proofs and identifying (and mostly resolving) problems that had previously escaped us.

Wider thanks are also due to our many supporters. The Sociology Department at the University of Manchester was the intellectual home from which this research emerged, and we would like to thank Beverley Skeggs, Alan Warde, Wendy Bottero, Nick Crossley, Colette Fagan – and others – for their interest in rethinking the meaning of class in our changed world. The support of the ESRC Centre for Research on Socio-Cultural Change (CRESC) – based at the University of Manchester and the Open University – has been fundamental in developing this project. We would like to thank particularly the team who worked on the Cultural Capital and Social Exclusion project (Tony Bennett, Elizabeth Silva, Alan Warde, Modesto Gayo-Cal and David Wright) which was a vital underpinning for the research here. More recently, the support of colleagues in the Department of Sociology at the University of York (notably Laurie Hanquinet and Roger Burrows), and, since 2012, in the Department of Sociology at the London School of Economics, has been essential in seeing this project through to fruition. We are grateful to the many London School of Economics students who displayed their characteristic energy and enthusiasm in responding to this work in seminars and classes as our thinking progressed. We have benefited from the outstanding administrative support of Louise Fisher (Departmental Manager), Attila Szanto (Research Manager) and Louisa Lawrence (Personal Assistant), who gave wonderful help in assembling the final version of the manuscript. We would also like to thank our London School of Economics colleagues John Hills (from the Social Policy Department), Niki Lacey (from the Law Department) and David Soskice (from the Government Department) for their ongoing enthusiasm for and encouragement towards this project. We are very excited that this book is published in the same year that the London School of Economics' International Inequalities Institute was launched, which will be a platform for further investigations of the themes we raise here.

This project would have been impossible without the terrific support of the BBC. They never told us how much of their money they invested in the GBCS, but it must have been considerable, and we hope that this book is testimony to the way that public social science is not confined to the academy, but can benefit from collaboration with the media. In particular, we would like to thank Richard Cable, Michael Orwell and Philip Trippenbach for their vital roles in keeping this project on the road, sometimes in circumstances when the going was hard.

Finally, we would like to thank Josephine Greywoode at Penguin for her support and excellent advice on earlier drafts of this manuscript, and Louisa Sladen Watson for her expert copy-editing, which greatly improved the book's clarity.

London, Manchester and York, April 2015

# The Great British Class Survey and the Return of Class Today

In the first quarter of the twenty-first century, inequality is firmly back in the public eye. In 2014 the World Economic Forum highlighted income disparity as one of the principal risks to economic and political security today. International non-governmental organizations such as Oxfam have drawn attention to the cycles of advantage transmitted across generations and pointed to the unequal opportunities that reinforce privilege. Longstanding problems such as poverty appear to be getting worse even though we live in more affluent times, and have, increasingly, been juxtaposed with the burgeoning fortunes of the super-rich.

This book shows, focusing on the British case, how these spiralling levels of inequality are remaking social classes today. It is one thing to point to growing economic inequalities, but we also need to know how people themselves understand these divisions. Do they overlap with wider social, cultural and political fractures? Can we identify distinctive social classes who share common lifestyles, identities, social networks and political orientations as well as levels of income and wealth? Only in this case can we talk about 'class for itself' (i.e. class as composed of people who are class conscious), rather than 'class in itself' (i.e. class as a social group), to use Karl Marx's idiom. In this book we argue that classes are indeed being fundamentally remade. Away from longstanding differences between middle and working class, we have moved towards a class order which is more hierarchical in differentiating the top (which we call 'the wealth elite') from the bottom (which we call 'the precariat' which consists of people who struggle to get by on a daily basis), but which is more fuzzy and complex in its middle layers. We will show in this book how social classes arise from the concentration of three distinctive kinds of capital: economic capital (your wealth and income); cultural capital (your tastes, interests and activities), and social capital (your social networks, friendships and associations). Each of these is fully introduced and explained in a later chapter. Understanding class as based on these three capitals allows us to understand how growing economic inequality is also associated with growing class inequality between the top and the bottom. We can also avoid the tendency to see class as a throwback. to the old industrial era of blue-collar factory workers, coal miners and farm labourers, pitted against mill owners, professionals and managers. Our focus on economic, cultural and social capital offers our alternative to previous sociological analysis focusing on classes as groupings of occupations and which do not adequately illuminate the wider cultural and political significance of class. We can also restate the importance of class, given that critical commentators such as Owen Jones or Danny Dorling rarely use the concept of class directly,[1] while economists, who in recent decades have done most to demonstrate the growth of inequality, tend not to use the concept of social class at all, which they see as too crude to capture contemporary economic divisions.

Our perspective allows us to see how expanding economic inequalities are associated with class divisions more broadly. We can identify today's major social fractures, especially at the top and bottom, and understand the difficulties of social mobility into the most advantaged positions, the intensification of geographical divisions, and the growing power of elite universities.

## Introducing the Great British Class Survey

The current explosion of interest in questions of class came home to us in 2013 when we published findings from the BBC's Great British Class Survey, which was publicized by the media and provoked astonishing interest across the globe. When the BBC persuaded us to help them design their web survey, we truly did not know how much interest it would generate. Who could be bothered to give up twenty minutes of their time to answer a battery of arcane questions on their leisure interests, cultural tastes, social networks and economic situation? We were therefore gratified when within a few weeks the survey elicited over 161,000 responses – to become the largest survey of social class ever conducted in Britain.

Having downloaded the first wave of data from the BBC in April 2011, we spent nearly two years trying to make sense of its patterns. After several false starts, we elaborated a new sociological model in April 2013 which proclaimed the existence of seven new classes, which we discuss further in Chapter 5.[2] The BBC promoted our findings with an impressive set of visual infographics. These were then hooked up to an interactive 'Class Calculator', whereby people could spend less than a minute tapping in replies to a few questions about their income, savings and house value, their cultural interests and their social networks, and were then told which of our 'new' classes they fitted into.

The results were staggering. Within a week seven million people – roughly one in five of the British adult population – clicked on the Class Calculator to find out which 'new' class they were in.[3] Social media buzzed with debate and a tidal wave of popular and academic comment overwhelmed us. During our careers we have written extensively about social class for mainly academic audiences, but had never experienced popular interest on this scale. There was extensive blogging and media interest in the arguments on a level rarely – if ever – seen for sociological research.

This is a prime message of this book – that social class is now a very powerful force in the popular imagination once again. People in Britain are aware of, interested in and also upset about class. During the media storm associated with the launch of the Great British Class Survey, we heard of train passengers chatting about which class they were now in and schoolchildren talking in the playground about class. There were some very odd incidents. Demand for theatre tickets in London increased by an average of 191 per cent in the week after the GBCS launch. Louise Mullock, spokesperson for Seatwave, remarked: 'We recorded a near universal increase in ticket demand which we were at a loss to explain, until we realized that it corresponded directly with the BBC's Class Calculator becoming public.'[4] It seemed that large numbers of people responded to the Class Calculator's questions treating theatre attendance as an indicator of cultural capital by deciding to get out more.

Scientific experiments are normally expected to stand back from the research they are conducting in order to provide distanced and 'objective' results, for instance using randomized control tests when comparing which medical interventions are effective. However, in the case of the GBCS, we could not do this. Interests in class are themselves so highly loaded that if we try to stand back, then we miss the energies, intensities, but also the hostility and insecurity that are bound up with class. Indeed, this is a fundamental argument of our book. We like to think of ourselves as living in a democratic society where individuals are supposed to have equal rights. Yet we also know that people's economic fortunes can be strikingly different. Symbolically, class is a lightning conductor for the anxieties this discrepancy between economic realities and our beliefs provokes.

This issue is crisply demonstrated in the differential take-up of the GBCS web survey itself. It turns out that those who are interested in doing a twenty-minute web survey are far from being typical of the population as a whole. The map (Figure 0.1) shows the distribution of where people participated in the GBCS in numbers greater or lesser than we would have expected, given the population of the area. (We have taken that underlying population from the 2011 census.) So, if there was a perfect equality of participation across the entire country, all local areas would match the figure we *expected*, based on the census. However, that clearly wasn't the case and there were big disparities in levels of participation that we actually *observed* at the local level. So this map

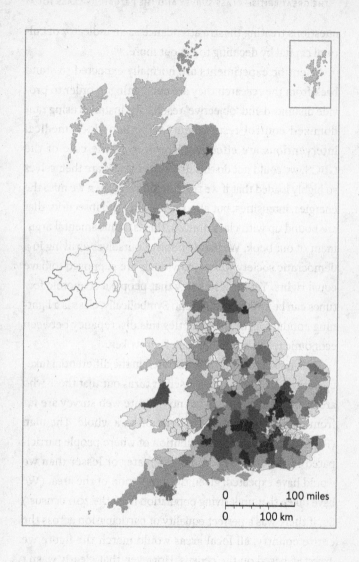

**Figure 1.1**

The geography of participation in the GBCS in relation to population

0    100 miles

0    100 km

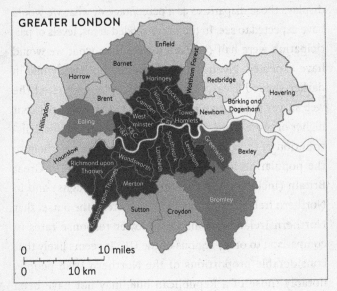

**GREATER LONDON**

Enfield
Barnet
Harrow
Haringey
Waltham Forest
Redbridge
Havering
Brent
Camden
Islington
Hackney
Hillingdon
Ealing
West minster
City
Tower Hamlets
Newham
Barking and Dagenham
K&C
H&F
Hounslow
Southwark
Greenwich
Bexley
Richmond upon Thames
Wandsworth
Lambeth
Lewisham
Merton
Bromley
Kingston upon Thames
Sutton
Croydon

0           10 miles
0           10 km

K&C    Kensington and Chelsea
H&F    Hammersmith and Fulham

**% of population 16–99 by unitary authority**

- 50 or less
- 75 to more than 50
- 90 to more than 75
- more than 90 to less than 110
- 110 to less than 125
- 125 to less than 150
- 150 or more

displays those disparities as a percentage of what we would have expected to see. In the white-shaded areas, levels of participation were half (or even lower) than what we would have expected, given the local population base, while in darker-shaded areas, many more people completed the web survey than we could have predicted, up to 50 per cent higher or more. Thus, the map reveals the geographical distribution of those who did the GBCS, comparing them to the population in different unitary authorities in Great Britain (including the Greater London boroughs) and in Northern Ireland by county.[5] We can note at the outset that Northern Ireland has markedly lower response rates in comparison to other regions of the UK. It seems likely that considerable proportions of the Northern Irish people, notably those of a Republican hue, may not have been attracted to a survey entitled the 'Great British Class Survey'. In this sense national identity may have trumped class and this may well also explain the lower response rates in swathes of western Scotland and even into the north of England.

At the other end of the scale, areas overcompensating in terms of response to the survey (indicated in darker shades), were heavily clustered in the west of London and to a large extent in the south-east of England more generally. These areas are the BBC's heartland. However, the geography is complicated. Edinburgh also had a very high response rate – and Glasgow residents were not far behind. Looking at a more refined spatial scale, university towns and cities were also over-represented, with Oxford, Cambridge and York all standing out from their hinterlands with particular clarity and Aberdeen, Brighton, Exeter, Canterbury, Aberystwyth and Norwich all being in darker shades.

The take-up of the GBCS is itself testimony to marked geographical divisions and poses a fundamental question as to the reasons behind such stark differences in why some people are interested in class, and others are not. It is the more affluent who seem more interested in the topic of class, even though they might also be sceptical of the survey results. Even the most basic indicator of the geography of GBCS respondents is itself indicative of the profound power of a class divide.

The plot thickens when we consider what the occupations were of people who were most likely to do the GBCS. Tables 0.1 and 0.2 demonstrate major differences. A huge 4.1 per cent of all those replying to the GBCS were chief executive officers (CEOs), which turns out to be twenty times more than we would expect, given the total number of CEOs in the labour force. We also see a dramatic over-representation of business and related finance professionals, and also all kinds of scientists, researchers and professionals. Experts, of all kinds, were drawn in droves to the GBCS.

Contrast this, however, with a list of those who did *not* hasten to the BBC's Lab UK website to complete the GBCS, as displayed in Table 0.2. This opposite group consist of people in largely unskilled manual occupations. Out of the 161,000 respondents, not a single cleaner or worker in the elementary (basic) services or plastics processing answered. There were also very few glaziers, fork-lift truck drivers or the like. In comparing these tables, the stark power of a class divide is clear.

These are very simple findings, but they display, in miniature, the power of class divisions in Britain, which divide an

| OCCUPATION | % OF GBCS | AMOUNT OVER-REPRESENTED |
|---|---|---|
| CEOs | 4.1 | × 20.4 |
| Business, research and administrative professionals | 0.9 | × 5.8 |
| Business and related finance professionals | 1.5 | × 13.7 |
| Natural and social scientists | 1.2 | × 8.3 |
| Physical scientists | 0.4 | × 5.9 |
| Barristers and judges | 0.4 | × 4.8 |
| Actuaries, economists and statisticians | 0.5 | × 4.8 |
| Engineering professionals | 1.3 | × 4.8 |
| Journalists | 1.2 | × 4.5 |

**Table 0.1**

Over-represented Occupations in the GBCS

| OCCUPATION | % OF GBCS | AMOUNT UNDER-REPRESENTED |
|---|---|---|
| Elementary service occupations | – | – |
| Elementary cleaning occupations | – | – |
| Plastics process operatives | – | – |
| Forklift-truck drivers | 0.01 | × 0.3 |
| Glaziers, window fabricators | 0.01 | × 0.3 |
| Roofers, tilers and slaters | 0.02 | × 0.4 |
| Rubber process operatives | 0.02 | × 0.4 |
| Vehicle/paint technicians | 0.02 | × 0.4 |
| Packers, bottlers, canners and fillers | 0.02 | × 0.4 |

Table 0.2

Under-represented Occupations in the GBCS

affluent, educated, professional and managerial group living in west London and the Home Counties on the one hand, from a group of manual workers, more likely to be living outside the south-east of England on the other. Such is the imprint of class that it is marked in the very conduct of the research tool designed to reveal its significance.

But the issue is even more complicated than this, for the GBCS is not only about class, it is also about being 'British'. We have already seen that Northern Irish and Scottish residents were less likely to respond to the GBCS than those in England. There was also a high skew in which ethnic groups, and the kind of members of different ethnic groups, who did the GBCS. Table 0.3 shows that the proportion of black and Asian ethnic minorities is considerably fewer than we would expect, if the sample is representative of the British population. Why was this the case? It might be that these ethnic groups are more likely to be in the lower levels of the class structure, members of which we have already seen are unlikely to respond to the GBCS. It is also possible that the connotations of 'Great British' might be taken to be 'white British', and hence of little relevance to ethnic minorities. Among those ethnic minorities who did do the GBCS, a high proportion were students or university graduates, indicating again that the GBCS is skewed towards the proportionately better educated from within these groups. Comparing Asians with white people, for instance, will largely turn out to be a comparison of the well-educated members of both groups. Thus, we can't simply assume there is only a class skew at work in the GBCS, as the biases in the data run in several different

| ETHNIC GROUP | % OF THE ETHNIC GROUPS WHO UNDERTOOK THE GBCS | % OF THE POPULATION WHO UNDERTOOK THE GBCS (2011 CENSUS, ENGLAND AND WALES) | % OF EACH GROUP'S GRADUATES WHO UNDERTOOK THE GBCS |
|---|---|---|---|
| White | 90.14 | 85.97 | 63.4 |
| Black | 0.90 | 3.32 | 59.9 |
| Asian | 2.18 | 6.81 | 68.1 |
| Chinese | 0.94 | 0.70 | 71.9 |
| Mixed | 1.89 | 2.18 | 62.2 |
| Others | 3.96 | 0.10 | 65.0 |

Table 0.3
Ethnic Skew in the GBCS

ways and we need to be attentive to all of these when we report findings.

The GBCS certainly can't be used to report nationally representative findings. But in a sense, this is actually a very important point, for as we see it, this skew is highly revealing. We would be failing to recognize the power of class in contemporary Britain if we did not understand how people's engagement with forms of knowledge and expertise is implicated in class itself. This is a point which we will return to time and again as this book proceeds.

Nevertheless, this observation also poses fundamental challenges for our analytical strategy. Clearly, if we simply reported the findings from the GBCS, we would be relying on the voices of the most affluent and well educated, and could hardly do justice to class divisions, and their intersection with ethnicity, gender, age and suchlike. And indeed the problems of relying on a survey with such an intense sample skew have been amply discussed by commentators on the GBCS in previous publications.[7] This is why in this book we have used numerous other sources to allow us to redress this bias.

Firstly, once the extent of the sample skew came to light the BBC agreed to conduct a small nationally representative survey of 1,026 people, conducted by the market-research firm GfK, asking identical questions to those in the GBCS, allows us to provide benchmarks to correct for the biases of the GBCS[6]. We use this national sample to provide representative patterns where this is appropriate for our arguments, and use the larger GBCS when we want to mine down into more detailed analyses. We will make it clear which of the samples we are using.

Secondly, given the immense media and public interest in the GBCS, we decided to follow up with fifty additional qualitative interviews in order to find out more about what people think about class, in ways which go beyond survey response tick boxes. We directed some of these interviews at those kinds of people who did not tend to do the GBCS, namely those at the bottom of the class structure, in order to find alternative means of accessing groups who were not predisposed to complete the survey. We use these qualitative interviews and ethnographic vignettes to flesh out our account and bring out issues which are left hanging by the survey itself. We also use these interviews to zoom in on members of the elite class, who are of particular interest to us.

Thirdly, and very importantly, in reporting the results of the GBCS we also draw on extensive sociological research that underpins our long-term engagement with these issues. The authors of this book have extensive direct experience with numerous other projects examining the remaking of social class divisions and we will deepen and bring out the connections with other research as we proceed. A particular reference should be made to the Cultural Capital and Social Exclusion project which conducted a comprehensive national survey, created focus groups and undertook qualitative interviews to assess the nature of cultural engagement in Britain (and the findings of which were published in Bennett et al., 2009).[8] This pioneered many of the questions on cultural capital that we used in our GBCS project and offers much additional research bearing on the topics of the book.

The Great British Class Survey is, then, an experiment in the true sense of the word. Both the data itself, as well as the public interest in the research, give us an unparalleled opportunity to think about the new kinds of class divisions that exist in contemporary Britain. But in understanding the lessons from this study we need to stand back from the data to look at the wider dynamics of class which inform us whether people are likely to have completed the questionnaire itself.

This book provides our interpretation of the significance of class today. We do not attempt to summarize swathes of literature. Rather, drawing on and distilling the extensive research we have conducted in recent decades, we try to offer a provocative account, which we hope will generate discussion and reflection inside and outside academic circles. This book is thus not simply a report on our work with the GBCS, but represents a much wider engagement with sociological research on class.

Our analysis is based on the British case, on which we are experts. We do not claim that the British experience is typical or that it lays down a course which other nations will follow. Far from it. However, we do think that the issues discussed here are unlikely to be confined to this country alone and will have resonances around the planet, even while we fully acknowledge that as one of the wealthier nations in the world, the relationship between wealth elites and poorer classes will be very different in other countries. And the British case is symbolically important too. Over the past century, reflections on the nature of class relations in Britain have generated pivotal arguments on the changing nature of citizenship, welfare, poverty, cultural snobbery, political radicalism and reform across the globe. In all these cases, by recognizing the peculiarities of the British case, it is also possible for those in other locations to identify how class relations work in other contexts. If our book provokes reflections from other national contexts, then we will have had a positive influence.

The topic of class is far from being a dispassionate one. There are bitterly contested views about what classes are, how to measure and analyse them, and their overall significance for society. And we are far from being neutral in these debates. We have been at the forefront of a group of British sociologists who have insisted over recent years that class remains fundamental to sociological analysis. We have also championed the thinking of the French sociologist Pierre Bourdieu as offering the most perceptive approach to unravelling the complexities of class today, in a programme of work which has been labelled 'cultural class analysis'. In this book, we do not debate with other perspectives directly, so as not to be distracted from our main aim.

Our book has a logical form and is best read in sequence. In the first part we explain how existing thinking about class continues to focus on the divide between the middle and working classes, which we will show is outdated. Part Two argues for our multidimensional approach to class, in which we unravel how economic, cultural and social capital each contribute to inequality, and in Chapter 5 we show how we can link these different kinds of capital together to develop

a new approach to class which shows there is no neat dividing line between working and middle class, but a more hierarchical class order, in which the wealth elite stands clearly
above the rest. Part Three then shows how social class
impacts on social mobility, education and geography. Part
Four zooms in on our two extreme classes – the wealth elite
and the precariat – to demonstrate the profound class divide
that now exists. We draw out the political implications of our
arguments in the conclusion.

# PART ONE

# The History of Social Class

# Contesting Class Boundaries

## DIFFERENTIATING MIDDLE AND WORKING CLASS

In January 2011 the BBC launched their new inquiry into social class in Britain – the Great British Class Survey – with the following announcement:

> The labels 'working', 'middle' and 'upper' first appeared in the nineteenth century as a way of classifying the sharp social differences that arose in Britain as it led the world in the Industrial Revolution. But can a Victorian system designed to describe the relationship between industrial workers, managers and owners still be relevant today? It's clear that social divisions have far from disappeared, and the traditional language of class still pervades public affairs, shapes political thinking and influences our personal careers. So what does class really mean in Britain in the twenty-first century?[1]

Of course, many people have always resisted the value of thinking in terms of these class categories, which might be seen as divisive or simplistic. Historical and sociological studies have demonstrated long-term ambivalence about how far people see themselves as belonging to classes – of any kind. Our own in-depth interviews with two hundred Manchester residents in the early 2000s suggested that two-thirds of those we talked to were ambivalent in seeing themselves as belonging to any kind of class.[2] As long ago as the 1960s – when British class divisions have usually been seen as very strong – even then half the population did not see themselves as belonging to a social class.[3]

We should not think that the differentiation between 'upper', 'middle' and 'working' class has ever been straight-forward or uncontested. Nonetheless, in many nations, and certainly in Britain, there has been an enduring preoccupa-tion with the centrality of the boundary between the middle and working classes over the past two centuries. The upper class tended to stand outside this fundamental tension: although highly visible, their aristocratic affiliations mark them as a group apart from the rest of society, defined by their privileges of birth, and with their own social rules and etiquette. It seems to exist in and of itself, as a kind of special group.[4] By contrast, the terms in which the middle and work-ing classes understand themselves are more fluid and con-tested. This is all part of political battles between socialists seeking to mobilize the working classes, and conservative politicians trying to appeal to the middle and upper classes.

This uncertainty about what it means to be working or middle class has the effect of making these identities potent symbolic and cultural forces. Are these differences of income, morality and values, lifestyle, residence, politics? Can you move from a working class background to become middle class? What does it mean to be middle class? Does it mean you have a white-collar job? Or that you are 'respectable'? Or that you are well educated? All these volatile uncertainties are bound up with these differentiations between the middle and working classes which has fuelled, and continues to drive, our obsession with class over the past two centuries. *But it is the central argument of this book that this no longer helps to unravel the way that class operates today.* This obsession acts as a smokescreen for a more fundamental remaking of class at the top echelons of British society.

## Class identification in Britain

Historians have shown that class awareness has a long history in Britain.[5] Compared with other nations, it is the power and persistence of working class identities from a very early date, the later eighteenth century, which is striking.[6] Many other nations – such as France or the United States – give greater symbolic pride of place to farmers, peasants, or tradesmen, seen to be the backbone of their nation. However, Britain is unusual. A large class of independent farmers or peasants had disappeared at an early date.[7] The early onset of capitalist agriculture in the sixteenth century – associated in part with the enclosure movement – produced a large class of wage-earning farm workers, many of whom also moved into part-time handicraft production to eke out a living.[8] Therefore, even before the Industrial Revolution there were numerous wage-earners in agriculture, as well as in skilled and unskilled trades. These workers had a strong sense of independence, drawing on what E. P. Thompson famously defined as the culture of the 'freeborn Englishman'. This pride, associated with the skills of handicraft production, endured well into the period of the Industrial Revolution, and indeed into the twentieth century. These craft traditions could feed into a strong sense of confidence in manual-working class identities, which cross-fertilized with socialist movements and the development of the Labour movement during the nineteenth century.[9]

In contrast to this strong plebeian identity stood the strong and cohesive world of the aristocratic and gentlemanly upper class. Unlike most European nations, the power of this class was never shattered through revolutionary upheaval, and it proved unusually innovative and forward-looking, realizing at an early period that it could thrive through taking advantage of commercial opportunities. The British upper class was adaptable and confident, driving forward what economic historians have called 'gentlemanly capitalism', which was embedded in imperialist power and the development of a powerful commercial and trading infrastructure (based in London).[10]

As feminist historians have shown, these tensions were underscored by the way that women's labour might straddle these worlds. The largest source of employment for women was as domestic servants, which entailed their working in close proximity to middle- and upper-class men, hence leading to anxieties about the transgression of sexual and moral norms as they went about their work.[11] Women were seen by men therefore as reinforcing class hierarchies, but they also had the potential to challenge them, which made them a focus of anxiety and objects to be regulated.

These factors all meant that middle class identities in Britain were uncertain. The expanding middle classes of businessmen, managers, tradesmen and white-collar workers were confronted on the one hand by the aloof and confident aristocratic class to which it was hard to gain entry, and by an assertive group of proud male manual workers on the other.[12] As the historian Dror Wahrman has shown, the result was to position the middle classes as a kind of mediating force – a sort of football – between the small aristocratic upper class and the working class majority.[13]

During the nineteenth century these tensions played out, especially with respect to electoral reform. Before 1832, voting was generally confined to a small group of male property owners, with the vast majority of the male population, and the entire female population, having no right to vote. There was a fear from the upper classes that if the franchise was extended to the majority of the population, then they would end up challenging the social order, thus eroding 'civilized' values and their own authority. But in the face of intense protest and demands for enfranchisement articulated by radicals in the early nineteenth century and Chartists in the 1840s, it became politic to give wider sections of the male population the vote, in reforms in 1832, 1867 and 1885. Through this delicate manoeuvre, the middle classes became politically incorporated in ways which distinguished them from those below them, who remained outside the franchise, and also institutionalized this patronage from above.

We can readily identify the stakes and tensions this history produced. For some people, the working classes were a dangerous force of commoners who would drag down standards and lead to social and cultural decline if they were allowed too much influence.[14] Yet for socialists and those active in the Labour movement, the working classes spearheaded a more egalitarian and caring ethos, which in its turn would bring about a more genuine nation, one able to move beyond the hypocrisies of upper-class gentlemanly culture.[15] In terms of political belief, a lot rested on whether one sympathized with the working class.

In this context, the relatively insecure middle classes were caught up in a cultural forcefield in which their own place was uncertain. J. H. Plumb, Maxine Berg and John Brewer have examined how, from the later eighteenth century onwards, the middle classes sought to establish a clearer identity for themselves by championing forms of luxury consumption and display.[16] This emphasized their cultural differentiation from the working class beneath them, and could become a point of contact with the aristocratic establishment above them. The result was to lead to a cultural politics in which the meaning and nature of the boundary between the middle and working class was to become a major preoccupation.

The ambivalences produced by these dynamics are profoundly English – taking subtly different forms in Scotland, Wales and Ireland. Thus, the quintessential English socialist writer George Orwell famously railed against upper-middle class values, notably in his tirade against his private boarding school in his essay, 'Such, Such Were the Joys', and yet was also caught up in a controversy about his portrayal of the working class in his epic *The Road to Wigan Pier*. In drawing attention to the desperate housing conditions of miners during the 1930s recession he was accused of snobbery, a charge which he firmly rebutted: 'I not only did not say that the working classes "smell", I said almost the opposite of this. What I said, as anyone who chooses to consult the books can see, is that 20 or 30 years ago, when I was a child, middle class children were taught to believe that the working class "smell" and that this was a psychological fact which had to be taken into consideration.'[17]

Even though Orwell was highly sensitive to class prejudice, his own case reveals the impossibility of standing outside the cultural tensions around him. And such anxieties fed into numerous arenas of life, creating an all-consuming anxiety about whether one stood on the right side of the 'class' line.

It is therefore understandable how a fascination developed with the middle reaches of the class structure. Were relatively well-paid, skilled artisans working class, or were they an 'aristocracy of labour' who might ape middle class mores? Were deprived white-collar clerks, corner shopkeepers, or primary-school teachers really middle class, or were they actually some kind of a lower-middle class? Who was respectable, and who was not? For much of twentieth century these uncertainties fuelled the English preoccupation with class and classification around this axial divide.[18]

## Classifying class: early sociological paradigms

These sensibilities fed into the first attempts to formally classify the population from the early nineteenth century onwards, when identifying the central cleavage between the middle and the working class became the main object of interest. The upper class was a group apart: they knew who they were, they did not admit outsiders and their privileges were largely unchallenged. If anyone was in any doubt, they could consult *Debrett's Peerage and Baronetage*, which, from 1769 onwards, provided an exact listing of aristocrats. The situation was subtly different, however, for the ranks of the middle classes in the professions and in business who were not always sure whether their ranks differed from those of skilled tradesmen.

And it was precisely these sentiments which played into the first developed mapping of the class system from the early decades of the nineteenth century. A key inspiration here was a new impetus to understand the nature and dynamics of poverty, in the context of large-scale urbanization and population growth and fears about the rise of a new 'residuum' (made up of the potentially law-breaking and disreputable unemployed).[19] In the context of these worries, Charles Booth, the celebrated London shipping magnate, devised a minutely detailed social map of London in the 1880s, whilst B. Seebohm Rowntree, the Quaker chocolate industrialist, produced his famous study of poverty in York in 1901. Both of these used colour-coded mapping, which differentiated streets according to the moral standing of their inhabitants, as measured by professional observers. Crucially, these studies conflated class with respectability and morality, as the key to Booth's London map reveals all too clearly, with its scale running from black: 'Lowest class. Vicious, semi-criminal', through pink: 'Fairly comfortable' to gold: 'Wealthy'.[20]

It was from this fertile milieu, with concerns about respectability, pollution and the class divide, that the first formal measures of class were developed by the Registrar

General's Office in 1911 to classify households into social classes. In order to explain the differential health of various social groups, and notably the extent to which the poor were more subject to illness and early mortality, it was essential to find clear benchmarks to group people to classes. This allowed those who contested the idea that ill health and immoral behaviour from the lower classes was due to hereditary factors, to argue that it was actually produced by the poor social conditions of those in poverty – as measured by new social class divisions[21].

The Registrar General's class schema was the result (see Table 1.1). This clearly identified the main class boundary as associated with the difference between 'non-manual' and 'manual' employment. It also split the 'skilled' class 3 into two components (IIIN and IIIM).[22] This additional concern to separate out strands in the middle testifies to the cultural anxieties directed towards this central boundary, and the added stakes involved in sub-differentiating groups within it.

On the face of it, the Registrar General's class schema was based on the grade of people's occupations, placing professional jobs first, followed by managerial jobs, close to the top of the class structure, then wending down through skilled non-manual employment, and then discriminating between skilled, partly skilled and unskilled manual work. Class, here, is the product of occupation.

However, in fact, the classification was more complex than this, since occupations were grouped according to the 'culture' of the occupations, not directly on the nature of the work involved or because of their typical income levels. The originator of this scheme, the medical officer of health,

| CLASS DESCRIPTION | EXAMPLES OF OCCUPATIONS |
|---|---|
| **NON-MANUAL** | |
| I  Professional | Doctors, chartered accountants, professionally qualified engineers |
| II  Managerial and technical/intermediate | Managers, school teachers, journalists |
| IIIN  Skilled non-manual | Clerks, cashiers, retail staff |
| **MANUAL** | |
| IIIM  Skilled manual | Supervisors of manual workers, plumbers, electricians, goods vehicle drivers |
| IV  Partly skilled | Warehousemen, security guards, machine/tool operators, care assistants, waiters and waitresses |
| V  Unskilled | Labourers, cleaners and messengers |

**Table 1.1**

The Registrar General's Social Class Schema

T. H. C. Stevenson, was emphatic that his purpose was to capture this cultural aspect of class most effectively. This is because he saw cultural factors as paramount in explaining why some social classes had lower mortality rates than others. In 1927, he wrote that:

> the lower mortality of the wealthier classes depends less upon wealth itself than upon the culture, extending to matters of hygiene, generally on the whole associated with it. [. . .] But culture is more easily estimated, as between occupations, than wealth, so the occupational basis of social grading has a wholesome tendency to emphasize it.

He went on to say: 'It follows that when one speaks of the more or less comfortable classes one is thinking largely of the more or less cultured classes.'[23]

Thus, this 'occupational' measure of class was actually a way of making for cultural judgements about the ranking and social importance of jobs. They subtly hinted at the moral worth of different kinds of jobs and therefore the respectability which flowed from them. But how were occupations placed in these social classes in practice? Stevenson carefully explained that the number of rooms in one's house was not discriminating enough: 'The wealthy bachelor may occupy no more rooms than the cab-driver with six children.' In the end he declared it almost self-evident that 'we know that the barrister and the blacksmith are in different social grades.' But was there actually a consensus about which occupations are more reputable than others?[24] Is it a coincidence that a class schema which placed professional classes at the top was actually devised by professional civil servants and academics?

We can see how differentiating class became bound up with ways of demarcating morally suspect working class groups and identifying the scale of their deviation from respectable norms.

The origins of class classification, then, cannot be removed from this elitist concern to demarcate and map the boundary of respectability, seen predominantly to differentiate middle (non-manual) and working (manual) classes (though within each of these classes there were also more-and-less respectable fractions). Hence, the underlying concern was with the cultural and moral aspects of class. Yet, this also evoked a claim to superiority of some groups over others, which flew in the face of an increasingly democratic ethos that found it improper to make such overt distinctions.

The result was to lead to a fudging of the role of culture within the sociological measurement of class. Of course, most professionals were in no doubt of their own cultural superiority. However, to openly admit to this in an age of a militant and assertive trade-union movement, and in a period of mass unemployment and deprivation following the 1929 slump, could be seen as highly distasteful, especially within a polity that was becoming ostensibly more democratic following the extension of the franchise to all men in 1918, and to all women in 1928. The cultural dimensions of class thus went 'underground'. They could be admitted within the company of one's own kind but were not to be broadcast more generally.[25]

One result was that the justification for the Registrar General's class schema changed over time, with the reference to culture being changed to a focus on skill and the 'standing' of occupations in the community. This appeared to make the Registrar General's classification more 'objective' and less judgemental – though in practice most occupations remained in much the same classes as before. Ross McKibbin has shown how during the middle decades of the twentieth century these dividing lines between middle and working class were adapted, notably by Conservative politicians who sought to define the middle classes as bastions of national virtue against what they saw as the 'dangerous', left-leaning working class. In the post-war years the classification gained further impetus through a technocratic emphasis on the need for skilled and qualified 'human capital', which in turn played into the development of educational reform and managerialism from the 1960s onwards.[26]

Increasingly during the twentieth century further anxieties concerning this white/blue-collar line were forged around gender and immigration. Previous male 'sanctuaries' of non-manual work were increasingly entered by women, who had formerly been confined to the then female 'ghettos' of teaching and nursing. From the early decades of the twentieth century onwards, there was a marked increase in the number of women in white-collar jobs (such as jobs in banking or as assistants in shops), though nearly entirely at the lower levels. There were therefore concerns that these women were a 'white-collar proletariat', and even after the Sex Discrimination Acts of the early 1970s made it illegal to employ women on different terms from men, they generally remained at the lower levels of the occupational structure.[27] As Beverley Skeggs has shown, issues of femininity and respectability came to focus on the difficulty of women being accepted as exhibiting appropriate forms of middle class respectability.

Immigration caused further anxieties and mobilizations around this class boundary, with substantial numbers of black and ethnic minority men and women moving into manual employment from the early twentieth century, and at a somewhat later date also into professional occupations. Numerous ethnic minorities found a way of claiming a form of British identity by taking on the language of class, notably through proudly appropriating working class identities. This was especially the case for Afro-Caribbeans and Africans. For other, mainly later immigrants, claiming a form of middle class status could be a means of demonstrating they had secured a place – albeit often fraught – within British society. Some sociologists such as Annie Phizacklea and Robert Miles sought to recognize the significance of racial divisions within the working class by using the concept of 'class fractions' but later analyses of racialization found it harder to clearly associate ethnic with class divisions, even in subtle ways.[28]

We can therefore see how these forces preserved the historical focus on the middle reaches of society as the decisive terrain for drawing fundamental boundaries about who was, and who was not, respectable. This is nowhere marked so much as in the peculiarly British obsession with the 'lower middle class' – on the one hand, differentiated from the world of manual labour, and on the other hand, not fully 'middle class'. But the cultural ramifications are much wider. The legacy of this history has been to make the boundary between the middle and working class central to the British understanding of class. Whereas in most nations, the majority of people are content to define themselves as middle class – neither terribly affluent nor enormously deprived – in Britain, to be middle class can be, and often is, taken to mean to command claims to cultural snobbery and privilege.

## The sociological analysis of social class: 1960–2000

From the mid-twentieth century onwards, it was on this febrile and emotive ground that sociologists sought to find a more rigorous way of understanding the boundary between middle and working class, one which sought to remove moral judgements and place the study of class on a more objective footing. Given the tensions and stakes around defining class, this was an important move. The key figures were a post-war generation of sociologists, with John Goldthorpe as the key protagonist. From a working class Yorkshire background, and having been rejected as an undergraduate applicant to study history at Oxford, he turned to sociology with gusto as a graduate student. His pioneering research with David Lockwood in the 1960s on well-paid 'affluent workers' led him to insist on the recalcitrance of these workers from middle class norms. In strongly resisting the view that the working classes were in any way culturally or morally deficient, but highly sensitive to the actual differences in life chances which they experienced, he sought to place the study of class on a less culturally loaded and more 'sociological' platform. This led him to elaborate a new occupational class scheme in the 1970s, which in due course became the basis for the class categorization which is officially used today by the Office of National Statistics, the National Statistics Socio-Economic Classification (NS-SEC).[29] This has also been widely adapted internationally and most nations use a version of this approach today.

Before turning to consider Goldthorpe's arguments, we need to mention that one unintended consequence of his intervention was to weaken analyses of the relationship between the study of class, and the study of gender, race and ethnicity. Because Goldthorpe's concern was to place the analysis of class on a distinctive footing, relating it to employment and occupation, he was thus determined to distinguish it analytically from these kinds of inequalities.

Goldthorpe's schema was shown to be more sophisticated and effective in its own terms than the Registrar General's class model because it distinguished two different principles which differentiated people according to their work, and did not place them on a unitary grading principle as with the Registrar General's scheme.[30] Table 1.2 gives a breakdown of this class schema with the proportion of people in its ranks in 2014.

Goldthorpe argued that a fundamental divide lay between those who were employers and the self-employed (placed here in class 4, unless they were large employers, in which case they fell into class 1.1), on the one hand, and employees on the other. The reasoning here is that employers and the self-employed are occupied in distinctive kinds of employment relationships: they own and control their businesses, which might extend to employing staff. Their income takes the form of profits. This situation distinguishes them clearly

| | | |
|---|---|---|
| 1 | Higher managerial, administrative and professional occupations | 11.4% |
| | 1.1 Large employers and higher managerial and administrative occupations | 2.7% |
| | 1.2 Higher professional occupations | 8.8% |
| 2 | Lower managerial, administrative and professional occupations | 21.0% |
| 3 | Intermediate occupations | 10.8% |
| 4 | Small employers and own account workers | 8.0% |
| 5 | Lower supervisory and technical occupations | 6.2% |
| 6 | Semi-routine occupations | 11.4% |
| 7 | Routine occupations | 8.7% |
| 8 | Never worked and long-term unemployed | 4.5% |
| | Not classified: full-time students, or occupation not coded | 18.1% |
| | Full-time students | 7.3% |
| | Not classified: occupational information not present/adequate, or for other reasons | 10.8% |

**Figure 1.2**

**The National Statistics Socio-Economic Classification**

*Source:* Data based on the July–September 2014 quarterly Labour Force Survey, with 71,873 respondents aged 16–74. (The Labour Force Survey is the largest social survey in the UK and offers the most wide-ranging information about people's income; it is a sample of all private households (plus those in NHS accommodations or student residence halls).) Percentages are calculated using suggested survey weighting

from the majority of people who are employees and are paid a salary or wage.

The differentiation between employers and employees was only one part of the story. Within the ranks of those employed, he identified a further divide between a professional and managerial 'service class', now comprising around a third of the labour force, and an intermediate class and a working class. Here Goldthorpe made a distinction analytically between 'staff' and their manual 'workers', one which was strongly inscribed in British employment practices. Until the 1980s, many British firms had separate canteens and toilets for workers in each of these grades, and there were separate forms of remuneration, and a distinction made between monthly salary and weekly, hourly, or piece-based wages, and also with respect to pension entitlements. In some cases, these kinds of distinctions were directly identified with cultural markers, such as that between 'intellectual' and 'mechanical' grades in the civil service.

Many sectors of employment enshrined these boundaries in subtle ways. Within banking, promotion to managerial positions involved moving into a manager's house, taking responsibility for one's staff, being prepared to be culturally differentiated from one's juniors and wearing a suit. These points are important, because from the 1950s onwards, as sociologists increasingly sought to find a more sophisticated understanding of class divisions, they picked on these differences in what David Lockwood calls the work, market and status situations as underpinning class relations.[31]

Goldthorpe argued that this association between salary and wage could be formalized more rigorously, to distinguish those employed in a 'service relationship' and those who are on a contract for their labour. Most people fall into the latter category: they are paid a 'spot wage', i.e. a sum which offers a market price for the specific work they do. This can take the form of an hourly rate, or may also be aggregated into a weekly or even a monthly sum. However, some employees play a more diffuse role, and one that is difficult to monitor directly. Their employers therefore are prepared to grant 'prospective rewards', such as an incremental salary, pension entitlements and other 'fringe benefits' which are designed to instil a longer-term commitment to their employers. Typically, these are workers with high degrees of skill or expertise, or who command managerial control by being supervisors of others.

Goldthorpe's was therefore a highly sophisticated framework, more attentive to the nature of people's employment than its predecessors, and appeared to completely take out cultural or moral dimensions. A range of studies from the 1980s showed it offered a much more satisfactory basis on which to place occupations into larger class groups than that which simply distinguished manual from non-manual employees.[32]

Nonetheless, this approach to class was still part of a longer-term history. First and foremost, the upper classes remained outside the purview of these class measures. Even though they were thought to command power and authority they did not figure explicitly in these measures of class. Partly, this is because they are small in number and do not show up on any large-scale survey.[33]

Secondly, we see a persistent emphasis on the divisions within the middle reaches of the class structure. This was no longer a straightforward divide between non-manual and manual labouring classes, but rather a tripartite one between the service class (1 and 2), the intermediate class (3, 4, 5) and the working class (6 and 7). Here, the 'service class' can be seen as clearly middle class, and the intermediate classes occupy an ambivalent position within this divide – just as they did over the past two centuries, through ideas of 'the lower middle class' or class 3. The NS-SEC still exhibited the ongoing concern with the boundary between middle and working class, and indeed it was precisely its capacity to offer a more sophisticated way of rendering this distinction which was an important part of its appeal.

The success of the NS-SEC lay in offering a more rigorous account of divisions between occupations, and in apparently placing the study of class on a scientific footing, one which needed no reference to the kind of cultural or moral judge-ments that pervaded previous classifications. This approach has been the basis of internationally significant work on social mobility and continues to be important today.[34] However, it comes at a certain cost. We have, in recent years, seen the proliferation of cultural markers of class which do not – at least on the face of it – appear to be directly linked to these occupational classes.[35] We believe we need to seriously grap-ple with these to understand class today. We argue that a new kind of snobbery has emerged, one which does not overtly claim that some people or lifestyles are superior to others – since that would fly in the face of our sense of democratic equality, which we genuinely hold dear. Instead, the new snobbery is based on being 'knowing', and in displaying an awareness of the codes which are used to classify and differ-entiate between classes. It distinguishes those who are skilled in exercising judgement, in a knowing and sophisticated way, against those, whoever they may be, who are deemed unable to choose effectively. This is a kind of snobbery which proliferates in a market-based consumer society such as ours, where our display of taste is paramount and mundane. But this is not the kind of snobbery which is easily attributed to classes as bundles of occupations, such as registered in the NS-SEC schema above. To find the best handle for grasping the codes which underpin this new snobbery, we offer our own framework for unpicking the class structure of Britain today.

## Bourdieu, inheritance and cultural class analysis

We have traced the contorted British obsession with class over the twentieth century which has crystallized the boundary between middle and working class as an enduring concern. This distinction carries moral and cultural, as well as economic, political and social characteristics. It is the contention of our book that we need to rethink class today on a different basis, which recognizes the profound ways in which British capitalism is now a different beast from its predecessors. Let us set out the fundamental features of our approach here.

Class is fundamentally tied up with inequality. But not all economic inequalities are about class. Consider the case of someone who wins a million pounds on the National Lottery. They would be propelled, overnight, into the top percentile of the wealthiest people in the country. However this does not, by itself, put that person into a different class. What allows inequalities to crystallize into classes is when advantages endure over time in a way which extends beyond any specific transaction. Thus, when our lottery winner invests her or his fortune in property, or buys a small business, we might then say that her or his economic resources are being accumulated and s/he is now implicated in different class relationships. Social classes, we contend, are fundamentally associated with the stored historical baggage and the accumulation of advantages over time.

This perspective has been most illuminatingly elaborated by the French sociologist Pierre Bourdieu, undoubtedly the greatest sociologist of the second half of the twentieth century. Born the son of a rural French postal worker, he ended his career in the most illustrious post in France, as a professor in the Collège de France. His own social mobility and awareness of the profound difference between the cultural worlds he had experienced was central to his own vision. He was interested in the symbolic power of class, and the way that shame and stigma were bound up with forms of domination. For him, class was associated with how some people feel 'entitled' or 'dominated', and it is in recognizing these cultural as well as economic and social aspects of class that his work is so powerful today.

Bourdieu saw class privilege as tied up with having access to what he called 'capital', which he defined as having 'preemptive rights over the future'. Some resources permit groups the ongoing capacity to enhance themselves (which is denied to those without access to them). Theoretically, this perspective has been labelled the 'capitals, assets and resources' (or CARs) approach to class analysis.[36] The fundamental argument of the CARs perspective is that class is not to be conflated with the division of labour (as with the idea that it can simply be defined according to what job you do), or with concepts such as exploitation, which also become loaded and moralistic, but instead focuses on the processes by which resources are unevenly accumulated. Bourdieu's own account of the significance of capital is abstract, but worth reproducing:

> The social world is accumulated history, and if it is not
> to be reduced to a discontinuous series of instantaneous
> mechanical equilibria between agents who are treated as
> interchangeable particles, one must reintroduce into it the
> notion of capital and with it, accumulation and all its
> effects. Capital is accumulated labour (in its materialized
> form or its 'incorporated', embodied form), which, when
> appropriated on a private, i.e., exclusive, basis by agents or
> groups of agents, enables them to appropriate social energy
> in the form of reified or living labour. It is a *vis insita*, a
> force inscribed in objective or subjective structures, but it
> is also a *lex insita*, the principle underlying the immanent
> regularities of the social world. It is what makes the games
> of society – not least, the economic game – something
> other than simple games of chance offering at every
> moment the possibility of a miracle. Roulette, which holds
> out the opportunity of winning a lot of money in a short
> space of time, and therefore of changing one's social status
> quasi-instantaneously, and in which the winning of the
> previous spinning of the wheel can be staked and lost at
> every new spin, gives a fairly accurate image of this

imaginary universe of perfect competition or perfect equality of opportunity, a world without inertia, without accumulation, without heredity or acquired properties, in which every moment is perfectly independent of the previous one, every soldier has a marshal's baton in his knapsack, and every prize can be attained, instantaneously, by everyone, so that at each moment anyone can become anything. Capital, which, in its objectified or embodied forms, takes time to accumulate and which, as a potential capacity to produce profits and to reproduce itself in identical or expanded form, contains a tendency to persist in its being, is a force inscribed in the objectivity of things so that everything is not equally possible or impossible. And the structure of the distribution of the different types and subtypes of capital at a given moment in time represents the immanent structure of the social world, i.e., the set of constraints, inscribed in the very reality of that world, which govern its functioning in a durable way, determining the chances of success for practices.[37]

This is a fairly long explanation, but it perfectly illustrates the stakes involved in understanding class *historically*, rather than as economists and sociologists often do, as a series of transactions or relationships taking place in a rapidly moving world of successively flashing-past times. Taking a society as a series of rapidly moving snapshots, we can see only a world of agents, each trying their best to maximize their position, equalized, as it were, by all being placed in the same moment without the 'baggage of history'. However, Bourdieu insists that in any one moment we come to social life with different endowments, capacities and resources, and therefore we can see how classes are being historically forged.

Economic inequalities are fundamentally important. Thus we will examine the nature of economic capital in Chapter 2. However, economic capital is not enough by itself to define class. Bourdieu also insists on the symbolic power of what he terms cultural capital. It is important for us to lay out his argument fully here. Part of Bourdieu's reflections on the role of cultural capital arises from his interest in how inheritance takes place in modern societies. For much of human history, inheritance has involved the passing over of economic capital to one's kin: property, savings, tools, heirlooms. But Bourdieu argues that it is supplemented by another kind of inheritance, one associated with cultural capital in the form of educational qualifications. Well-educated parents pass on to their children – knowingly or not – the capacity for them to succeed at school and university, and thereby get the sort of qualifications which help them to move into the best jobs. This is not a direct inheritance; one cannot give one's degree certificate to one's daughter or son. But it is a probabilistic one, where there is a strong tendency for this kind of inheritance to be at work. This depends on certain cultural tastes and preferences being seen as superior – more 'legitimate' – than others.

The fact that this inheritance is not direct means that its significance can be misrecognized. No one is in any doubt about the value of economic capital. But the power of cultural capital depends on its not being recognized directly. Part of Bourdieu's thinking here comes from his background in anthropology, in which much attention has been given to the topic of gift giving.[38] Here, for Bourdieu, the gift is a 'reality that denies reality'. The minute we refuse to see gifts as altruistic and voluntary presents, but as self-interested devices to make us feel grateful to the gift-giver, then the gift loses its power. If we think someone is giving us flowers as an inducement to prepare a nice meal for them, then we discount it as a gift (we might be more likely to see it as emotional manipulation or even as a form of domination). Bourdieu pursued this line of thought through his concept of symbolic violence. Here violence does not depend on physical coercion, but can take place when we accept domination tacitly. It marks the 'naturalization' of historical forces.

And this, for Bourdieu is precisely how cultural capital works. We can immediately recognize the inheritance of property. We can readily imagine relatives gathering to listen to the lawyer reading out the will. The transmission of cultural capital, however, is opaque, and is necessarily masked in a language of meritocratic achievement and hard work. The importance of culture is therefore apparently denied in the very same moment that it operates. For Bourdieu, this opacity is a necessary feature of the ability of cultural capital to operate as a form of capital at all. The minute it is actually seen as a form of overt privilege, then it can be contested and its power can be challenged.

Let us consider an example, and one which also provides a platform for the argument about how meritocracy allows a new kind of snobbery, which we will make in this book. It can certainly be argued that in old educational curricula, certain kinds of canonical knowledge – of classical literary works, music and so forth – was prized over knowledge of popular culture: Shakespeare rather than *Hello!* magazine, to put it crudely.

This permitted those schoolchildren brought up in homes in which families went to the theatre and talked about literature to gain advantages over those who did not. However, as soon as it became apparent that these educational curricula benefited advantaged social groups – that is to say, as soon as cultural capital became recognized as such – educational reform movements campaigned to change the curriculum. And indeed, these have largely been successful. Thus, the current 'A-level' curriculum in English literature now has set texts including the poetry collections *And Still I Rise* by the black feminist Maya Angelou, the *Feminine Gospels* by Carol Ann Duffy and *Skirrid Hill* by Owen Sheers, which now sit alongside established canonical works such as those of Lord Tennyson and the Brontës.[39]

The point here is to recognize how cultural capital cannot be construed as a fixed set of tastes but as a much more mutable phenomenon. We will show in this book that the nature of cultural capital has changed, so that it now takes cosmopolitan and ironic forms which appear to be pluralist and anti-elitist. However, we should not take this at face value. It is one's ease and grace in moving between different genres, playing with classifications and typologies, which might count as cultural capital today. Well-educated people feel confident in dealing with institutions, in advancing their cause and in being assertive, and hence are often better able to get the best services from schools, the health service and suchlike. Those without such educational resources may feel underqualified and or even ashamed, unable to clearly and effectively make themselves heard. They may blame themselves for their own lack of confidence. These inequalities in senses of entitlement are not just peripheral, and not simply a matter of personality, but are fully implicated in the operations of class today through being accumulated and institutionalized.

Finally, we should remember that Bourdieu also elaborates upon the importance of social capital. This is the range and nature of people's social networks, which can affect people's life chances. Here again, contacts can accumulate over time, and may be a resource which can be mobilized to gain information about jobs, accommodation, exciting opportunities and so forth. Just as with cultural capital, this is an arena where there can be pervasive misrecognition. We may define a 'best friend' as someone who we care about, come what may, and hence someone from whom we do not expect return favours. In fact, however, such a friendship also needs to have a degree of reciprocity for it to persist. We get fed up with even our best friend when s/he doesn't reply to our text messages after several prompts.

This general approach can be applied in several ways. We can understand the 'moralization of place', the way that neighbourhoods evoke powerful cultural connotations based on the characteristics of their residents: stigmatized, respectable, posh and so forth.[40] Class thus becomes etched on to the landscape in powerful and evocative ways. Youth cultures and identities – defined using terms such as 'chavs', 'nerds', 'geeks' and suchlike – also demonstrate associations between class and cultural values.

In these terms, classes are the product of myriad processes of accumulation and sedimentation. They form in combination with other inequalities, such as those which exist around age, gender, race and ethnicity, as distinctive crystallizations of advantage, derived from the accumulation of these different capitals. But the proof of the pudding is in the eating: and, in the rest of this book, we will now turn to see what insights this approach might generate. Our argument is straightforward. Previous understandings of class have focused primarily on one's occupation and the relationship between middle and working class, and this is the social divide which has caused most anxiety and concern. Today, we place the focus on forms of capital and their capacity to allow accumulation and inheritance. We will show that if we look at class in this way, we can detect a very different structure, one in which a small, wealthy elite class is pitted against a precariat with few resources, and between these two extremes there exist a patchwork of several other classes, all of which have their own distinctive mixes of capital, but none of which comes close to reaching the boundary which demarcates the top rank of the class hierarchy.

# PART TWO

# Capitals, Accumulation and Social Class

# Accumulating Economic Capital

# The paradox of inequality

We live with a fundamental paradox. The growth of economic inequality has been dramatic in recent decades. Britain is now more unequal than most comparable nations. Before taxation and welfare transfers, only Portugal and Ireland were more unequal among developed nations. Even after the mildly redistributive effect of taxation and welfare provision, Britain is still more unequal than most of its peers. Surveys show that this shift does not reflect popular perceptions about the legitimacy of inequality. Most people tend to be critical of inequality: 78 per cent of Britons are in favour of at least some forms of redistribution.[1]

However, when it comes to viewing their own lives, British people do not straightforwardly, or even at all, place themselves as winners and losers in this intense economic competition. We asked our in-depth interviewees as to how they ranked themselves economically. Three characteristic replies are reported below:

Q: In terms of money, there are obviously some people in Britain that tend to have more than others. On a scale of one to ten, with one being the top, where would you put yourself in terms of money?

"Oh in the middle... Yeah, I can cope and I don't have big demands, I don't have computers, I don't have this, you know, and I don't travel, so I'm, just have enough to survive."

**JANE'S HOUSEHOLD INCOME: £6000; SHE HAS NO PROPERTY AND HER SAVINGS ARE £5,000**

"Erm... I'd say—, oh, I don't know. I would say wanting to be... Definitely—, I don't know, like a kind of midsection, like a five. My instant reaction was five, so five."

**JEREMY'S HOUSEHOLD INCOME: £60,000; HIS PROPERTY VALUE IS £250,000, BUT HE HAS NO SAVINGS**

"Erm, I'd probably put myself at about a six. I've got the house but you want to see my car, do you know what I mean? I don't have a lot of material goods and what I tend to get I tend to keep for a very long—, you know, like flog to death for a very long time. Yeah, six, maybe a seven, yeah."

**FIONA'S HOUSEHOLD INCOME: £60,000; HER PROPERTY VALUE IS £700,000, AND SHE HAS SAVINGS OF £100,000**

Jane, Jeremy and Fiona all saw themselves as being clearly in the middle of the spectrum, despite actually being in fundamentally different economic positions. Jane has a very low income, being reliant on a state pension. She does not own a property, and lives in sheltered accommodation, though she does, however, have some modest savings. Even though Jane is actually hard up, for instance having no computer and no capacity to travel, she nonetheless sees herself in the middle of the income distribution.

At the other end of the spectrum is Fiona, who, by contrast, enjoys a good income as an IT project manager which easily puts her in the top 10 per cent of earners, has a house with a substantial price tag and very high savings. Yet Fiona also puts herself in the middle range of the scale and emphasizes her modest needs and thrifty spending habits. She certainly does not boast and was even a bit embarrassed by her considerable economic capital. She does not go about flaunting her income and wealth. Jeremy, whose position on the scale lies between Jane and Fiona, and has a good income, but a lower-priced house and no savings, also rates himself as at about a 'five'.

What is going on here? Scrape beneath the surface and a different picture emerges from these interviews. Although people tended to place themselves in the middle of the economic class structure, it was clear that those who had only modest amounts of money were nonetheless aware that this had shaped and often constrained their lives in the past – and in the present. Alison, a poor pensioner from Yorkshire, constantly referred to money throughout her interview – whether the jobs she did over her lifetime paid 'good money'; of not having 'enough money' for her daughter to go to university; of needing to make sure she had 'some money' coming in (after her divorce) to support her and her daughter; of choosing things to do with her friends that didn't 'cost too much money'. She talked about how she was someone who had learned 'to get by . . . I can manage, I've learned how to manage'.

By contrast, the stories given to us by the affluent were very different. Louise was at the high end of the spectrum of wealth. She had an income of £225,000, a house worth just under £2 million and other assets worth over £100,000. Initially, when we asked Louise our question about where she was on the economic scale, she answered dismissively: 'I don't know, see, money's not a big thing for me . . . I've never done anything for money, I've done it for the love of doing it, so if you said to me, where do I sit, I don't know.' She downplayed the importance of money in her life and emphasized that it was acquired – almost by accident rather than design – as a consequence of loving her job. Those who have money, it seems, care less about it. Yet actually money was important to Louise and in subtle ways she recognized its importance. Coming from a working class background and having been in debt in the past, her good economic position allowed her to reflect from a position of ease on the acquisition of money itself:

> You know, so I mean at thirty I was earning over £100,000 a year . . . I think, you know, from where I've come from, from having no food in the cupboard to the life that I've lived and I think, how did I get here?

So, those with modest means found their lives constrained by necessities which they could not pay for. Those who are more affluent and with greater 'distance from necessity' (as Bourdieu puts it) are able to stand back from the brute power of money itself. Both these people might say they are in the middle of the income distribution – but for very different reasons. The stories of two women of different ages, with similar incomes but very different circumstances, bring this out. Lorraine was aware of the lack of money in her life, having divorced from her husband and moved out of the family home into private rented accommodation with her two teenage sons. Her employment as a fork-lift truck driver gave her 'a low wage, not the lowest, but it's not great', which she later disclosed as around £11,000 per year. Lorraine wanted to own her home again, but she worried about her options. With some decent savings to fall back on – £40,000 – but with a limited income, the 'bottom line is you just don't earn enough, you just don't earn enough' to buy somewhere. Lorraine's case is an example of the 'shocks' that can be experienced, due to things like changes in family circumstances, when economic position can change dramatically.

Charlotte, a retired schoolteacher, thought that her annual income drawn from her pensions and 'various other bits and pieces' was around £12,000 – only slightly more. But she had a very different perspective on her circumstances. She was also divorced, but she had grown-up children, enough savings that she could describe them as a 'cushion', and she owned her home outright. Charlotte felt able to claim a confident moral standing from her ability to get by, which was actually afforded to her by her assets, but which she presented as a result of her simple standard of living: 'I don't actually have a lot of money coming in, but then I know how to manage, you know. I always say I can live on a shoestring.'

One of the key differences between Lorraine and Charlotte is not only their ages and family circumstances, but their position on the 'property ladder'. Lorraine has lost her own property and cannot get back on the ladder; Charlotte is comfortably positioned, having the asset of her own home. They are juggling different components of economic capital – in a way which demonstrates how people might not easily place themselves on a simple ladder, which goes from one to ten. And we can also see them both comparing their present economic position with that of their past lives and making sense of their current economic situation in the context of their previous experiences.

We can identify, even in these few cases, the complexity of how economic divisions stamp themselves decisively in people's identities. However, the way they do this is complex, and not simply a matter of identifying using terms such as 'rich', 'poor', 'middle income' or 'low income'. Simply noting that Britain is highly unequal, and getting more so, is not enough to put a handle on how people experience these inequalities in their own lives and how they understand the divisions they see around them. We can see lots of different forces at play even from these few vignettes. People do not want to show off. Nor do they want to recognize the shame and stigma of being at the bottom. Yet, despite people's hesitancies about identifying themselves economically, we will insist on the centrality of such inequalities in shaping people's lives.

# The power of income inequalities

Income inequalities in Britain are very high, and have been rapidly increasing. In their highly influential book *The Spirit Level*, Richard Wilkinson and Kate Pickett use the standard metric to measure inequality between countries – the Gini coefficient – in the fifteen states who were members of the European Union prior to its major enlargement in 2004 and also the major industrial English-speaking countries of Australia, Canada and the USA.[2] Figure 2.1 gives an indication of the inequalities within nations as they reflect the relative differences between countries in terms of earnings. The UK is a country of high gross income inequalities between households, coming second only to Ireland in the list of eighteen nations. Figure 2.1 shows also that those inequalities increased between 2008 and 2010 in the UK, as indeed they did in the vast majority of countries surveyed by the Organization for Economic Cooperation and Development (OECD). This clearly points to the impact of the financial crisis in exacerbating inequalities within the UK and across the globe.

Why is income inequality so intense in Britain? There is clearly a gulf between those wealthy households benefiting from Britain's centrality in global trading, corporate, professional and financial networks, when compared to poor households, which have been affected by the decline of manufacturing jobs and the proliferation of poorly paying jobs at the lower ends of the service economy. This is also associated with a powerful regional divide. Individuals working in the City of London earn huge sums of money in terms of

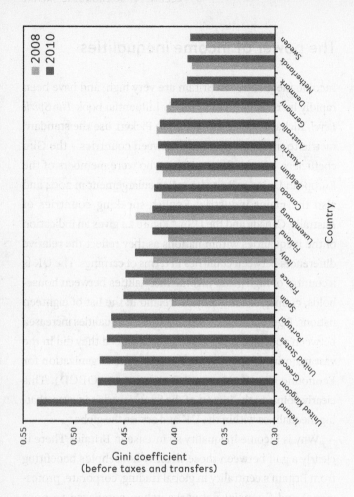

**Figure 2.1**

Income inequality in the EU15 and major Anglophone nations in 2008 and 2010 before taxes and transfers

*Source:* Social Protection and Wellbeing – Social Protection – Income Distribution and Poverty: this data comes from the Office for Economic Cooperation and Development (OECD)'s statistics website, accessed 22 May 2015. (See https://stats.oecd.org/Index.aspx)

both base income and additional bonus payments. At the other end of the economic spectrum, the UK also has an increasingly large number of people working in low-paid, long-hours, service-sector roles.[3] There are powerful biases, therefore, in the structure of the UK economy, that tend towards greater income inequality over and above other nation states with more balanced employment frameworks.

Are such stark income differences linked to a meritocratic system in which incentives are offered to those who are skilled and energetic enough to take on the most demanding and responsible jobs? If so, we might see these differences – intense as they are – as reflecting the need for a skilled and dedicated workforce in highly competitive conditions. Perhaps, following the logic of the NS-SEC, which we discussed in Chapter 1, the more highly skilled jobs in the professional and managerial classes command a higher premium.[4] Table 2.1 examines the extent of income inequality between the different NS-SEC classes (which we defined in Chapter 1), in 2011.

Table 2.1 shows that there is some difference in the levels of income between these classes. Thus the highest-paid occupational class, those at 'higher managerial and professional' levels, earn just under three times as much as those in the lowest-paid 'routine occupations'. This may sound a big difference, but when one realizes that the top 10 per cent of income earners earn nearly 17 times more than the lowest 10 per cent (an average of £67,566 versus an average of £4,018 in the latest Labour Force Survey data), and the top 1 per cent earns nearly 124 times as much as the poorest 1 per cent, this is actually not very striking. Secondly, we see a huge

| OCCUPATION | AVERAGE ANNUAL EARNINGS (£) |
| --- | --- |
| Higher managerial and professional | 45,362 |
| Lower managerial and professional | 29,419 |
| Intermediate | 18,178 |
| Small employers (with own accounts) | (no income data) |
| Lower supervisory and technical | 20,874 |
| Routine | 14,944 |
| Semi-routine | 13,389 |
| Never worked, unemployed, uncategorized | 9,857 |

**Table 2.1**

Occupational Class and Differences in Annual Incomes:
January–April 2011

*Source:* Labour Force Survey, 2014

differential between the higher managerial and professional class and all other classes. This class earns £15K more than the next best paid class – lower managerial and professional classes. But, the differential between lower-level managers and professionals and the worst-paid group – semi-routine workers – is only slight. What seems to be happening, therefore, is that the top class stands apart from all the others.[5]

Table 2.2 shows what proportion of earners in each of the occupational classes are in the top 20 per cent, bottom 20 per cent or middle 20 per cent of income earners. It shows that, actually, there is no perfect match between income and occupational class. Even the lowest-paid 'semi-routine occupations' have 3 per cent of their members in the top 20 per cent of earners, and 3 per cent of the higher managerial and professional class are among the bottom 20 per cent. We are dealing here in the world of probabilities and tendencies – income is not in any direct way a product of your occupation alone.

Levels of income are related to occupational class even more imperfectly at the top end of the income distribution and here GBCS data (gathered from responses to a question about the income of all household earners after tax and other deductions) can be used to differentiate between specific occupations' income in unusual detail.[6] Table 2.3 shows that CEOs earn nearly twice as much as scientists. Broadly, even within the most economically prosperous 'higher professional and managerial' category (NS-SEC classification 1), we can therefore distinguish a group of especially well-paid occupations. CEOs, doctors, lawyers and financial intermediaries have an average income (which includes

| | WITH INCOMES IN THE: | | |
| --- | --- | --- | --- |
| | BOTTOM 20% | MIDDLE 20% | TOP 20% |
| Higher managerial and professional | 3 | 10 | 59 |
| Lower managerial and professional | 8 | 19 | 33 |
| Intermediate occupations | 18 | 28 | 8 |
| Lower supervisory and technical | 10 | 25 | 15 |
| Semi-routine occupations | 36 | 19 | 3 |

**Table 2.2**

Occupational Class and Levels of Income

*Source:* Labour Force Survey, 2014

| OCCUPATIONAL GROUP | MEAN AGE | AVERAGE SALARY IN £S (FOR ALL IN THESE ELITE OCCUPATIONS) |
|---|---|---|
| Scientists | 36.1 | 47,928 |
| Engineers | 37.2 | 51,237 |
| IT professionals | 38.3 | 55,296 |
| Doctors | 36.9 | 78,221 |
| Other medical professionals | 38.0 | 58,924 |
| Higher-education teachers | 45.2 | 62,640 |
| Education professionals | 44.5 | 57,901 |
| Lawyers, barristers, judges | 34.3 | 79,436 |
| Public sector (outside health) | 39.9 | 53,163 |
| Accountants | 36.4 | 59,118 |
| CEOs, directors, presidents | 44.9 | 93,881 |
| Other senior business personnel | 38.6 | 63,233 |
| Financial intermediaries | 38.2 | 74,130 |
| Journalists | 35.8 | 50,168 |
| Other NS-SEC category 1 occupations | 39.6 | 54,738 |

Table 2.3

Average Income by Occupational Group and Age

the combined incomes of all those in their household) of over £70k after tax, whereas scientists, public sector professionals, journalists, IT professionals and engineers earn below £60k. We also see that age differences do not seem very important in explaining these differences: lawyers are relatively young, but are among the best paid of these occupation groups, whereas teachers tend to be older, but earn relatively less. In short, if we are to understand who is doing best in terms of income, especially at the top end, we can't simply rely on occupational class to measure it. Certain occupations at the 'top end' seem clearly to have pulled away from other occupations of supposedly equivalent skill, expertise and authority in terms of their relative economic rewards.

In later chapters we will probe these differences further to examine what factors may affect an individual in order to reach the highest income brackets, but for now we need to move on to consider other aspects of economic capital associated with the wider distribution of wealth.

## Bringing wealth in

We have shown how income alone is highly divisive, but there is more to inequality in economic capital than this. Economic capital is also affected by other assets we may be able to call on, such as savings, pension rights and potential financial resources tied up in house values. These sums have rarely been taken seriously into account in previous analyses of class, but they are fundamentally important. Piketty, for instance, has shown that capital tied up in housing is now the single major component of national capital as a whole, composing well over half of it in 2010.[7] It is also important to note that high amounts of wealth are not necessarily associated with high income.[8]

Using somewhat old data, Sierminska et al. show that the average net worth – accumulated assets – which British households possessed in 2000 was £173,641.[9] This is a sizeable sum, equivalent to five times the average annual household income. And in considerable numbers of cases, net worth today is much higher. Recent calculations suggest that as many as two million Britons are 'dollar millionaires', that is to say, they own this equivalent sum as a net asset (and after any debts are discounted). In light of this, we can better appreciate why our interviewees were highly aware of these aspects of their economic situation. Net worth in Britain is somewhat lower than in Italy and considerably lower than in the United States and (especially) Luxembourg, but it is higher than in Germany or (especially) Sweden. In reflecting on the significance of these sums, we need to introduce a very important distinction between what we might term absolute wealth: the total stock of capital in society – and relative wealth – which is how that total amount is distributed between the households which make up society. On the former point, there has been a remarkable revolution in recent decades. The amount of personal wealth – i.e. savings, housing and possessions – in Britain has tripled from £2,000 billion in 1980, to over £6,000 billion by 2005 (in constant prices which are controlled to include inflation).[10] The proportion of wealth as a percentage of GDP has doubled in the same period from less than 300 per cent to over 500 per cent.[11]

The collective accumulation of wealth over the past three decades is therefore enormous, and testifies to the massive accentuation of the sheer volume of economic capital in British society.

Why does this matter? It effectively means that in any one year collective current income is increasingly being over-shadowed by wealth assets accumulated from the past. When people reflect on their own economic situation their current income is significant, to be sure, but it is likely to be only one part of a much wider sense of their economic situation which is also based on their accumulated wealth from the past. We should not be deceived by dramatic rags-to-riches stories of highly unusual entrepreneurs, such as Mark Zuckerberg, founder of Facebook, to think that gaining a billion-dollar fortune can take place within a few years. As Bourdieu and Piketty remind us, accumulation is a long-term process.[12]

This absolute increase in wealth is divisive. It means that those who start with no wealth now have a much larger hill to climb in order to reach the top, or even the middle range of wealth-holders, compared to thirty years ago. This overall and absolute increase in wealth thus has knock-on implications for social inequality. This is especially the case given that wealth is also becoming more unequally distributed. In constant 2005 prices, the average marketable wealth of the top 1 per cent more than tripled from £700,000 in 1976, to £2,230,000 by 2005. By contrast, the average wealth of the bottom 50 per cent rose from £5,000 to only £13,000 in the same period.[13] The absolute gap between these two figures has risen from £695,000 to £2,217,000. If an individual were to move from bottom to top, they would have to amass three times as much money as they used to. The 'wealth mountain' is so much higher these days.

Bringing wealth into our analysis has three major implications. Firstly, it makes us aware that income is not the only, or even the main, way that economic capital matters to people, especially at the upper reaches of society. We have already found this to be the case when discussing our interviewees earlier in this chapter, and now we can see why. Secondly, the absolute gap between those with and without economic capital is getting larger. The successful self-made person needs to acquire even more resources to climb to the top of the mountain than they used to. Thirdly, given this trend, accumulation over the longer term is more important if one is to reach the top. Perhaps help from parents as well as a person's own efforts earlier in life becomes relatively more significant if they want to reach the top. (This is an issue we will look at in depth in Chapter 6.) If so, we need to understand economic capital in terms of a consolidation of previous advantages. The most obvious example of this comes from the transfer of resources from old to young people.

Parental support, especially from the affluent, is highly significant for young people. Twenty-nine per cent of parents give financial support to their non-resident children, a figure which rises to 45 per cent for those parents aged between forty-five and fifty-four (the age period when their children are likely to be leaving home).[14] Significant amounts of money are now being inherited among the majority of the population and it would be erroneous to see inheritance as confined to the very wealthy. Nonetheless, those in the top 20 per cent of wealth-holders are both more likely to inherit wealth themselves, and the amount they receive tends to be greater (an average of £59,000 as against £27,000 for those in the bottom 20%).[15] Through this mechanism, wealth tends to accumulate more intensely among wealthy households. John Hills and his colleagues conclude that there are 'long-lasting advantages for children from wealthier family backgrounds'.[16]

Having established the importance of wealth in general terms, we need to say a few additional words about the single most important component of wealth: housing. In the British case, it has moved from being about equivalent to average national income in the 1920s to around 300 per cent of that same amount today. In the UK, housing assets comprised 76 per cent of total net worth in 2000, a higher proportion than other comparable nations (the figure is 54% in the USA). What are the implications of housing wealth for economic capital?

## The property market

Owner-occupied housing is now thoroughly implicated in the accumulation of economic capital. This has three major effects: (a) it creates a powerful categorical divide between those who are tenants and those who are owners, (b) it accentuates the significance of age in the possession of economic capital and (c) it tends to spatially differentiate wealth and hence economic capital according to the buoyancy of local housing markets. To link these points together, those who are tenants are deprived of a major source of capital accumulation, and given that these tend to be younger people, and this process is especially intense in the buoyant housing market of the south-east of England, housing dynamics are now fundamentally implicated in processes generating inequality.

The broad story of housing wealth in Britain is well known. Over the course of the twentieth century, there was a long-term trend towards more people owning their own homes.[17] Margaret Thatcher certainly promoted Britain as a nation of home owners. The flip side has been that there is growing stigma attached to social housing across much of the UK.[18] One of Thatcher's most popular policies was the sale of council houses to tenants. This was presented as an agenda of rewarding aspiration, and many aspiring council tenants were able to buy their homes, which in many cases provided them with cut-price assets, particularly those tenants who lived in parts of central and inner London where house prices have increased so much in recent times.[19] There is a stark divide between those who own, and those who do not. Furthermore, new council houses were certainly not built at a rate to replace old ones, because central government would not allow local authorities to spend the money raised from the scheme on new house building. The long-term consequences of this policy have been huge. Coupled with spiralling house prices, home ownership fell for the first time in 100 years from 69 per cent in 2001 to 64 per cent in 2011.[20]

The significance of housing as a source of wealth is that it generates a powerful categorical divide towards the bottom of the economic distribution between those who rent and those who own property. This is an important point, because it suggests that a powerful fracture can be found among the bottom ranks who share very small amounts of economic capital. It is partly for this reason that we might be inclined to place the key economic division, not between manual and non-manual workers – as with the classic middle/working class divide – but between a smaller group of the 'precariat' at the bottom of the scale, whose paucity of economic capital and their frequent reliance on rented housing is a defining feature of their insecurity and disadvantage and prevents any realistic prospect of getting on to the housing ladder.

Of course this divide is also associated with age. It is becoming increasingly clear that age differences are widening, as most young people cannot afford to buy. In July 2014, a report by the homelessness charity Shelter found that nearly two million young adults between the ages of twenty and thirty-four were still living at home with their parents as part of what has been dubbed the 'clipped-wing generation'.[21] There has been a further outcome of these long-term policies which goes beyond the private housing sector. The squeeze on social housing expenditure since the 1980s has increased pressure for more affordable social housing, and one of the 2010–15 Coalition government's responses to this problem has been the introduction of the so-called 'bedroom tax' as a penalty on tenants for residing in council properties which are deemed to have surplus space.[22] The objective of the policy was to encourage these tenants to vacate these properties and move to smaller ones, but only 4.5 per cent of them had downsized within the first six months, while 59 per cent of those affected by the new rules had fallen into arrears with their rent.[23]

Housing wealth is critically associated with location, and

notable in that it distinguishes the metropolis of London from other parts of the UK.[24] This is because housing values depend not simply on the size and state of individual properties; they also reflect the market attractiveness of the neighbourhoods that surround them. Properties in more desirable areas will command higher prices than similar ones in less attractive places, even if there is little physical difference between the actual homes on offer. Therefore, property is inextricably linked to geography and the attractiveness of particular places to live. A home is not just somewhere to lay your head; for the advantaged, it can also be a strategic investment choice.[25]

In recent years local planning policy has adapted to respond to increasing fears of social segregation between the rich and poor in our towns and cities, with requirements for developers to include a proportion of 'affordable' housing in their private housing schemes. In a fascinating example of the techniques some developers will use to ensure the rich and poor are kept apart in such schemes, it was reported in July 2014 that some apartment blocks were now being built with separate lobbies and entrance points for those who could pay market prices as opposed to social tenants.[26] In a city where the extremes of poverty and affluence already lie cheek by jowl, such initiatives are a portentous statement in relation to future trends.

Tables 2.4 and 2.5 show the property values of the top and bottom twenty unitary authorities, using data from the Land Registry. Table 2.4 shows that all the highest values are either within London or in very close proximity to it. Standing out in this regard are the central London boroughs of Kensington

| | RANK | PROPERTY VALUE (£) |
|---|---|---|
| Kensington and Chelsea | 1 | 1,581,747 |
| Westminster | 2 | 1,387,151 |
| Camden | 3 | 808,061 |
| City of London | 4 | 754,138 |
| Hammersmith and Fulham | 5 | 753,911 |
| Elmbridge | 6 | 647,992 |
| Richmond upon Thames | 7 | 646,016 |
| Islington | 8 | 580,041 |
| Wandsworth | 9 | 568,319 |
| South Buckinghamshire | 10 | 532,208 |
| Chiltern | 11 | 501,446 |
| Merton | 12 | 471,566 |
| Southwark | 13 | 455,625 |
| Barnet | 14 | 451,287 |
| Haringey | 15 | 451,050 |
| Windsor and Maidenhead | 16 | 444,132 |
| Kingston upon Thames | 17 | 443,518 |
| Ealing | 18 | 437,209 |
| Waverley | 19 | 435,451 |
| Hackney | 20 | 428,970 |

## Table 2.4

### Property Prices in the most Expensive Unitary Authorities

*Sources:* England and Wales: UK Government Land Registry: Table 581: Mean house prices by district (second quarter, 2013); Scotland: Registers of Scotland, quarterly statistics (second quarter, 2013); Northern Ireland: Northern Ireland Neighbourhood Information Service (NINIS): Average capital values of domestic properties (administrative geographies), 2013.

| | RANK | PROPERTY VALUE (£) |
|---|---|---|
| Knowsley | 367 | 114,814 |
| North-east Lincolnshire | 368 | 114,685 |
| East Ayrshire | 369 | 114,202 |
| North Lanarkshire | 370 | 112,269 |
| Barrow-in-Furness | 371 | 111,190 |
| Rhondda Cynon Taff | 372 | 110,835 |
| Middlesbrough | 373 | 110,764 |
| North Ayrshire | 374 | 110,569 |
| West Dunbartonshire | 375 | 110,219 |
| Bolsover | 376 | 106,657 |
| Pendle | 377 | 105,705 |
| Neath and Port Talbot | 378 | 105,132 |
| Blackpool | 379 | 103,444 |
| Merthyr Tydfil | 380 | 103,066 |
| Kingston upon Hull (city) | 381 | 102,995 |
| Stoke-on-Trent | 382 | 99,281 |
| Hyndburn | 383 | 99,090 |
| Eilean Siar/Western Isles | 384 | 98,446 |
| Burnley | 385 | 83,982 |
| Blaenau Gwent | 386 | 83,437 |

### Table 2.5

### Property Prices in the Cheapest Unitary Authorities

*Sources:* England and Wales: UK Government Land Registry: Table 581: Mean house prices by district (second quarter, 2013); Scotland: Registers of Scotland, quarterly statistics (second quarter, 2013); Northern Ireland: Northern Ireland Neighbourhood Information Service (NINIS): Average capital values of domestic properties (administrative geographies), 2013. Data for Northern Ireland shows annual rather than quarterly valuations; Northern Ireland data (for its five counties and the Belfast metropolitan urban area) is aggregated to the GBCS geographies

and Chelsea and the City of Westminster, where the astronomical property values are a reflection of their status as domiciles for a 'global elite'.[27] The mean values here are £1.5 million, nearly twenty times as much as housing in the cheapest areas. And we can also see how the 'top end' boroughs are outliers, exponentially higher than those beneath them. Values in Kensington and Chelsea are almost twice as much as in third-placed Camden and three times as much as eleventh-ranked Chiltern.

Table 2.5 shows that property of low value is scattered much further afield, with clusters in South Wales and the north of England. These include Port Talbot in South Wales, which was a town once dominated by the mining and steel industries which have more or less collapsed and been subject to major restructuring in recent decades. Blackburn, in the north of England, which has a Muslim population from South Asian countries of 26 per cent, the highest proportion of Muslims from this area outside London, was once the heart of the British cotton textile industry that is now long gone too. The average house value in Knowsley (on Merseyside), is less than 10 per cent of that in Kensington and Chelsea. These are radical differences, which show the interplay between geography and the accumulation of economic capital.

Finally, age itself is associated with one's economic capital. Figure 2.2 depicts the distribution of economic capital by age, and shows a picture of 'relentless accumulation' over the life-course. Figure 2.2 shows clearly how all the different components of economic capital have similar age profiles. Income, savings, and wealth from property are lowest during the mid-twenties and highest in later middle age. Those who

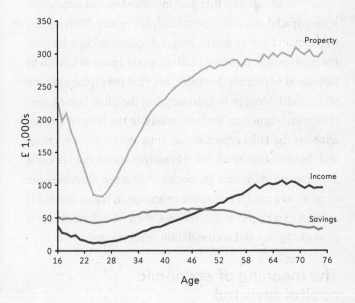

**Figure 2.2**

The distribution of economic capital by age

*Source:* GBCS data

are in their early twenties, even if they are from well-off backgrounds, might not enjoy much economic capital, whereas large groups of those who are thirty years older might see themselves as altogether more advantaged. The acquisition of capital is fundamentally tied up with one's age.

Economic capital is therefore multifaceted, and comes with strong spatial, age and generational differences. With respect to the main housing assets, geographical variation is intense. Parental savings, combined with property assets which can be liquidated as retirees downsize, are vital in helping children and grandchildren go to university, buy their first homes, start their own businesses, and, ultimately, in the form of inheritance. As the Hills report noted, thus 'economic advantage and disadvantage reinforce themselves across the life cycle and often on to the next generation'.[28] Because the possession of economic capital takes time to acquire, it is also inevitably associated with the ageing process, even when inheritance is at work. Ageing and accumulation reinforce each other.

## The meaning of economic capital revisited

We are now in a position to return to our earlier reflections about how people perceive economic inequality. It follows from our argument about the relative significance of wealth compared to income, that people's perceptions of economic inequality might not involve comparing themselves with those in other occupations or forms of employment, but rather with those in different geographical locations or age groups. In this way, the effects of economic capital can be naturalized, so that monetary differences are associated with a range of personal, social and spatial factors which may make them appear 'natural' in the minds of many.[29] And in particular, the amount of time needed to accumulate a high amount of economic capital, especially in absolute terms, explains why people place their situation in the context of their life histories, rather than draw direct 'relational' contrasts with the very wealthy or poor. People thus see their economic fortunes as tied up with their own specific lives, rather than as also the product of global social forces.

Such life experiences might take several forms. Partly, they can be reflections on geographical location. Roger, a lecturer in the north-east of England, had moved away from south London with his family in the late 1980s. Even then, the differences between the capital he had from the sale of his former property and what he was able to buy in the north was considerable, and it was something that he still reflected on twenty-five years later:

> I'm obviously an incomer . . . At the time we were selling
> relatively dear and buying relatively cheap so we were able
> to buy a house . . . So you might have supposed that people
> would resent the fact that here we were, we're rolling up,
> we've done nothing to deserve this apparent wealth
> and luxury.

This sense of dissonance was also felt by Stuart, a retired nurse who had latterly worked as a manager for the local drug and alcohol team in a large, fashionable town on the south coast of England. He had not inherited any wealth personally (although his wife had been given her late mother's flat), but had a decent pension along with his wife's salary. After buying his house for £109,000 in 1992, a similar house down his road had recently sold for £850,000. Stuart was rather bewildered by this situation, calling it 'madness', 'nonsense' and 'bonkers'. He spoke about it with his friends (who had houses worth over half a million pounds), about how weird it was to be in this position, which he saw as a matter of luck. This did mean, however, that Stuart would be able to pass his accumulated wealth on to his adult sons, something that he saw as increasingly necessary:

> We're secure 'cause we've got this property that's worth a huge amount of money, ridiculous amount of money, but where are our kids going to live? I mean, we look at Frank . . . we could look at perhaps having to support him and I'm aware of all that stuff about male children on average stay with their parents now till they're about thirty-six so some are clearly never leaving home, which is an interesting one . . . But at the same time, you know, it makes us very secure and it makes us secure for the kids, and I think the kids appreciate we have that level of security behind us.

In the minds of our respondents, therefore, property was a very important component of economic capital, especially as a form of accumulated wealth that could be passed on to the next generation.

In a similar way, we can see how people with high savings can interpret their lives in terms of their ability to manage their choices and options. Craig, a nightclub security worker, was aware of not overstretching his finances, especially during the recession. He did not carry a credit card and always paid in cash. As with his immigrant parents from the Caribbean, it was important to him that he was able to pay off the mortgage on his house and accumulate some savings too. He was keen to teach his children the value of managing their money well so they put some aside for difficult economic times. Similarly, Monica, a retired teacher, spoke of how she and her husband had made plans for their retirement and that they had money and choices. As she explained, 'Yeah, I think we always kind of wanted to retire at about fifty-five or so, so we saved money for that and we also paid into our pensions obviously . . . I suppose we were fairly moderate while we were working and we did save as much as we could. I mean we did inherit some money when my husband's parents died, so that kind of helped a little bit, quite a bit actually.' People's preoccupations ranged from covering a month or two of mortgage repayments to planning for a long and comfortable retirement. The individuals' different levels of economic capital facilitated very different constraints and opportunities.

A case in point is the effect that gentrification has on local property markets and the cultural and social make-up of cities. Imogen, a bohemian, self-employed rebirthing therapist, lived in a gentrifying area of central London. She had never been wealthy and described her upbringing as a 'struggle', but had taken out a 100 per cent mortgage to buy a flat for £55,000. She now thought that it was worth getting on for £420,000. So, while Imogen had a very modest income (her business had a turnover of £21,000 the previous year), her economic capital tied up in her property had become considerable. One result of this gentrifying trend has been that people buying into Imogen's neighbourhood have had to have much more money that she ever did to be able to do so. It meant that Imogen felt out of step with her more recent neighbours, who 'have so much money'.

People's subjective understandings of class are also influenced by understandings of cultural and social capital, as well as economic capital. People can be 'classy' without necessarily having money, and conversely, having money does not necessarily 'give' you class or make you better than anyone else. We will explore these ideas – that 'everyone is as good as everyone else' – in more depth in Chapter 11, when we look at class identities. Sometimes people use terms such as 'old money' and 'new money' to talk about the differences between people with differing amounts of economic, cultural and social capital:

> You know, you've got, like the royalty and the very rich and the old —, what I call 'old money' and then you've got the new money, which I call the 'common' rich [*laughs*] in my opinion . . . Footballers and that kind of thing and pop stars and, you know, they . . . they come from probably the working class and yet they've got bags of money.

## Is there a new aristocracy?

What does the accumulation of wealth entail? Are we seeing the formation of a new wealth elite? And how similar are those people with high amounts of economic capital? The work of Katharina Hecht offers some powerful indicators here.[30] She has used the GBCS to look at those who have extremely high incomes, savings and wealth, and shown that, as we might expect, there is a strong overlap between them. Seventy-five per cent of those with households earning over £200k also live in a property worth £500k or more. Sixty per cent of these very high earners also have savings of over £200k. This seems a very powerful indication of the strong overlap between these different dimensions at the top end.

In social terms, however, Hecht shows that those with the most economic capital are not always very distinctive: they are only slightly more likely to have degree-level qualifications (whether undergraduate or postgraduate). However, those in households earning over £100k are much more likely to come from traditional professional (nearly twice as likely) and senior managerial (three times as likely) backgrounds, compared to the sample as a whole. These figures appear to demonstrate that those who have the most economic capital do indeed have the most privileged backgrounds. This is an issue we take a closer look at in Chapter 6.

Hecht also shows that the very wealthy tend to have an unusually crisp awareness of themselves as either upper or upper-middle class. The proportion of those earning over £200k who think of themselves as upper class is still only 8.4 per cent – but this is fourteen times the rate for respondents in the GBCS as a whole. Well over half of them think of themselves as upper-middle class, four times the rate in the sample as a whole. They are also marginally more likely to feel they belong to a class than other members of the GBCS. Whereas we have seen that most people feel reluctant to place themselves at the top or bottom of the economic hierarchy, this does not seem to apply as much to those at the very top. Those who are in the most affluent positions do identify as being in the upper-middle, or even upper class. Similarly, those in the highest income brackets, earning over £200k a year, are markedly more likely to know an aristocrat (38 per cent do) compared to 27 per cent of those earning £150k to 199k, and less than 10 per cent of the GBCS sample as a whole. By contrast they are much less likely to know a postal worker. They are three times more likely to go to the opera than those in the sample as a whole and are markedly more likely to go to the gym and the theatre.

Those with the highest levels of economic capital are not only very well off – but they also seem to have distinctive social and cultural characteristics too. Being very well off is also associated with having more exclusive networks, being much more likely to think of themselves as upper-middle or upper class, and being more likely to come from advantaged class backgrounds.

The accumulation of economic capital, therefore, has profound implications for class today. This does not mean that economic inequality translates itself directly into social-class identities or antagonisms. We need to understand these trends sociologically; that is, in more subtle – and in some ways more unsettling – terms. Four main points stand out in conclusion to this chapter.

Firstly, an absolute increase in economic capital goes hand-in-hand with a more complex and elaborate hierarchy of economic positions in the middle ranges of society which clouds over the kinds of boundaries between middle and working classes that we might traditionally have expected to find. The sheer absolute increase in economic capital over the past three decades means that those in the middle are found further apart from those at the top (in particular) and, to a lesser extent, from those at the bottom as well, but also that within any part of the economic hierarchy there is considerable variation. This argument partly repeats the older claims of Max Weber and Pierre Bourdieu on the 'gradational' qualities of economic differences, but there are important twists. Although economic capital may be fuzzy in the middle, it is much more coherently organized at the two extremes: the top and bottom of contemporary society. In the latter case, tenants, often with no savings and with poor incomes, are likely to form a coherent group. At the top end, although there are great differences between the very wealthy and those within the top 1 per cent, the GBCS suggests a strong overlap between the different forms of economic capital – income, savings and house value – which is likely to give some coherence to this group, and also distinctive attitudes and identities. So, we have a picture of growing cohesion at the top and bottom, but within the middle ranks – which are the majority of the population – a much more complicated picture.

Secondly, economic capital is not organized along a unitary occupational axis. For instance, income is not as strongly associated with occupation as we might imagine, so that one cannot make simple judgements about wealth on the basis of employment alone. We have seen how geographical location, family and household situation, and especially, age, are associated with the accumulation of stocks of different kinds of economic capital.

Thirdly, we can only understand economic capital, following Piketty as well as Bourdieu, as the crystallization of long-term forms of accumulation. Being surrounded by stories of bankers and thrusting, dynamic industrialists making quick fortunes on the back of global trading and business takeovers should not blind us to the fact that the main beneficiaries of the accumulation of economic capital are the product of much longer-term historical processes. In every dimension of historical social advantage, the better-off are more closely associated with historically resonant forces: whether those are social (knowing aristocrats); cultural (going to old-fashioned activities, such as the opera), or coming from a senior managerial background. What we see here is how present-day wealth, in the form of economic capital, can best be viewed as the product of long-term investments.

Fourthly, the growing relative proportions (of wealth vis-à-vis income) in people's economic capital might well reduce general awareness of where they stand compared to other people. In a situation where earned income is the main source of economic capital, it is likely that people will be looking to compare themselves with those in other kinds of occupations which are doing better or worse than the ones they are in. That is a world in which class antagonism is directly linked to employment relations. However, when another kind of income or wealth is a bigger component of total wealth, then such relational awareness changes its form, and tends to take on spatial and age-specific dimensions, as people compare themselves with those living in different parts of the country – where house prices are different – and with different generational groups.

# Highbrow and Emerging Cultural Capital

Most people are well aware that economic capital is a resource which they need to get by, and which shapes their lives in fundamental ways. But on the face of it, cultural tastes and interests seem to follow from our personal enthusiasms and don't obviously seem to be an asset which can be accumulated and exchanged. However, for Bourdieu, and for us, the key issue here is whether one's tastes and interests are seen to be *legitimate* – socially approved – and seen as respectable and worthy. For, while there may be limitless types of cultural activity, ranging from gardening through to visiting the British Museum, watching *Big Brother*, or playing computer games, not all are valued *equally*. Some forms carry a cachet that is cultivated and reinforced by influential people and institutions. And, where such forms are legitimate, they can generate resources and advantages.

Traditionally, three factors have cemented a widely shared notion that forms of 'high' culture are more valuable than popular forms. First, what is sometimes called 'high' culture has been deeply promoted by the state. The vast majority of the Arts Council budget, for example, is spent subsidizing 'high' art forms such as theatre, dance and visual art, with only the cryptically titled 'combined arts' representing a funded form of popular culture. This is consistent with the idea that business interests can sustain popular culture (in the form of popular music, for instance), and hence that 'high' culture rises above grubby commercial considerations. Secondly, the value of 'high' culture is also perpetuated by the education system, where arts and humanities subjects such as English literature, music and art history traditionally promote canonized 'high' art forms. It is not possible to take examinations in playing *Grand Theft Auto*, for instance. Finally, the 'high' arts also derive legitimacy from the influence exerted by cultural critics and other taste-makers whose job it is to make very public judgements about the quality of culture, and who largely (although not always) tend to elevate the avant-garde over the popular. What lies behind these observations is the idea that some kinds of cultural taste and activity are a form of *capital*.

## What is cultural capital?

The concept of cultural capital picks up on the fact that our cultural preferences are not only a marker of our personal preferences, but also highly social. When we dress, we want to impress other people. Our passion for certain kinds of music goes hand-in-hand with disparagement of the music that we don't like. This invariably slides into a dislike of the people whom we assume *do* like such music. As the famous German sociologist Georg Simmel pointed out over a hundred years ago, our style of life is therefore deeply social and is a marker of who we want to be, which simultaneously indicates who we do not want to be. We wheel around in social circles which distinguish us from some and align us with others.[1]

This basic insight was elaborated by the French sociologist Pierre Bourdieu into a major statement about the power of what he called 'cultural capital'.[2] He claims that certain kinds of culture have the prospect of generating social advantage and are hence forms of 'capital'. But how does this happen? Bourdieu argued that the appreciation of hallowed forms of music (such as classical music), or the visual arts, depends on valuing their abstract qualities – not seeking immediate indulgence or pleasure, but instead being able to appreciate them 'at a distance', more cerebrally, in a way which permits their application across different contexts. Thus, when roaming in the British Museum, there are no games machines or gimmicks, but instead only 'great' artistic and archaeological exhibits that are seen to have universal status. And by learning to appreciate culture in this abstract way, certain other advantages can be accumulated. It gives access to what Bourdieu calls 'legitimate culture', which is respectable and socially approved, being consecrated in public forums such as museums, galleries and in the educational system. As we have already seen, this goes hand-in-hand with a sense of entitlement and authority. It follows that those steeped in this culture are better placed to understand their school curriculum and are trained in the skills of abstraction, which might help them to get better qualifications which can also be a platform for more successful careers. This might explain, for instance, why it is those with 'analytical skills' whose earnings seem to have increased the most in recent years.[3]

This idea led Bourdieu to claim that in France, in the 1960s, cultural capital involved an appreciation of what has been termed 'highbrow' culture: enjoying art galleries, museums and venerated stately homes, appreciating tasteful literature, classical music, the visual arts and suchlike. And, importantly, for Bourdieu, this set of appreciations involves an opposition to the world of the popular and vulgar. In his hugely important work *Distinction*, Bourdieu studied the tastes of French people in the 1960s to show that there were major cultural divisions between 'intellectuals' and the popular classes. The working classes avoided overtly 'artistic' activities – going to museums or reading classical literature – and preferred 'honest' entertainment and escapism. The well-educated, however, were drawn precisely to these cultural arenas which marked off their status and cultural prowess.

Bourdieu saw cultural capital as not simply a reflection of how much money you had. Within the upper and middle classes he showed that there were important differences between those with more or less cultural capital. He thus contrasted 'industrialists', who might enjoy a lavish display of their money through having expensive holidays or posh cars, with 'intellectuals', who wanted to show their discerning gentility through a tasteful acquisition of antiques.[4] This argument is essential for Bourdieu to claim that cultural capital has its own significance which is different from economic capital.

Our interviewees clearly articulated the power of this cultural capital, though in complex ways. To be blunt, the people we spoke to who had highbrow cultural tastes also had much more cultural confidence, or what the sociologist Shamus

Khan has identified as 'ease'.[5] We were struck by the sense of pride and assurance they exuded. References to favourite works of art, architecture, music and so on abounded, often offhandedly dropped into conversations about entirely unrelated issues. Thus Paul's commute passed by a church 'much admired by [John] Betjeman', whilst Anthony connected professional interests in microbiology to the painting style of Salvador Dali. These remarks were not self-conscious displays of snobbery, but instead signalled the ease with which these more privileged people were able to deploy cultural reference points in casual conversation.

Such striking conviction was also evident in the way respondents linked their cultural interests to the public domain. Charlotte, for example, a retired maths teacher, explained that one of her interests was food, and specifically making jam. Making jam is not unusual, but what was striking was the way Charlotte had developed this hobby. Rather than just making jam for her own family, she had decided many years ago to start selling her jam at craft fairs. Underlying this decision was an unwavering belief in her own taste. 'I get a lot of fun out of it, but I suppose I'm also on a one-woman crusade to show the world what proper food should taste like!' she told us, before explaining how her hobby had even extended into publication of books on jam-making: 'One of my daughters stood there one day looking at my stall, and said, "Mother, you can't die and take all this [knowledge] with you." And yes, so I've written two books [on jam] now.'

This distinctive self-assurance was also evident in our discussion with Fraser, a retired primary-school headteacher.

Fraser was a prodigious cultural enthusiast, with strong interests in opera and classical music. But what was particularly significant was the way Fraser had attempted to disseminate his cultural interests during his professional life. At various points in our interview he described how he had deliberately 'inflicted' his taste on his pupils in an attempt to 'broaden their horizons'. Yet despite using the word 'inflict', Fraser was unapologetic about this practice of culture-pushing. Here he describes his routine of playing classical music while the children were filing into morning assembly:

> I never felt guilty about it. The best example was when I was a class teacher and we had a new child who the parents had moved from a pub in [northern England], where he had been bullying kids. He was a big thickset lad, Michael – you remember the names. So I had a word with him and said, 'Michael, you can't do that, we don't do that in this school.' And I was doing a lesson on beauty and I had pictures of Sophia Loren and all sorts and I said, 'I'll now play you a bit of music which I think is beautiful,' and it was Tortelier playing 'The Swan' on the cello. And Michael is sitting crying. I said, 'What's the matter?' 'I've never heard anything so lovely in my life,' he said. I've never forgotten that. Again that was me inflicting my taste on the kids, but that's the impact you can have.

What is striking here is Fraser's remarkable belief in the innate and redemptive qualities of his highbrow cultural tastes. His were not only a set of private passions, but also part of a social concern to spread good taste more widely. To put this in another way, culture becomes a wider social currency in which people differentiate between those with it, and those without it – and who could do with more of it. Rather like money . . .

Yet, though it seems clear that cultural tastes carry with them a loaded set of signifiers, we also need to be cautious about relying on Bourdieu's concept too closely today.[6] This is for four reasons. Firstly, Bourdieu's criticisms of 'elitist' culture hit home, to the extent that it has generated worries among those working in the arts themselves in relation to their role as cultural policy-makers. Cultural institutions have themselves become much more aware of their own elitism and snobbery and have taken steps to counteract these things. Museums and galleries are now full of interactive devices to facilitate more accessible forms of visitor engagement and to encourage children to enjoy museums even if they are not used to them. Entry to the major national museums is free. There is more effort to show off a wider diversity of cultural works, rather than just those of the 'great old men'. There are now, for instance, museums of football, sex and rock music. The National Trust does not only look after grand aristocratic homes, but also displays Glasgow tenement houses, the family homes of John Lennon and Paul McCartney and old industrial factories.

Secondly, we now live in a much more intensely 'cultural' world. When Bourdieu conducted his surveys for *Distinction* only half of French households had television sets, and certainly no computers, smartphones or iPads. Just as we have seen the absolute increase in economic capital, so the sheer volume and availability of art, literature, music, film and television has risen sharply. Perhaps the proliferation of media devices over the past four decades has made all cultural forms more accessible? Do we still live in an age of such marked cultural divisions compared to the era when you could only hear opera by actually going to an opera house? Is it still elitist to like opera when people can now freely download opera music on Spotify even if they can't afford to go to Covent Garden?

Thirdly, we have also seen the rise of a whole series of cultural activities which don't seem 'highbrow'. A good example would be stand-up comedy, which has moved from being a marginal and largely disparaged taste, to being a mainstream of entertainment, via the Edinburgh Festival or primetime TV.[7] Aren't there key style icons who have little or no cultural capital in the way that Bourdieu talks about it? What about David Beckham, the upwardly mobile lad from Essex, who has defined new standards of masculine style over the past twenty years, but hardly on the basis of highbrow cultural capital?

Fourthly, in recent decades cultural appreciation has been massively transformed by globalization and flows of immigration which have eroded the appeal and significance of older classical forms of culture which used to be held up as the markers of national excellence. We are no longer so much in thrall to specifically national beacons defining the boundaries of legitimate taste, ranging from the Royal Opera House to the National Theatre. It has become 'cool' – up to a point – to be interested in black culture.[8] Where, if at all, do world music, jazz, bhangra and reggae fit in the hierarchies of today? Isn't it rather old fashioned to just be interested in Shakespeare, Austen and Britten these days?

Our research, drawing also on numerous other studies conducted on cultural capital in recent years, allows us to present the most comprehensive account of cultural capital in Britain today.

# The primary cultural divide: engagement

The GBCS endorses the view – consistent with numerous other recent studies[9] – that cultural capital can still very much be found today, but that it has changed its form. We can reveal these patterns most easily by reporting the results of a 'cultural "capital" mapping' exercise.[10] This analysis takes a wide number of different cultural activities and tastes and considers which of them *are most rarely done together*. This is telling because if some activities, such as going to the opera, are hardly ever done with some other specific activity, such as playing darts, they might reveal clear cultural oppositions which could be a sign that these activities are organized hierarchically.

Figure 3.1 is a summary, revealing which cultural practices lie in opposition to each other most directly. These are not to be seen as simple pairings, but more as two 'families' of orientations standing in opposition to each other. This having been said, the item in the first row is the most 'loaded' cultural activity, the one which is least likely to be done in combination with those activities listed in the other column. Before interpreting Figure 3.1, readers are invited to reflect on whether either column is more socially respectable than the other. The principles of the cultural mapping should

| CULTURAL ORIENTATIONS: FAMILY A | CULTURAL ORIENTATIONS: FAMILY B |
| --- | --- |
| Liking fish and chips | Going to the theatre |
| Eating out rarely | Going to the opera, ballet and classical music concerts |
| Not going to restaurants | Going to museums and art galleries |
| Not liking pop music | Going to the gym |
| Disliking Indian food | Going to rock gigs |
| Not going out with friends | Playing sport |
| Disliking jazz | Going to arts clubs |
| Disliking world music | Liking French and Italian restaurants |
| Not going for a walk | Watching live sport |
| Disliking reggae music | Liking world music |

## Table 3.1

### Primary Cultural Oppositions[1] in the UK

*Source:* Derived from multiple correspondence analysis of GfK (nationally representative) data.
1. The ten activities/tastes listed contribute the most to the variance on the first axis, with those activities contributing most to this variance listed in the top row

mean that it is likely your choice of activities will fall into one of these columns or another, rather than finding that you have equal numbers of items from both columns.

Perhaps the most striking difference between these two columns is that on the right-hand side the orientations involve actively going out into the public world of cultural institutions, restaurants, music and sports venues, whereas the left-hand side reveals an aversion to these public activities. Affiliated to this division, those who find themselves in the right-hand column are active and engaged – in music, the arts, theatre – whilst those who find themselves in the left-hand column have aversions to music and eating out. Our suggestion is that most readers would see the orientations on the right-hand side as more socially approved of – more legitimate – than those on the left-hand side – indicating the subtle social pressures and assumptions at work.

The findings from Figure 3.1 are in fact similar to those which have been found in other studies and they suggest a strong cultural divide between those publicly engaged in what Bourdieu might term 'legitimate' culture, which is socially approved of and supported, against those who abstain from it.[11] But it is also important for us to realize that this divide does not differentiate between 'highbrow' and 'popular' activities. In fact, on the right-hand side we can see some highbrow activities (going to art galleries and museums) interspersed with more popular and commercial activities, such as going to the gym and to rock gigs, and liking world music.

So, are these differences in Figure 3.1 symptomatic of a kind of cultural capital? There is in fact a very clear divide according to income and education. Those who earn the highest income and who are well-educated tend to have the cultural tastes listed in the right-hand column whilst those with much lower qualification levels and income tend to have preferences in the left-hand column. This is a stark indication that cultural divisions *do* map on to fundamental social divisions. It is not simply a private matter if you like going to (for instance) the British Museum or not. It also indicates how much of a foothold you have in legitimate and socially approved culture.

Most of the activities in column B demand considerable amounts of money, and this is true whether attending ballet or going to rock gigs. All the activities in column A demand little or no money. Those with more money and good educational qualifications are much more extensively involved across a range of leisure pursuits compared to those without these resources. How do we understand these patterns as a form of cultural capital? We are not implying that those who are less well-off and have few qualifications have no cultural interests, or simply sit passively at home all day. Rather, their cultural engagement is likely to be more informal, more neighbourhood-and-kinship-based, and is hence less likely to be something based around particular leisure activities such as going to a museum.[12] However, for those who are highly educated and better-off, attending such formal activities can become associated with a sense of being active and engaged, adding to their cultural confidence and assertiveness. This takes us back to the worlds of Charlotte and Fraser, whom we met at the start of this chapter: confident, assured, engaged in public cultural life, in the kind of activities which are also visible and respectable. By contrast, the lifestyles of those on the left-hand side, being largely conducted privately or in the close bosom of family and friends, have less of a public profile. Hence, without anyone necessarily intending it, the cultural differences revealed in Figure 3.1 are nonetheless likely to convey rather different sets of legitimacy and lend themselves to different kinds of opportunities.

Contrast the cultural confidence of Fraser and Charlotte with that of Imogen, a freelance rebirthing specialist based in south London. Unlike Fraser and Charlotte, Imogen had not been to university. She was from a working class background and earned less than £20,000 a year. She did not make lots of offhand comments about her cultural interests, and in fact seemed to be rather inactive. She rarely went to art galleries and museums, she didn't play sport, go to the pub or eat out, and she didn't listen to classical music or opera. Yet, in fact, Imogen was not culturally disengaged. Far from it. It was partly that Imogen's more informal and 'alternative' cultural interests fell outside the categories we asked about in the survey. She practised yoga, was interested in salsa and tango dancing and talked at length about her interests in colour consultancy as an alternative to 'normal' fashion. Nonetheless, although Imogen was very enthusiastic about her cultural interests, she clearly lacked the kind of confidence exhibited by Fraser and Charlotte. Indeed, when we first introduced the topic of 'cultural taste' during the interview, Imogen's instinctive reaction was to do herself down. 'Well it's one of my limits, it's possibly a weakness, I'm not someone informed, and sometimes I think I suffer [from this].'

The key issue at stake, then, between people like Imogen and those like Fraser and Charlotte, was their differing degree of conviction in the *legitimacy* of their own cultural activities. This comes out when reflecting on people's confidence and assuredness, as revealed in what our interviewees said about the idea of 'good taste'. Those with fewer educational credentials and on lower salaries were markedly more tentative about what good taste was, even when they had a lot of keen cultural interests. Pauline, an antiques dealer, was a case in point. Pauline's house was a veritable treasure trove of culture. She had a red telephone box in her front garden, a gypsy caravan in the back garden, and her house was packed to the rafters with porcelain busts, vintage advertisements and other antiques. She even had a tuk-tuk taxi shipped over from Thailand, which now sat jostling for space among the other unusual objects in her living room. Yet despite spending her working life surrounded by cultural artefacts, Pauline nonetheless rejected the idea that she had good taste. Like many others from modest backgrounds, she viewed her taste as a personal matter, random almost, and certainly not, like Fraser, something to inflict upon others. In fact, she seemed acutely aware that her taste might be seen as 'sentimental', 'over the top' or lacking minimalist sophistication. 'It's the sort of thing you either love or hate. I mean, if you like what I like you'll enjoy it, but if you like everything minimalistic you'll find it horrendous to come and see all these things.'

Pauline's uncertain attitude stood in sharp contrast to those in more privileged social positions. These respondents were certain they had 'good taste'. As George, a lobbyist, told us: 'I think it's probably a bit false to say that there's just different "types" of taste because I think there is some objective level [to good taste].' Pushed further on what such 'objective' good taste looked like, he (like many) settled on the idea of discernment, about making the 'right' choices about what you consume. George continued: 'I would say it certainly requires a level of understanding, that a judgement's based on some evidence rather than just saying "Yeah, that's good" without having thought about it.'

The significance of this cultural divide is therefore associated with legitimacy, confidence and ease. Substantial numbers of people – those who choose the activities on the left-hand side of Figure 3.1 – are not engaged in activities which are prominent and legitimate in wider society, and are less likely to be webbed into wider networks of 'like-minded' people, as well as public approbation and recognition. In contrast, we can see that the cultural capital accumulated by those whose activities fall on the right-hand side of the table comes not just from doing and consuming particular forms of culture, but from the sense of confidence that seems to flow from this participation. As our interviews illustrated, such familiarity with formal, 'legitimate' and often state-sponsored culture seemed to breed a striking sense of certainty in the 'right' to speak about *cultural value*, to ordain what is and what isn't good taste, and then to communicate this conviction in public.

# The secondary cultural divide: highbrow versus 'emerging' cultural capital

There is more to our cultural mapping, however, than this one contrast alone. We can also detect other, secondary but still powerful oppositions. Figure 3.2 reveals this second set of oppositions, over and above those revealed in Figure 3.1. The lists here are intriguing and readers are also invited to reflect on whether one column reveals activities which are more socially approved of than the other.

What Figure 3.2 shows: on the right-hand side we see a liking for going to stately homes, museums and art galleries, and the theatre, and preferences for ballet, opera and classical music, as well as a disliking for rap, reggae, pop and rock music. These are indeed all consistent with a form of 'highbrow' taste, which we can also see goes along with a disliking of aspects of contemporary music. This is much as Bourdieu argued in *Distinction*, even though his study is thirty years old.

In the left-hand column, by contrast, we can see a range of activities which show indifference to highbrow activities (such as listening to classical and jazz music) and the embracing of fast food, vegetarianism, rap, Spanish holidays and sport.

We would expect that readers will be more divided about which column they think is more legitimate than they would be in relation to the primary axis of cultural division shown in the previous figure (3.1). Older readers would probably

| CULTURAL ORIENTATIONS: FAMILY C | CULTURAL ORIENTATIONS: FAMILY D |
| --- | --- |
| Liking fast food | Going to the opera, ballet and classical music concerts |
| Liking rap music | Disliking pop music |
| Being indifferent to classical music | Going to stately homes |
| Being indifferent to heavy metal music | Going to the theatre |
| Not going for a walk | Liking classical music |
| Liking vegetarian restaurants | Going to museums and art galleries |
| Being indifferent to jazz music | Disliking reggae music |
| Playing sport | Disliking rap music |
| Taking holidays in Spain | Not going to fast-food restaurants |
| Watching live sport | Disliking rock music |

Table 3.2

Secondary Cultural Oppositions in the UK

*Source*: Derived from a multiple correspondence analysis upon nationally representative data for the GBCS (conducted by the market-research company GfK)

feel that the right-hand column is clearly more prestigious, but younger readers might be less sure. Indeed, our further analysis shows that these differences do map on to a stark age division, with younger people tending to have the tastes listed in the left-hand column (Family C) and older people in the right-hand column (Family D). This age gap is ore profound and significant than Bourdieu realized, but seems strongly etched into contemporary British culture.

What this indicates, then, is a picture of cultural differences which have a very direct generational, as well as class-based, dimension. The kinds of highbrow activities discussed by Bourdieu are now predominantly associated with older Britons, those who are middle-aged and above. This finding is corroborated by ample other evidence about how enthusiasm for classical music is becoming a more age-based phenomenon. The average age of listeners to BBC Radio 3 is now sixty-two. Looking at attendees at classical music concerts and ballets, one is confronted by a predominantly elderly audience. Listening to hip-hop music, however, is very different.

Our point here is that these oppositions are not neutral 'lifestyle choices', but are also hierarchical in the way they differentiate from each other. And we are especially interested in the power of the age division among the well-educated. The younger middle class generation are highly engaged – in the world of contemporary music, computer games, the social media and sport – but are much less active in the world of 'highbrow' culture. Their passions lie elsewhere. This seems a striking shift compared to their older peers. This leads us to argue that there are two modes of cultural capital, one which we term 'highbrow' and the other 'emerging'. The former is more established. It is historically sanctioned and institutionalized in the educational system, via art galleries and museums and such like – but it is also an ageing mode of cultural capital. We are witnessing the rise of a kind of 'hip' (or hipster) cultural capital associated with younger people. It too has its own infrastructure – social media, and in the bar, club and sporting scene, and might also be seen to be institutionalized in new professional workplaces and lifestyles which emphasize the ability to be flexible and adaptable. This is a kind of 'emerging' cultural capital which could become more powerful in the coming years.

This significance of age in relation to cultural capital is in contrast with economic capital. We saw in Chapter 2 that there is a systematic tendency for higher amounts of economic capital to be concentrated among the old. Young people have rarely had the chance to accumulate massive amounts of income and savings, or to have accrued assets in their housing. However, with respect to cultural capital, younger people are not obviously disadvantaged compared with their elders: a higher proportion of young people have been to university and enjoyed advanced education, and, as we have seen, they also partake extensively in emerging cultural capital and are highly engaged. What we see, however, is a generational clash between the forms of cultural capital.

And, indeed, our interviews shed light on how cultural capital in Britain is changing. Among older generations of the privileged the traditional divide between high and low culture discussed by Bourdieu has retained an important significance. For example, Nigel, a sixty-year-old scientist, described the fact that he doesn't have a television in his house. This is very much a conscious decision, he told us, born out of the fact that there's 'nothing ever on it!' This blanket rejection of popular media was also echoed by others like Fiona and Alison, who described similar aversions to tabloid newspapers, Facebook and electronic or rap music. Yet the drawing of such sharp boundaries was relatively rare, even among the older interviewees. Most were keen to demonstrate the *eclectic* nature of their taste and to thus proclaim themselves as cultural egalitarians.

In recent years a number of sociologists, particularly those working in the USA, have found that those in high social positions increasingly enjoy both high and popular culture. They have subsequently proclaimed the rise of the 'cultural omnivore' and have argued that this confirms the beginning of the end for the traditional cultural hierarchy. We are now entering an era characterized, they argue, by increasing cultural tolerance where the new currency of 'cool' is an explicit rejection of snobbery and a celebration of diversity.[13]

This is a long way from what we think is happening. For those we talked to, the ethos of eclecticism did not necessarily imply cultural openness. Certainly, we were struck by the effortlessness with which the wealthy and better-educated talked about their interests in a broad range of cultural activities. But at the same time there was a distinctive *knowingness* to this engagement, particularly in terms of making reference to popular culture. Taste in these areas was often highly intricate and discerning. Even Fraser, whom we met at the start of this chapter, expressed a preference for pop music and some Hollywood films amid his gamut of largely highbrow interests. However, Fraser was keen to point out that these were reserved only for certain 'obscure' artists, the reasons for liking each of them were meticulously explained and thereby shown to be compatible with his more highbrow interests. Popular culture was acceptable when its relevance could be justified. Whereas Fraser's preferences for classical composers like Phillip Glass and Shostakovich were named nonchalantly and without further explanation, the aesthetic capacity of Diana Ross or *Gladiator* needed immediate validation. Popular cultural consumption was also not always about simple enjoyment. Elizabeth read the *Daily Mail* not because she liked it, but in order 'to know what most people in Britain are reading'. Similarly, Georgia described a 'weird fascination with pop music' which was more ironic and playful than sincere.

Emerging cultural capital is therefore not about liking popular culture per se, but rather demonstrating one's skill in manoeuvring between the choices on the menu, and displaying one's careful selection of particular popular artists; through one's ability to pick, choose and combine the 'very best' of popular culture. Moreover, this type of popular discernment was not just about *what* you like, but *why* you like it. For example, Benedict, an IT consultant, seemed at first to be a classic cultural omnivore. He had strong interests in traditional high art – particularly visual art and literature – but was notably more animated when discussing his taste for pop music. Here his taste was incredibly selective. He strongly rejected the 'overly produced', 'formulaic' and 'commercial' pop music of the charts and instead explained at length his interests in 'indie', 'post-punk' and 'electronica'. He was unapologetic about having a 'pop sensibility', but at the same time was clearly looking for a certain type of popular music, where there was a 'combination of originality *and* familiarity', or which was both 'conventional' but also 'a little unhinged'. The 'perfect example' of this complex aesthetic match, he explained, was the American synthpop band Future Islands:

> It's fairly conventional, but the singer's got a very unusual vocal style, he's really odd. When I first heard him I actually hated him, thought, 'That's bloody ridiculous – he sounds like a crooning French academic.' He's got these two registers, falsetto and quite deep, but at the same time just enough of a normal pop sensibility.

Especially among the younger generation, for the better-off and well-educated, then, no art form or cultural activity was out of bounds. Anything was possible to like, though in championing it, it was necessary to be able to explain why it was enjoyable, through recognizing the different taste registers at play.[14]

This openness was also paradoxically exhaustingly selective. Every cultural option must be weighed up and a set of aesthetic principles applied in order to assess quality and value. Thus George (a lobbyist) valued Twitter more highly than Facebook because it contributed to a more 'meaningful intellectual conversation' and Georgia (a communications director) thinks Detroit house music is 'far superior' to drum 'n' bass. The point here is not so much the similarities in exactly what popular culture these people valued or liked, but more the manner in which it was expressed. Nothing escapes critical scrutiny. As Benedict explained, 'It's about making a choice in almost any situation. We don't like fast food, but we would choose Burger King over McDonald's – we still exercise choice even at the low end, you know?'

This performance of emerging cultural capital is best summed up with Henry, a nineteen-year-old law student from the most privileged background of all the people in our study. Throughout his interview, Henry proudly outlined the range of his cultural interests, from game-shooting in rural Cheshire to watching stand-up comedy in Edinburgh. Attempting to drive home his omnivorous credentials, at one point Henry pulled out his iPod to show us his 'recent[ly] played [music]'. 'So we have everything here,' he said proudly. 'From Phil Collins to Puccini, Deep Purple, Jay-Z – there's no cohesion at all, it's such a broad church.' Henry thus moved effortlessly from the elite to the popular, refusing to create fences and eagerly engaging with a broad range of tastes. But again there was a clear knowingness to this playlist. Some music tastes were described as 'ironic', some 'obscure', some just 'hopelessly poppy'. And what was perhaps more important was what Henry did with this knowing taste, how it informed his everyday life. In particular, we were struck by how Henry connected music to his social network. Every night in his halls of residence the main topic of conversation was culture. 'So it's about always having material to add to that discussion,' he explained, 'whatever that is.'

Herein lies the power of emerging cultural capital. This may be expressed by consuming the 'right' kind of pop culture, legitimate pop, so to speak, but equally it may be about consuming the 'wrong kind' of (vulgar) pop culture in the *right* way. You only have to think of the image of the contemporary 'hipster', for example, whose tastes are a veritable assemblage of 'ironic' and 'kitsch' cultural consumption, to get a sense of what the successful execution of this emerging capital may look like in practice.[15] In any case what is most central here is a particular style of aesthetic appreciation, a certain detached, knowing orientation to popular culture that demonstrates both an eclectic knowledge and a privileged understanding.

## Ways of Seeing

Cultural capital does not simply involve pointing to differences in cultural activity between various kinds of people. Market researchers routinely profile consumer products by noting that they appeal to different 'segments' of the market. We also need to see how such activities might be valued in different ways, with some being seen as more legitimate, while others are denigrated. This is where we can observe a telling difference between the way some activities were seen as discerning, while others were seen as immediate and sensuous.

Discernment involves the ability to range across genres and activities, being able to come to judgements rapidly, and being able to justify these. These are skills which are increasingly instilled in education and valued in fast-moving professional and corporate work environments. But these are not neutral skills – they operate as a form of cultural capital because they also denigrate other kinds of orientation. When we conducted our interview we found that there was also an inherent suspicion of more immediate, sensual reactions. It wasn't that these respondents didn't report such experiences, but more that they were framed as 'guilty pleasures', exceptions to the rule, when, as Paul noted, 'you're knackered and your energies are dissipated'. These confessions of guilty pleasure were revealing. The overriding idea here was that one should have to 'work at' appreciating culture, and that through carrying out this aesthetic labour it was possible to reach a higher level of appreciation. As Elizabeth concluded, 'I don't just want to consume, I want to be stretched.'

This way of seeing is important because it can be directed, implicitly or explicitly, against those who are less well-off and who have less formal education. For such respondents cultural enjoyment was not something that needed labour or detachment, or which required a display of judgement. On the contrary, culture was there to be completely and unapologetically immersed in, for instance, as a kind of escapism which allowed you 'time out'. Imogen, for example, explained her interaction with dance, music and fashion as fundamentally about 'celebration', with pleasure as the main goal. Similarly, Jane's passion for soap operas was related directly to her ability to 'connect' emotionally with the characters. 'Well, it's life, isn't it, it's about life,' she told us before explaining her bond to a character in *Coronation Street*, who had, like her, recently been diagnosed with Alzheimer's.

This way of seeing could also be used against those working class respondents who reported consuming highbrow culture, but possibly not in a 'discerning' way. Tina, for example, a factory worker and adult carer, had well-developed interests in ballet, theatre and classical music. However, the style of appreciation remained telling. What was intriguing about Tina was that her appreciation of highbrow culture remained quite different from that of those from more privileged backgrounds. Tina didn't talk much about what she 'got' from ballet or theatre, but instead simply described an insatiable, autodidactic thirst for cultural knowledge. She was thus more interested in collecting new experiences than in developing an aesthetic account of her interests.

Tina's example shows that even though highbrow culture is not confined to the well educated, subtle differences in how it is enjoyed can become axes upon which snobbery might be exercised. In some cases, there was actually a clear rejection of the highbrow academic aesthetic, which was recognized to be socially differentiating. Alan, a chemical salesman, was from a working class background and had a degree in communications from a new university. Interestingly, though, Alan was ambivalent about his degree. Not only had it 'not really helped' his career, but he had also rejected the more abstract ways of evaluating culture that the academy had tried to encourage:

> I don't think it's the case that it's above me; 'I'm incapable of liking that', sort of thing. It's just something that doesn't really interest me. In terms of highbrow film, I studied

it a lot at uni so I've watched *Battleship Potemkin* and all that sort of thing. And, you know, some of them were OK, but I think by the end of my course I got programmed into analysing them rather than watching them, to the point that after that I kind of . . . I just want something to just entertain me, something I can kind of switch off to.

Snobbery is therefore being redrawn alongside cultural capital itself. As forms of culture which used to be restricted to the educated middle classes actually filter down to wider sections of the population, the dividing lines are being redrawn so that it is *how* specific cultural activities are enjoyed which matters. It is now a badge of honour for the well educated to *refrain* from being overtly 'snobby', and distinctions are more subtle – but all the more powerful for this.

## Cultural Snobbery

People in higher class positions usually distance themselves from any suspicion of snobbery. There was an explicit awareness that talking about taste could inadvertently imply snobbery or judgement and most therefore qualified their preferences with disclaimers such as 'I don't mean this in a snobby way . . .' or 'I know this might sound snobby, but . . .'. This self-conscious rejection of snobbery also frequently went hand in hand with the assertion of cultural eclecticism described earlier in this chapter. 'I would never ever condemn other people's taste,' Fraser told us. 'If it's their taste, it's their taste, live and let live I always say.'

Yet despite this apparent laissez-faire attitude, people

frequently contradicted themselves on the issue of snobbery. Fraser was a case in point. Having just told us that he would 'never condemn' the taste of others, he then went on the offensive about, first, bingo-goers ('It's not sort of an intellectually absorbing pastime – other than if you're a greedy person and hope to win') and, second, those who dislike opera ('I feel sorry for them because if you don't appreciate the beauty of something like opera, you're missing out in life').

This type of brazen contradiction is surprisingly common. It was as if people felt that as long as their judgements were expressed towards a lifestyle, rather than directly to a person who belonged to a certain 'type', this made it more socially acceptable. Such aesthetic judgements were often directed toward particular art forms, genres or artists that were seen as inherently deficient. Reality television and TV talent shows were frequently mentioned, as were certain pop artists and cultural activities like bingo. Aesthetically, this kind of popular culture was seen as 'banal', 'mundane', 'obvious' or lacking in 'substance'. As Elizabeth summed up chick lit – 'It just lacks a raison d'être!' Another common arena for drawing boundaries was fashion, which was often the focus of discussions of 'bad taste'. Here the issue of 'branding' was key. For the better-educated, heavily branded clothes were 'naff' and 'gaudy'. As Georgia, a communications director, outlines:

> I've got friends in Essex and they're quite into labels
> and to them that's status. Now I'm into labels too, but
> I'd like people to know because they know the designer,
> not because I've got a great big logo on it. I don't like

the obvious. If you've got it, you shouldn't have to shout about it.

Underpinning this dislike for 'logos' and 'branding' was a wider dislike for culture that was seen as mass produced, 'lowest common denominator', its creative potential contaminated by the homogenizing effect of the free market. Yet what was also striking about these judgements was that although people started with cultural objects, they often unwittingly moved on to particular types of people. For example, Fiona felt that audiences for reality TV or pop music somehow lacked the ability to make autonomous decisions about their taste and therefore were somehow co-opted or duped into consuming:

> I would say there are people who look for originality and tend to cherry-pick things and put them together in a way that's their own, whereas on the other side there is [sic] people who buy mass-produced things because they think – that's what they've been told to do without actually thinking.

Cultural snobbery often extended beyond aesthetic judgement into the realm of personhood. Our wealthier and better-educated respondents often considered cultural tastes as powerful indicators of pathological identities, expressing a tangible sense of contempt and even disgust. Taste was thus a crucial way to judge the 'worth' of others. Such judgements invariably appeared towards the end of interviews, when people were feeling more relaxed and began to let their guard down. Among countless instances, here we focus on two examples: first, Paul discussed his frustrations with the 'phil-istines' at his local walking club:

> There's a bit of – contempt is too strong a word. People who've never taken the trouble to look at the best in things, because that's what it's about, if people just take the easy way out and just listen to whatever's on. But that's a bit priggish really, isn't it? But you can't sort of entirely eradicate these character traits, can you? And that's who we're happy with, people who appreciate the better things. And it's all about choices, isn't it? . . . if income isn't limitless, and for most people it isn't.

Benedict the IT consultant spoke at length about multiple dislikes – for TV shows like *X-Factor*, soap operas, celebrity, even fake tan. Asked what united these things Benedict thought for a moment and settled on the idea of 'bad choices':

> *Benedict*: There is this saying that you should never judge on appearance; actually, I think you should always judge on appearance. Because people haven't arrived there by accident, it's not like the colour of your skin. Everything else they have completely chosen, so I would always completely judge people.
>
> *Questioner*: What do you think you're judging them on?
>
> *Benedict*: I suppose it's a lazy default. Yeah, what gets me about that is that it's the lazy default. In other words, they're just being . . . it's more than influenced. What they're doing is being determined by things outside of themselves, so the external pressures of the market, of

media, I suppose the money culture, in a way. So all of those things that we've described there, it's people who are submitting really to the default thing. So the judgement is on people's thoughtlessness.

It is therefore pervasive to appeal to sophistication, plural and flexible tastes and so forth as a means of differentiating people from those with unitary or simple tastes. This is a new class snobbery that is pervasive, even if not overt.

Cultural activities, therefore, are not simply private enthusiasms, but bring with them social baggage. Some people are energized by modes of cultural consumption which bring them into contact with others, and which empower them. Such people also tend to be aware of the 'legitimacy' of their activities and see them as being appropriate to 'inflict' on others. Others, by contrast, may be culturally active, but may nonetheless feel disempowered and unconfident.

Our argument in this chapter has been simple. 'Old style' – what we have called 'highbrow' – cultural capital is still very much with us, but is increasingly confined to an older age group. But we can also detect a new kind of 'emerging' cultural capital. Here, it is the fast-moving, hip and fashionable that counts. This is in an intense world, fuelled by media coverage, where interests, enthusiasms and excitements multiply and bounce off each other with great intensity. And, as we explained in Chapter 1, it is precisely this milieu which explains the appeal of the BBC's Great British Class Survey itself, the massive public take-up to which testifies to the ongoing fascination which the topic of class still has in Britain today.

Processes of accumulation therefore work differently with respect to cultural capital compared with economic capital. Rather than replicating the acute generational gap in which younger people tend to have much less economic capital than their parents, younger people have their own kind of distinctive cultural capital which jostles with that of their elders. This can betoken a cultural confidence and assertiveness. And indeed, this kind of emerging cultural capital embodies new kinds of sophistication. It is marked less in terms of the actual activities people enjoy, but more in the way that they enjoy them, and talk about them. And in this respect, whilst appearing critical of the snobbery which might be seen as latent in 'highbrow' culture, it also embeds its own subtle forms of hierarchy, as we discuss further in later chapters of this book.

# CHAPTER 4

# Social Capital

NETWORKS AND PERSONAL TIES

We do not need to be reminded about the significance of social networks in our lives. Many of us use social media which allows us contact with people at a tap of a phone. We meet and socialize with people at work, in our neighbourhoods, in following our leisure interests, and many of us have an extensive range of family ties. On the face of it, these networks allow us to meet a range of people, and many of us pride ourselves on having contacts from all walks of life. Yet despite this apparent democratic potential, social capital also has an exclusive character which benefits those in the most advantaged situations.

Many of our interviewees were all too familiar with this ambivalent aspect of our social ties. One of them explained that he comes into contact with all kinds of people, including millionaires, as part of his work in security, and said, 'I've got friends that [have . . . ] got their own business as a solicitor and stuff like that.' However, he then went on to say that he 'never had a lot friends that were white-collar workers' and that the people he mostly socializes with were:

manual workers, yeah. 'Cause I'm a manual worker myself [. . .] You know, work hard, do what we have to do, and but on percentage we try to meet up every now and again and have a good time, you know. [ . . .] And that's as life's gone on [. . .], you get on really well, with manual workers.

At the other end of the social ladder, Fraser, the retired head-teacher, was keen to let the interviewer know that one of his closest friends 'came from what you would call a real working class background', and had had to 'leave school before he did A-levels 'cause his father said, "You have to get a job."' But he was also very keen to make it clear that this friend was not (stereo-)typically working class. He said: 'You would call him working class if you had any sort of survey, but he's the brightest working class person you will ever see, let's put it like that.' He went on to describe hobnobbing with politicians, business leaders and even being selected to represent his area in a luncheon with the Queen.

These kinds of accounts exemplify the new snobbery we talked about in Chapter 3. It is not the 'done thing' to say that you only mix with certain kinds of people – this might mark you as limited and aloof – or vulgar. But this does not mean that people are as genuinely democratic as they might think. And in fact, people are also aware that their contacts are not socially random and that there are strategic values in knowing certain kinds of people. This generates a kind of 'knowing' and 'reflexive' awareness which is consistent with the 'emerging cultural capital' we unravelled in Chapter 3.

The most widely known application of the concept of social capital is explained by the American political scientist

Robert Putnam in his book *Bowling Alone*. Putnam has the benevolent view that when people are collectively engaged, when they join clubs and have extensive social networks, then the social fabric as a whole is itself stronger.[1] His arguments feed into policy endeavours across numerous nations to build social capital through encouraging civic engagement, and there is considerable evidence that they do foster better health and wellbeing.[2] British Prime Minister David Cameron's advocacy for the 'Big Society', or that we need to support 'sustainable communities', draws on these motifs.

Bourdieu's concept of social capital is different from Putnam's view, however. Rather than seeing social networking as benefiting society in general, he sees it as a means of allowing the privileged and powerful to use their connections to help each other and protect their interests – and thereby shut out those who lack such social capital. Of course, this idea is also familiar to us. We are well aware of how the rich and powerful can 'look after their own'. For example, one of our respondents told us how her son was the first in his family to attend university. He studied law, and looked for law jobs after he graduated. His girlfriend also studied law, took a first-class degree and was second-ranked in her entire year. The mother thought that since her son had worked two jobs all the way through university, potential employers would recognize him as a good worker. But after they graduated, neither of them could find a job in law. They reported that one person from their class went on to further education in order to become a solicitor, but this mother told us that her son had said, 'The only way you'd get in a law job is if you'd got a parent or family within a solicitors' who would take you on. [. . .] Otherwise, you've no chance.' The mother was understandably very unhappy about this, and saw her son's university education as nearly a total waste.

However, we should not get too hung up on this 'pulling of strings'. In one of the most famous pieces of sociological research ever conducted Mark Granovetter emphasized the 'strength of weak ties'.[3] Although we might think that it is those who are closest to us – our family and intimate friends – who matter most in affecting our lives, Granovetter argued that in fact it was those whom we know in passing who are more likely to convey benefits to us. This is because, by being more removed from our daily activities, they are more likely to have information which will assist us and which we otherwise would not know about.

This basic idea has now been studied in a number of settings and been shown to be highly robust. The American sociologist Roland Burt shows that in the business world, those who have the most social capital are those who have social ties which bridge what he calls 'structural holes', i.e. people in the organization or sector who otherwise would not know each other. In a different context, Stephen Ball has drawn attention to the significance of weak social ties for parents thinking about which school to send their children to.[4] Often it is those parents who are known slightly but have a telling experience to impart who matter most. In a similar vein, most parents are aware of the power of 'school-gate' networks (when parents exchange crucial information when waiting for their children after school). Bonnie Erickson has discussed how the most successful managers are often able to talk easily about sports or TV in a way which allows them to communicate, not only with their peers, but with anyone in their organization, regardless of status.[5]

The power of 'weak ties' might be linked to the idea that there is a powerful 'Establishment'.[6] The argument here is not that upper-class people know all other upper-class people intimately (though they might know a few of them very well). Rather, the claim is that they are linked by an extensive series of weak ties. They might vaguely recall someone who was at a boarding school or at Oxford with them, or someone they meet in their West End club, and such contacts can be mobilized to provide information or assistance when needed. Indeed, one might even think of the entire aristocracy of past centuries being a kind of association of weak ties, in that within it everyone would know many people with titles, if only by repute.

In the age of social media weak-ties networking is now much more common throughout the social structure. Many young professionals engage in a form of 'network sociality' as part of their job in which their portfolio of contacts from different walks of life is a key resource in their jobs. If this is true, then perhaps social capital has become more diffuse and been democratized across the social spectrum. Perhaps people of all walks of life know a range of other kinds of people these days.

The GBCS is the first survey to analyse this issue in depth, using the most sophisticated version of the Lin Position Generator, which has become a widely used method for assessing the extent and range of people's social networks. (It is named after sociologist Nan Lin, who developed it in the 1980s.)[7] It is simply a set of questions asking survey respondents whether they know, socially, someone from a series of occupations. By asking if respondents knew people in different social positions, we could assess how far they had ties stretching across the social structure. This set of questions can be used to ask whether an individual knows someone with different ethnicity, or in a different geographical location. However, we are using it in the form developed by Lin to find out whether respondents know someone socially (in our case, from one of thirty-seven different occupations).

The occupational positions in the GBCS were deliberately chosen to exemplify jobs of very different status, ranging from that of aristocrat to domestic cleaner. The idea was to see whether we can distinguish people who know lots of people via their different occupations, suggesting a wide range of social ties, from those who know only a few. And, over and above this, whether people are more likely to know others from high-status or low-status occupations. This is therefore an unusually sophisticated way of unravelling the structure of social capital in Britain today to allow us to see how our networks are linked to social class.[8]

## Who knows whom?

Table 4.1 shows the results for both the nationally representative sample and the GBCS web survey in terms of the kind of occupations that are identified there. We discovered that GBCS respondents were far more likely than those from the nationally representative GfK survey (who were asked exactly the same set of questions) to know people in more professional, managerial and higher-paid positions, and far less likely to know people in working class occupations. This is in line with GBCS respondents' overall differences from the UK population which we have discussed above. Table 4.1 also includes information from the Labour Force Survey (LFS) about how common such jobs are in the UK as a whole, so we can see if respondents are disproportionately more or less likely to report "knowing people" from their ranks.

Table 4.1 suggests that if one works in a public-facing job one is more likely to be known socially across the board, with high numbers of such workers being known compared to the proportion of such jobs in the labour force. And when people are employed in specific occupations this effect is even more striking. Nearly two-thirds of people know a teacher, a nurse, an electrician or a shop assistant, the kinds of people one expects to run across in daily life. By contrast, it is unusual to know a train driver. This is largely because there are simply not nearly as many train drivers as a percentage of the workforce when compared to nurses (see their positions in the third column of Table 4.1), which we can understand (once we take this into account) as showing that actually train drivers appear to be identified as social contacts relatively frequently (see the last column of Table 4.1). Few people actually know aristocrats or chief executives. People in the most privileged occupations are indeed less likely to be known more widely, though there are some exceptions. We should also note that since our question asks whether you 'know' someone in a different occupation, there might be ambiguity about what this entails (friendship or simply being on 'nodding terms'?).

| | GFK (OF RESPONDENTS WHO SAY THEY KNOW SOMEONE IN THESE OCCUPATIONS) | GBCS (OF RESPONDENTS WHO SAY THEY KNOW SOMEONE IN THESE OCCUPATIONS) | LFS (OF WORKFORCE IN THESE OCCUPATIONS) | DEGREE OF REPRESENTATION |
|---|---|---|---|---|
| Teacher | 63.4 | 84.2 | 3.8 | 16.9 |
| Sales/shop assistant | 62.9 | 51.4 | 3.7 | 17.2 |
| Student | 62.8 | 68.5 | 5.9 | 10.6 |
| Electrician | 59.5 | 39.4 | 1.0 | 62.6 |
| Nurse | 58.3 | 64.4 | 2.0 | 29.9 |
| Cleaner | 56.0 | 28.7 | 1.9 | 29.8 |
| Bus/lorry driver | 50.8 | 24.4 | 2.1 | 24.8 |
| Factory worker | 50.8 | 23.7 | 1.6 | 31.7 |
| Secretary | 49.7 | 43.9 | 1.6 | 31.7 |
| Receptionist | 49.7 | 34.3 | 0.8 | 60.6 |
| Accountant | 48.9 | 67.6 | 0.8 | 61.1 |
| Office manager | 48.2 | 55.7 | 0.7 | 73.0 |
| Never worked | 47.5 | 31.0 | N/A | N/A |
| Gardener | 44.2 | 29.9 | 0.6 | 76.2 |
| Civil/mechanical engineer | 41.6 | 52.9 | 1.5 | 28.7 |
| Member of the armed forces | 40.7 | 43.2 | 0.28 | 146.9 |
| Solicitor | 39.9 | 56.7 | 0.4 | 99.8 |
| Medical practitioner | 38.6 | 59.9 | 0.8 | 46.5 |
| Postal worker | 38.1 | 19.8 | 0.6 | 61.5 |

Table 4.1

Percentage Who Report Knowing People in Chosen Occupations

*Sources*: GBCS data (January 2011–July 2013), and as a percentage of the total working population represented by the Labour Force Survey, 2014

| | GFK (OF RESPONDENTS WHO SAY THEY KNOW SOMEONE IN THESE OCCUPATIONS) | GBCS (OF RESPONDENTS WHO SAY THEY KNOW SOMEONE IN THESE OCCUPATIONS) | LFS (OF WORKFORCE IN THESE OCCUPATIONS) | DEGREE OF REPRESENTATION |
|---|---|---|---|---|
| Clerical officer | 36.2 | 49.0 | 1.4 | 25.5 |
| Artist/musician/performer | 35.6 | 58.7 | 0.5 | 78.6 |
| University/college lecturer | 35.0 | 57.1 | 0.9 | 39.3 |
| Publican | 34.7 | 21.3 | 0.1 | 247.9 |
| Catering assistant | 31.6 | 19.1 | 1.4 | 22.3 |
| Call-centre worker | 31.2 | 28.3 | 0.4 | 84.3 |
| Machine operator | 31.1 | 12.1 | 0.5 | 66.7 |
| Restaurant manager | 28.9 | 23.0 | 0.4 | 74.1 |
| Farm worker | 28.6 | 23.6 | 0.2 | 136.2 |
| Scientist/researcher | 27.8 | 61.4 | 0.6 | 45.3 |
| Security guard | 27.3 | 14.5 | 0.6 | 44.0 |
| Software designer | 26.8 | 49.1 | 0.8 | 34.8 |
| Finance manager | 26.4 | 41.1 | 1.2 | 21.5 |
| Travel agent | 25.0 | 15.5 | 0.1 | 178.6 |
| Chief executive | 23.3 | 35.6 | 0.2 | 111.0 |
| Bank manager | 22.5 | 20.0 | 0.3 | 72.6 |
| Train driver | 12.5 | 7.0 | 0.1 | 156.3 |
| Aristocrat/noble | 7.9 | 11.3 | N/A | N/A |

Table 4.1 does not say anything about the distribution of social capital or its relationship to advantage. All we can see is that people are the most likely to say they know teachers, shop assistants and students; and that the least commonly known people are in these positions: bank manager, train driver and aristocrat/noble. We can see some striking differences, by comparing the proportion of respondents who know people in these occupations with the proportion of people in these occupations nationally. On the other hand, those in education (teachers and students), health and care (nurses, medical practitioners and cleaners) are under-represented. The position generator does not capture the *number of people* a respondent knows in each position or group, only *whether or not* they know anyone in that position; a respondent who knows eight finance managers but no aristocrats, CEOs, scientists, lecturers, software designers, bank managers or solicitors would only be recorded as knowing one of these *positions*, even though she knows eight people in one category.

## The structure of social ties

Sociologically speaking, what matters is not how many people from different occupations are known, in general terms, but rather the patterning of who it is that you know. So, if you know an aristocrat, are you also more likely to know a chief executive? If you know a train driver, does this make you less likely to know a finance manager? An examination of this patterning is equivalent to the cultural capital mapping which we provided in Chapter 3. If there are no social differences in social capital, then we would expect there to be a random distribution in knowing people from different occupations. If, however, it is proportionately more likely for teachers to know nurses, or doctors to know solicitors, for instance, then this indicates that we are seeing some kinds of differentiation at work.

Table 4.2 reports the occupations that people are most and associate with are another, so we get a sense of 'families' or 'clusters' of occupations.[9] These are ranked in opposition to each other, indicating that those who report knowing an aristocrat (at the top of the table) are least likely to know a machine operator (at the bottom). The occupations listed in the middle are the least differentiated in this way. Knowing a nurse is not very discriminating: you might be just as likely to know someone in an occupation listed higher or lower in this list. We added a column comparing occupation by status rank according to the Cambridge score, which largely correlates with our findings.[10] We have also listed the ranking of these occupations within the NS-SEC system which we discussed in Chapter 1, so that we can see how far the differences we find here overlap with that system's occupational class divisions.

Table 4.2 shows a slight tendency here for those in the higher NS-SEC professional and managerial groups (1 and 2) to be at the top, and those in the semi-routine and routine manual worker groups (6, 7 and 8) to be at the bottom. However, there is no perfect correlation with the Cambridge rank and NS-SEC by occupational social class. Clerical

|  | RANK: OUR ANALYSIS | STATUS RANK: CAMBRIDGE SCORE | OCCUPATIONAL RANK: ACCORDING TO THE NS-SEC |
| --- | --- | --- | --- |
| Aristocrat/noble | 1 | N/A | N/A |
| Scientist/researcher | 2 | 6 | 1.2 |
| Finance manager | 3 | 8 | 1.1 |
| Chief executive | 4 | 5 | 1.1 |
| University/college lecturer | 5 | 1 | 1.2 |
| Software designer | 6 | 13 | 1.2 |
| Bank manager | 7 | 9 | 2 |
| Solicitor | 8 | 4 | 1.2 |
| Clerical officer (in local or national government) | 9 | 16 | 3 |
| Medical practitioner | 10 | 2 | 1.2 |
| Artist/musician/performer | 11 | 15 | 2 |
| Accountant | 12 | 11 | 1.2 |
| Teacher | 13 | 3 | 2 |
| Secretary | 14 | 14 | 3 |
| Civil/mechanical engineer | 15 | 7 | 1.2 |
| Office manager | 16 | 10 | 2 |
| Nurse | 17 | 18 | 2 |
| Student | 18 | N/A | N/A |
| Restaurant manager | 19 | 23 | 4 |

## Table 4.2

Differentiation of People in Certain Occupations According to their Chances of Contact with Each Other

|  | RANK: OUR ANALYSIS | STATUS RANK: CAMBRIDGE SCORE | OCCUPATIONAL RANK: ACCORDING TO THE NS-SEC |
|---|---|---|---|
| Call-centre worker | 20 | 22 | 3 |
| Electrician | 21 | 24 | 5 |
| Travel agent | 22 | 19 | 2 |
| Member of the armed forces | 23 | 12 | 3 or 1.1[1] |
| Receptionist | 24 | 17 | 6 |
| Train driver | 25 | 34 | 5 |
| Sales/shop assistant | 26 | 20 | 6 |
| Gardener | 27 | 26 | 4 |
| Postal worker | 28 | 25 | 3 or 6[2] |
| Publican | 29 | 21 | 4 |
| Farm worker | 30 | 30 | 6 |
| Cleaner | 31 | 33 | 7 |
| Never worked | 32 | N/A | N/A |
| Bus/lorry driver | 33 | 29 | 7 |
| Catering assistant | 34 | 27 | 6 |
| Factory worker | 35 | 31 | 7 |
| Security guard | 36 | 32 | 6 |
| Machine operator | 37 | 28 | 6 |

1. Depending on rank
2. Depending on role

officers are placed in class 3 in the NS-SEC system, but rank ninth in our list, for instance, and above many occupational positions ranked NS-SEC 1 or 2. Travel agents, on the other hand, are classed in NS-SEC 2, but in our analysis rank below many occupations in lower NS-SEC classes, because positions are ranked based on how likely it is that the same person within the given occupation knows someone in each position.

Table 4.2 does, however, reveal the power of a class divide. If we look at Table 4.2 from top to bottom, we range down from the higher-status positions, with more power, generally requiring more education, commanding more respect, and/ or earning higher incomes, to those which garner a great deal less. Table 4.2 looks, in fact, like a clear map of social classes. Our social networks are differentiated by class. If you know people in some professional and managerial occupations – such as that of scientist or finance manager – you are likely to know others in these sorts of occupations, and fewer working class ones. The inverse also operates. If you know a machine operator, you might also know a factory worker and a security guard, but you are much less likely to know an aristocrat.

## Social ties and inequality

The differences revealed in Table 4.2 relate to other aspects of people's lives in powerful ways. It is this which makes those differences a form of capital. We can show this by grouping these thirty-seven positions into five smaller groups so that the patterns between them can more easily be seen. Table 4.3 shows that actually most people know at least one person from each of the clusters. For instance, 73 per cent in the nationally representative sample know at least one person from the most advantaged elite cluster, and the figures rise to around 90 per cent for all the other clusters. Table 4.3 demonstrates that most people in our sample know someone in a top-ranking occupation and someone in a lower-ranking occupation. Although there are tendencies towards selective social networks, this should not detract from the fact that nowadays most people have wide-ranging ties. This is a very different situation from fifty years ago, when classes and their cultures would have been more sealed off from each other. There is no class apartheid at work. The chances are that we know someone in both routine employment and in an exclusive job.

But there is more to it than this. In all kinds of subtle ways, our networks are socially differentiated and convey different kinds of advantages. Figure 4.1 shows the relationship between someone's family income and how many people in each group they know (based on the nationally representative GfK data-set). Starting on the left, it shows that people in the bottom income quintile know an average of just over one person in one of the eight elite positions (aristocrats, chief executives, etc.). This compares to people in the highest income quintile, who know, on average, someone in more than three of those eight positions. The differences between the top and bottom of the income distribution are nearly as steep with regard to the positions in the professional group.

So, wealthy people are considerably more likely to know

| OCCUPATIONAL GROUPINGS | NUMBER OF POSITIONS ALTOGETHER IN GROUP | AVERAGE NUMBER OF POSITIONS KNOWN BY ONE PERSON IN THE GFK[1] SAMPLE | IN THE GFK SAMPLE WHO KNOW AT LEAST ONE PERSON IN THESE GROUPS | AVERAGE NUMBER OF POSITIONS KNOWN BY ONE PERSON IN THE GBCS SAMPLE | IN THE GBCS WHO KNOW AT LEAST ONE PERSON IN THESE GROUPS |
|---|---|---|---|---|---|
| Elite<br>Aristocrat/noble, Scientist/researcher, Finance manager, Chief executive, University/college lecturer, Software designer, Bank manager, Solicitor | 8 | 2.1 | 73 | 3.3 | 92 |
| Professional<br>Clerical officer, Medical practitioner, Artist/musician/performer, Accountant, Teacher, Secretary, Civil/ mechanical engineer | 7 | 3.1 | 89 | 4.2 | 98 |
| Intermediate<br>Office manager, Nurse, Student, Restaurant manager, Call-centre worker, Electrician, Travel agent, Member of the armed forces | 8 | 3.5 | 93 | 3.4 | 96 |
| Skilled<br>Receptionist, Train driver, Sales/shop assistant, Gardener, Postal worker, Publican, Farm worker | 7 | 2.7 | 88 | 1.9 | 77 |
| Routine<br>Cleaner, Never worked, Bus/lorry driver, Catering assistant, Factory worker, Security guard, Machine operator | 7 | 3.0 | 88 | 1.5 | 64 |

Table 4.3

Frequency of Contact Between People in Different Occupational Groups

1. GFK = nationally representative sample taken by the market-research firm of that name

several people in high-status occupations; they might be said to have the 'bridging social capital' to allow them a greater range of bridging contacts there. They have the kind of weak ties to other elite people which might indeed allow them more potential for sharing useful information, gossip etc.

By contrast, the 'skilled' group is not at all socially distinctive: people across the income spectrum report knowing on average people in just under three of the seven positions in this group, which is high and shows they know a wide range of people. This is because many of the jobs in this category are public-facing ones (and lots of people tend to know someone in this group), and this category also consists of other occupations (such as that of train driver) in which the worker is not in the public gaze (and very few people know someone in that sort of occupation). The routine occupations group, however, is more isolated. Those with the highest income levels are less likely to know someone from this group compared to those who earn less.

To summarize Figure 4.1, we can see that the most 'sloped' line is for the elite group, indicating that this is the most socially differentiated of all the five clusters of occupations. *It is the elite occupations which are most socially exclusive.* So there are clear differences in the connections people have across the income spectrum. People who are financially well-off know fewer people in working class jobs than do people who are less well-off. Poorer people know far fewer people in high-status jobs than do their better-off neighbours. This matters because since it is high-status people who are likely to have useful contacts, their advice will be socially

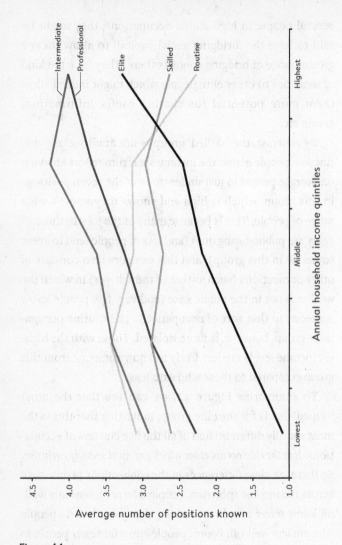

**Figure 4.1**

Income and who you know

(A 'quintile' divides the population into five equally sized groups, so that the top quintile here consists of the 20 per cent of households with the highest income, and so on.)

exclusive – even though they may personally think that they talk to everyone and are not being preferential. And it turns out to be the very wealthy (with household incomes over £200k) who have more distinctive social ties compared to everyone else. They are much more likely to know people from most of the elite occupations. They are the only group of people who know more members of the elite occupations than of the professional occupations. Here we see evidence of how the very wealthy are not only economically distinctive, but also seem to have specific kinds of social ties.[11]

One final way to look at the relationship between income and social networks is to look at just a few of the occupations individually. Figure 4.2 shows the percentage of people in each income category of the GBCS who know someone in each of six occupations we have chosen. Very few people report knowing an aristocrat/noble, for example; only about 10 per cent of those earning £50,000 per year or less – the majority of people in the UK – know one, and there's little difference by income below that level. Above £50k, the percentages of people who know an aristocrat start to rise, so that for those with incomes around £100,000 about twice as many people (20 per cent) report knowing one. But the steep upward curve starts after that point, with nearly 40 per cent of people in the top income bracket saying they know an aristocrat. The percentage of people who know a chief executive also increases steadily across the income spectrum, starting at about 20 per cent for those earning the least, and rising to over 80 per cent of those earning the most: high-income people know chief executives at four times the rate of low-income GBCS respondents.

The percentages of people who say they know a sales/ shop assistant or factory worker, conversely, decline across the income spectrum: the richest people are as unlikely to know a factory worker (or a catering assistant or call-centre worker or people in a few other positions not mentioned above) as the poorest are to know an aristocrat, despite the fact that there are far more low-income workers than aristocrats in the UK.

What we are seeing here is a kind of 'outlier' effect. Rather than the key differences lying in the middle of the social structure, between middle and working class, the most arresting differences are at the extremes. The affluent appear very different from those below them, since they are much more likely to know aristocrats and chief executives than even established professionals do. And the same effect is evident, in a less marked manner, at the bottom, where the poorest groups are much more likely to know a shop assistant.

These findings show that the very wealthy are distinctive in their social ties. They are not simply an economically advantaged group who nonetheless blend into the wider population in terms of whom they associate with. Instead, they are systematically much more likely to have acquaintances drawn from their own elite world.

So far we have looked only at income. However, Figure 4.3 shows clearly that the more educated you are, the more likely it is that you know someone from the elite and professional groups, and these slopes are both very steep. Postgraduates on average know well over three people in the elite occupations, whereas those with no educational qualifications know only one. The slope is far less steep for the other occupational clusters, showing that university graduates, those leaving schools with A-levels, vocational qualifications or GCSEs don't vary that much in terms of the number of people they know in any of the intermediate, skilled or routine job categories. But the big exception here is those without educational qualifications, who know considerably fewer people from any of these clusters. They are markedly more isolated.

Our social networks are patterned, but not closed. Many of us know people from across the social hierarchy. However, at the top and bottom we can detect much more distinct profiles in which more affluent and better-educated people are considerably more likely to know people in elite occupations, and those who are in the bottom income bracket and have no qualifications know fewer people from any other social group.

## Why does social capital matter?

Let us finish this chapter by showing that knowing more elite and professional people is not simply an idle fact. Social networks are also associated with different kinds of backgrounds and therefore accumulate over time.[12] Figure 4.4 shows how social ties are considerably affected by our family background. Figure 4.4 groups people's backgrounds into three broad categories: those who had parents who were professionals or senior managers and therefore come from the most privileged backgrounds; those with parents who had mid-range occupations in clerical work, technically skilled work, or lower management positions, and might therefore

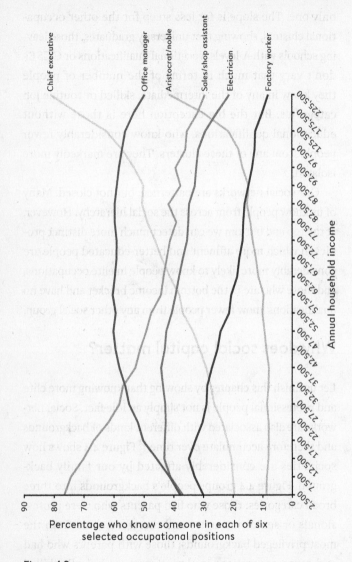

**Figure 4.2**

Income and social networks

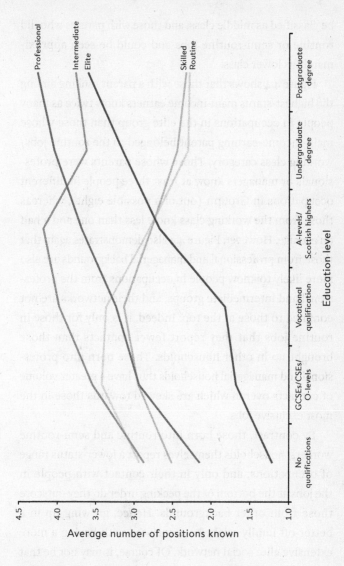

**Figure 4.3**
Education and who you know

be classified as middle class; and those with parents who did routine or semi-routine jobs and could be seen approximately as lower class.

Figure 4.4 shows that those with a parent ranking among the highest-status main-income earners know twice as many people in occupations in the elite group than those whose main-income-earning parent belonged to the routine jobs/ working class category. Those whose parents were professionals or managers know at least three people in different occupations in Group 1 (out of a possible eight), whereas those from the working class know less than one and a half on average. However, Figure 4.4 also demonstrates again that those from professional and managerial backgrounds are also more likely to know people in occupations from the professional and intermediate groups, and their networks are not confined to those at the top. Indeed, it is only for those in routine jobs that they report fewer contacts than those brought up in other households. Those born into professional and managerial households thus have a greater volume of contacts overall which are skewed towards those in the most exclusive jobs.

By contrast, those born into routine and semi-routine workers' households themselves report a lower-status range of occupations, and only in their contact with people in the jobs at the bottom of the pecking order do they outscore those from other backgrounds. Hence, growing up in a better-off family might be associated with having a more extensive elite social network. Of course, it may not be that people from professional and managerial families get to know a higher number of aristocrats or chief executives

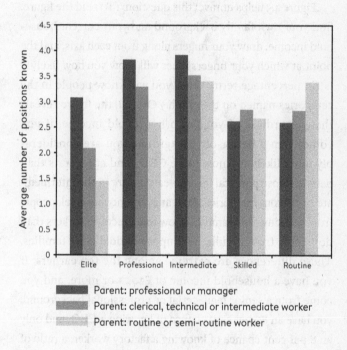

**Figure 4.4**

Differences in social contacts by family of origin

*because* of their families; but maybe their family backgrounds help them go to university and to get jobs and have leisure activities in which they are more likely to meet CEOs and aristocrats.

Figure 4.5 helps unravel this question. (To read the figure, find your own family background and your current household income, draw your fingers along from each axis, and the point at which your fingers meet will show you how likely it is (in percentage terms) that you will know people in the categories named on the graph.) Overall, the figure reveals that, regardless of your own household income, if you come from a better-off background you are considerably more likely to know more CEOs and aristocrats than people whose parental income-earners are in the intermediate or bottom categories. And, at every income level, people from working class families know more factory workers than do people from middle- and upper-middle class families. These differences are extreme among the top earners. If you have a household income of £200k or more, and you come from a senior managerial or professional background, you have an 80 per cent chance of knowing a CEO, and only an 8 per cent chance of knowing a factory worker: a ratio of ten to one. However, if you are equally well-off, but come from a working class background, then the ratio falls to under four to one (you have a 75 per cent chance of knowing a CEO, but only a 21 per cent chance of knowing a factory worker).

Our final theme – age – is an important one. We have seen how economic capital is strongly skewed towards older people, whilst cultural capital is differentiated between a (socially more legitimate) highbrow form which is oriented towards older people, and an upstart emerging cultural capital which young professionals are more likely to possess. Social capital is rather less affected by age (see Figure 4.6), except for the older groups (over seventy years of age), in which the number of contacts become much lower (probably because people over seventy mainly mix with retired people). This having been said, there is a tendency for GBCS respondents to know more people in the elite and professional occupations as they get older, presumably because they are more likely to be in that group themselves and hence mix with people like them. Similarly, for those in the older groups, their number of contacts with those in the intermediate group falls, presumably because these jobs tend to be occupied by younger people. The contacts of those in the skilled and routine job clusters vary less by age. Social capital is therefore relatively age-invariant, a striking contrast to both the other two forms of capital.

In Britain in the early twenty-first century, as in other nations, our social networks are tied up with our social class. But this is not to say that there is a simple association in which we know only people like ourselves. Bourdieu's concept of 'misrecognition' and the gift exchange that we introduced in Chapter 1 aids our understanding of this. Just as we see gifts as freely given tokens of esteem, so we tend to value our friends for their own qualities, and not because they 'open doors'. If we just saw them as means of gaining advantages, we would no longer really see them as friends. Bourdieu's point is that precisely for this reason, advantage can nonetheless be bestowed from such relationships in

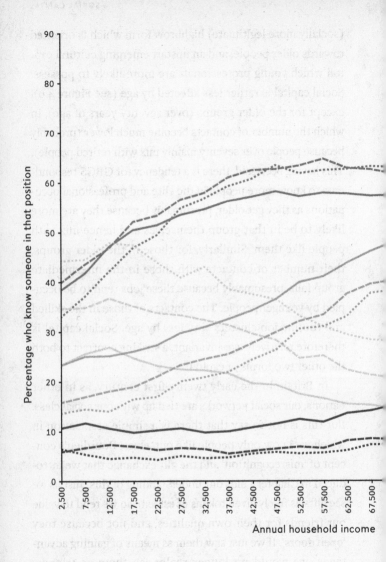

**Figure 4.5**

Differences in social contacts by family of origin and income

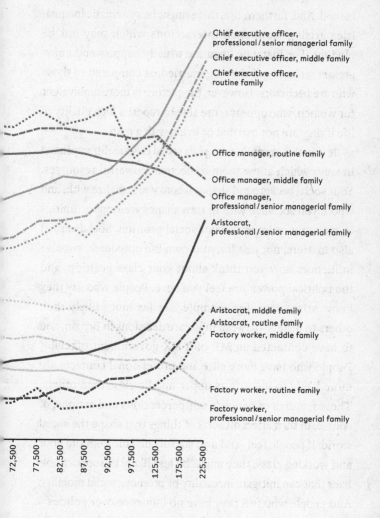

Chief executive officer,
professional / senior managerial family

Chief executive officer, middle family

Chief executive officer,
routine family

Office manager, routine family

Office manager, middle family

Office manager,
professional / senior managerial family

Aristocrat,
professional / senior managerial family

Aristocrat, middle family

Aristocrat, routine family

Factory worker, middle family

Factory worker, routine family

Factory worker,
professional / senior managerial family

72,500
77,500
82,500
87,500
92,500
97,500
125,500
175,500
225,500

ways which might not be recognized directly by those concerned. And, furthermore, there might be systematic inequalities arising from such interactions which may not be obvious. For instance, men are usually happier and enjoy greater wellbeing if they are married, as compared to those who are bachelors. However, the picture is more ambivalent for women, who appear more able to report a high quality of life if they are not married or living with a man.

It is in this spirit that people's social ties are differentiated in ways which allow them to become powerful resources. Your social background shapes whom you socialize with, and whom you socialize with in turn shapes your opportunities to maintain or improve your social position. Social capital also matters, not just for your own life outcomes, but also influences how you think about your class position, and the political power you feel you have. People who say they know aristocrats, for example, are far more likely than others to believe they can influence decisions in Britain, and to have contacted an MP or a UK government official.[13] People who have more elite and professional contacts are more likely to identify as upper middle class than others. These features of people's self-perceptions and actions, of course, in turn affect all sorts of things that shape the social world: if people feel (and are) socially distant from the poor and working class, they might be less likely to support policies that can mitigate inequality or promote social mobility. And people who feel they have no influence over politics – disproportionately lower-income people and especially people without elite and professional contacts – are not likely to try to effect political change for their own benefit,

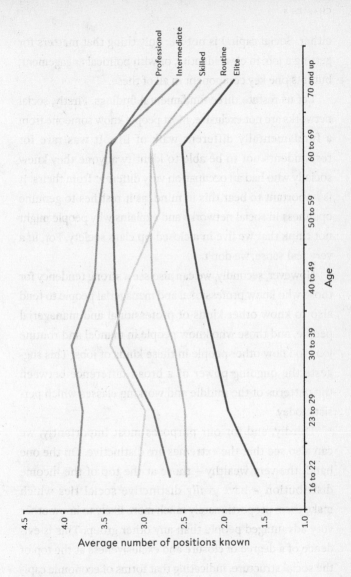

**Figure 4.6**

Differences in number of social contacts by age group

either. Social capital is not the only thing that matters for getting a job, in class identity, or with political engagement, but it is one key component in all of these.

Let us restate three fundamental findings. Firstly, social networks are not exclusive. Most people know someone from a fundamentally different walk of life. It was rare for respondents not to be able to identify anyone they knew socially who had an occupation very different from theirs. It is important to bear this in mind, as it testifies to genuine openness in social networks and explains why people might not think that we live in a closed-up class society. For, in a very real sense, we don't.

However, secondly, we can also see a strong tendency for those who know professional and managerial people to tend also to know other kinds of professional and managerial people, and those who know people in manual and routine jobs to know other people in these kinds of jobs. This suggests the ongoing power of a broad difference between the patterns of the middle and working classes which persists today.

Thirdly, and for our purposes most importantly, we can also see that the extremes are distinctive. On the one hand, the very wealthy – those at the top of the income distribution – have *really* distinctive social ties which make them proportionately much more likely to know other very advantaged people than any other group. This is evidence of a degree of closure and exclusiveness at the top of the social structure, indicating that forms of economic capital intersect closely with social networks and social capital to produce a pulling-apart from the rest at the highest levels of the social hierarchy. And we can also see that those who have no educational qualifications are much less likely to know anyone from any of the other occupational clusters. And so it is that our social networks are tied into wider patterns of class differentiation.

# The New Landscape of Class

We have seen how economic, cultural and social capital are associated with inequities tied in to the processes of accumulation associated with them. Yet we can't just leave the story here. To say that we live in a complicated world with lots of different kinds of inequalities is true enough, but we also need to draw the threads together. We need to understand the interplay between these sorts of capital so that we can identify how certain forms of advantage and disadvantage build up across them. It is these overlaps which generate the kinds of cumulative advantages and disadvantages which may fuse together in social classes more broadly.

Drawing links between these three kinds of capital is complicated because we have shown that the three strands of capital are organized on different principles. Economic capital has accumulated massively in recent years, in ways which have most advantaged those at its higher reaches. On the other hand, it is difficult to *see* cultural and social capital accumulating in this sort of way. Perhaps people have more cultural interests and more social contacts than they used to as result of technical innovation, but it is likely that any increase in either sort of capital (made via online activity) will affect the quality of the relationship. Do we have the same intense knowledge of our Twitter followers or of down-loaded music from Spotify compared to that gained from friends whom we hang around with every day or music which we make a special effort to listen to by attending concerts? Economic capital is remorseless, in that a thousand pounds can buy pretty much the same amount of something, regard-less of whether it is your first thousand or your hundredth thousand that you spend. This is not true in relation to cul-tural and social capital: your tenth favourite leisure interest can rarely be pursued as vigorously as your first.

Economic capital has therefore been subject to massive *absolute* accumulation, whereas the key forces affecting cul-tural and social capital are *relative* – that is to say, dividing people with different kinds of cultural interests and social ties. But these relative differences are also hierarchical. People with certain new cultural interests – highbrow and emerging cultural capital, in our terms – are hostile and snobbish to those without. Similarly, these kinds of cultural capital also intersect with other kinds of advantages. We are in a world of virtuous and vicious circles – though distin-guishing whether these are virtuous and vicious depends on where you stand. This is the stuff out of which classes are built.

In thinking about how these sorts of capital intersect, we can pose two possible scenarios. On the one hand, perhaps the three kinds of capital are completely independent of each other. For instance, an individual might be rich, with lots of economic capital but not have many social contacts – limited social capital. The reclusive millionaire Howard Hughes would be such an example. If this *is* the case, and we can't identify any obvious ways in which advantages reinforce each other, this will surely make it harder to define classes. On the other hand, we might imagine that these three different sorts of capital largely coincide: that those who are wealthy might also be likely to have high amounts of cultural capital and extensive social networks. If this is so, then we could identify mutually reinforcing processes which link these three sorts of capital together and link people into distinctive social classes.

Bourdieu himself tended towards this latter view; that there was a 'homology' between these capitals, that is to say, a tendency for them to coincide, but he also thought that this fit was not perfect. For instance, he identified 'intellectuals' as those with extensive cultural capital, but relatively little economic capital (think of the poor artist working in her/his attic), as well as 'industrialists' who were well-off but not necessarily very 'cultured', in his terms (think of an upwardly mobile executive who had not been to university). And these kinds of subtle distinctions are often the ones that we are aware of when reflecting on those around us. We think of 'self-made business people' who have made a fortune without necessarily knowing the 'right' people or having a high amount of cultural capital. We think of wealthy footballers who have not necessarily had an advanced education, people who seem to have extensive cultural interests but don't hold down a steady job, and so forth. It is often the lack of fit between these kinds of capital which intrigue and interest us.

In fact we already have clues from the previous three chapters that the various sorts of capital are not independent of each other. We have shown that people's social networks are associated with their income, that their cultural capital is linked to their occupation, and so forth. But in this chapter we want to consider more systematically what kind of interplay we can identify between them so that we can identify different social classes in the twenty-first century.

## A new model of social class?

Our first analysis of the GBCS in 2013 was extensively reported in the media and in academic discussion, since it suggested a new way of thinking about class which goes beyond the difference between upper, middle and working class which we are familiar with. We won't rehearse the actual details of the analysis itself, which are freely available for anyone interested, but the key elements of its class schema are important and have wider implications.[1]

We used a method called 'latent class analysis' to group measures of the three kinds of capital to show how they clustered together to reveal distinctive social classes. We thus used data on people's household income, their savings and house value, alongside scores for their highbrow and emerging cultural capital, and information on the number and status of the social ties they had. Table 5.1 indicates the amounts of capital each of the seven classes had, and lists the names we gave to each of the classes (which we explain more fully below).

Table 5.1 shows that these seven classes do not form a neat hierarchy. It seems somewhat arbitrary from the classification itself whether 'new affluent workers' should be placed higher or lower in the social structure than the

| | ELITE | ESTABLISHED MIDDLE CLASS | TECHNICAL MIDDLE CLASS | NEW AFFLUENT WORKERS | TRADITIONAL WORKING CLASS | EMERGING SERVICE WORKERS | PRECARIAT |
|---|---|---|---|---|---|---|---|
| Household income | £89k | £47k | £37k | £29k | £13k | £21k | £8k |
| Household savings | £142k | £26k | £66k | £5k | £10k | £1k | £1k |
| House value | £325k | £176k | £163k | £129k | £127k | £18k | £27k |
| Social contact score[1] | 50.1 | 45.3 | 53.5 | 37.8 | 41.5 | 38.3 | 29.9 |
| Social contact number[2] | 16.2 | 17.0 | 3.6 | 16.9 | 9.8 | 14.8 | 6.7 |
| Highbrow cultural capital[3] | 16.9 | 13.7 | 9.2 | 6.9 | 10.8 | 9.6 | 6.0 |
| Emerging cultural capital[4] | 14.4 | 16.5 | 11.4 | 14.8 | 6.5 | 17.5 | 8.4 |

## Table 5.1

### Classes and their income

Source: GBCS data.

1. The social contact score is the median value of the Cambridge scale score (see note 10, Chapter 4) of people in all these occupations known by respondents (i.e. higher value = higher status of social contacts)
2. The social contact number = the number of occupations that a respondent knows someone in all of the occupations listed) to 0
3. Highbrow cultural capital = frequency of participation in highbrow cultural forms (listening to classical music or jazz, attending stately homes, museums, art galleries, the theatre and French restaurants)
4. Emerging cultural capital = frequency of participation in emerging cultural forms (playing video games, interacting on social network sites, using the internet, playing sport, watching sport, spending time with friends, going to the gym, going to popular music concerts and showing preferences for rap and rock music)

'technical middle class'. This having been said, we have broadly tried to place them in order of rank according to their economic capital, which, as we have seen, is the most unevenly distributed of the three sorts of capital. The 'established middle class' is comfortably the second most well-off class after the 'elite', with higher incomes than the technical middle class, who, in their turn, also outscore the new affluent workers. Then, beneath these, we see that the 'traditional working class' and 'emerging service workers' have low economic capital (though they differ in the balance between their income and house values), whereas the 'precariat' are clearly at the bottom.

In this analysis, the two most clearly differentiated classes are the elite and the precariat, which score highest and lowest on most of our measures of the three capitals. The elite turn out to have incomes twice as high as any other class; they also have by far the largest house values and savings. And they also have the highest amount of 'highbrow' cultural capital – in the form of cultural activities such as going to museums, galleries and classical music concerts. Furthermore, they also have extensive social networks, generally with other high-status people. So at the top, we do seem to see Bourdieu's 'homology' principle working.

Our elite is also somewhat different from the '1 per cent' which has been identified by many commentators, in that it covers a significantly larger proportion of the population, about 6 per cent in our case. There is absolutely no doubt that, as Dorling, Piketty and others have shown, the super-rich are pulling away in economic terms from the rest of the population,[2] but we should also not lose sight of a somewhat larger group, who are also massively advantaged over the rest. Because of their importance, we discuss the elite in more detail in a later chapter, but here we simply note that the difference between this class and all the others is the most striking of any that we found.

The other exception is at the bottom, where we define a 'precariat', which consists of about 15 per cent of the population. We borrowed this term from the academic Guy Standing, who has done so much to promote the interests of the 'precarious proletariat' class at the bottom of contemporary societies. As we explain in more detail in Chapter 10, we used this term deliberately, in place of the more conventional 'underclass' label, which has been used to stigmatize the poor and deprived for decades. This class has by far the lowest household income, has little if any savings, and is likely to rent property. And it also has the smallest number of social ties, with few associates in higher-status occupations, and its cultural capital is more limited than that of any of the other classes. As we emphasize in Chapter 10, we should make it very clear that we do not see this as evidence that this group is somehow morally degenerate. Although their range of social networks may be more limited than those of other classes, they may still have extensive social networks and forms of cultural engagement.

However, the five classes in the middle of the spectrum are a much more complicated mix and don't form such a neat pattern. We can find two classes which have more economic capital than social and cultural capital. These are the new affluent workers, who are reasonably well off but don't report extensive cultural engagements, and the technical middle class, who are also relatively affluent but have surprisingly limited social networks. And at the lower end of the scale we also find the group of emerging service workers, who have extensive cultural capital and considerable social networks, but don't have that much economic capital. So around 40 per cent of people don't have consistent or homologous amounts of the three kinds of capital, but vary somewhat, having rather more of one or two of them. From this perspective, we can see why class boundaries might be difficult to draw in any kind of completely clear-cut way.

Then, we also have two other classes, who have more internally consistent amounts of economic, social and cultural capital, but considerably less than the elite (in the case of the established middle class) and more than the precariat (in the case of the traditional working class). These patterns suggest a fracture which makes it difficult to distinguish a clear, cohesive 'professional and managerial service class', or a 'working class' which embraces all kinds of routine workers. The overall findings are therefore that there is considerable fuzziness in the middle reaches of the social structure, that it is difficult to define coherent 'middle class' or 'working class' groups. In short, the class hierarchy which we distinguished separates out three main groups: a small elite at the top, massively better off than others, a somewhat larger 'precariat' at the bottom, who score lower than others in relation to all three kinds of capital, and then five other classes in the middle, who have a much more hybrid mix of sorts of capital and can't be put in a simple hierarchy.

Table 5.2 summarizes the seven classes which were

produced by this method, including the names we gave them, the proportion of the population which fell into each class, the proportion of the GBCS sample which fell into them (which is different, because the GBCS is not representative of the whole population), and an explanation of the differing amounts of capital that each of the classes had.

One of the striking features of this model of class was the way that it appeared to be 'intuitively attractive'. In the aftermath of the story coming out, we were told by numerous journalists that the results 'made sense' to them. People found it possible to reinterpret the classes in ways that made sense of how they saw British society today.

Our mapping of the class structure, with its very clear distinctions at the top and bottom, overlaps with other divisions which we know are salient, and shows how class is not a separate axis of inequality, but one which intersects with others. Table 5.2 shows this with respect to age and ethnicity.[3] Ethnic minorities are relatively under-represented among the elite – but are well represented in the established middle class beneath them. We also see that ethnic minorities are very well represented among the 'emerging service workers', the group of well-educated young people who have not yet procured large amounts of economic capital. So there appear to be some telling indications here as to how ethnicity is bound up with these new class categories, in that ethnic minorities have considerable amounts of cultural capital but have not been able to translate this into economic capital in the same way that white Britons have. This complex patterning of ethnic minorities into these different new classes is a further indication of the way that ethnic groups cannot be

| NAME OF CLASS | % OF POPULATION | % OF GBCS SAMPLE | AVERAGE AGE | % OF ETHNIC MINORITY |
|---|---|---|---|---|
| Elite | 6 | 22 | 57 | 4 |
| Established middle class | 25 | 43 | 46 | 13 |
| Technical middle class | 6 | 10 | 52 | 9 |
| New affluent workers | 15 | 6 | 44 | 11 |
| Traditional working class | 14 | 2 | 66 | 9 |
| Emerging service workers | 19 | 17 | 32 | 21 |
| Precariat | 15 | <1 | 50 | 13 |

**Table 5.2**

Summary of the New Social Classes from the GBCS
*Source:* GBCS data.

clearly positioned within the older middle/working class divide.[4]

The average age of those in the different classes varies considerably in a highly revealing way and shows how powerfully age divisions are associated with social classes. We can see that the emerging service workers, who do not have much economic capital, despite considerable cultural and social capital, tend to be much younger – average age thirty-two – than those in the other classes. Is this a sign that young people, even when highly qualified, are being locked out of affluent careers? And we also see that the elite has a very high average age – fifty-seven years. So here we can see how the accumulation of advantages is cumulative. But not all older people are in this fortunate position – the average age of someone in the traditional working class tends to be even older. So the seven classes are not simply a set of age groupings, but are nonetheless strongly associated with age.

In many nations the existence of fundamental cleavages between generations is widely recognized, nowhere better than in France, where Louis Chauvel has emphasized the difficulties of the younger generation compared to their parents.[5] Many Latin American societies have similarly drawn attention to the significance of 'emergents', new classes of the affluent young who have benefited from the neo-liberalization of these economies. In Britain, however, sociologists typically abstract age from class, seeing these as independent and separate issues. This is despite the fact that class motifs – from yuppie to dinky, hipster to chav – are often premised on certain kinds of age groups. 'Chavs' are quintessentially seen to be young, for instance. It is also clear that there are large age divisions among ethnic minorities, with younger generations being less disadvantaged economically, compared to white Britons, than their parents.[6] The result of this unfortunate separation of class from age in much of our thinking is that generational divisions have instead been subsumed into an anxiety about 'declining social mobility', which seeks to frame the issue of age as one of mobility between classes. In fact, as we will discuss further in Chapter 6, the evidence that social mobility is declining is, at best, mixed, but the fact that this nonetheless captures such public interest is indicative of the way that it serves as a proxy for mobilizing anxieties about the prospects of the younger generation.

Age is therefore much more strongly bound up with the organization of class than has been previously recognized. And this is not surprising, given the way that different sorts of capital are accumulated over time and hence those in particular stages of the life cycle may well be better placed to benefit from this. The age-related class differences are indeed telling. As we saw in Chapter 2, economic capital can be accumulated over many years and therefore it is not surprising that our 'elite' class tends to be older than any of the others. It is also not surprising that those who are in their twenties, who tend to have less income, fewer savings or any capital tied up in housing, are less likely to be in the established middle class or technical middle class.

Emerging cultural capital can be acquired early in life, especially arising out of interests in contemporary cultural life and linked to experience in universities, and therefore it is revealing that quite a lot of younger people have a lot more cultural than economic capital, especially those who fall into our class category of 'emerging service workers'. Furthermore, unlike economic capital, there is a limit to how much cultural capital an individual can possess – there are only so many hours in the day for someone to be culturally engaged, only so much time to surf websites, after all. The point here is that the balance of economic capital in relation to cultural capital tends to favour older people over younger ones. This is the reason why the emerging service workers form such an interesting group – being distinguished by their youthful age profile.

What this recognition points towards is a fundamental recognition of the intersections between age and class, which suggests that a very different problematic is now shaping our debates about British society than the older concern about the boundaries between middle and working class, and the associated assumption that these identities are transferred between generations.

A moment's reflection clarifies what the stakes are here. The younger well-educated age groups are dynamically championing new and emerging cultural forms which are much less steeped in the historical classics than are 'highbrow' forms of culture.[7] Bourdieu's model of cultural capital is premised on the weight of the 'canon' – the legitimated works of culture which are bequeathed over time and seen to define cultural excellence: Shakespeare, Mozart, the British Museum and so on. However many commentators have argued that the balance of historical forces has now changed. Most visibly, those proclaiming we live in 'postmodern' times argue that cultural forms are now implicated in ironic and 'knowing' references, which do not hark back to a 'grand tradition'. Although we do not need to subscribe to such claims in their entirety, we agree that this does indeed point to a powerful shift. The 'canon', defined in terms of socially approved and legitimated 'great' works of art and culture, is no longer constitutive of cultural excellence, moral certainty or tradition. The 'avant-garde', which used to define itself as cutting edge in competition with older and more established cultural forms has been replaced by themed and fashioned trends with no historical reference points, where the new and contemporary are automatically held to be the markers of excellence.

This is precisely the tension involved in our differentiation between 'highbrow' and 'emergent' cultural capital. And it also underscores the difference between old forms of snobbery and the newer varieties which we see as central to the remaking of class hierarchies today.

And indeed, this brings us on to our third point, regarding the way that expertise is directly involved in the organization of our seven-class model. To put this another way, skill, awareness and knowledge are bound up with class. How? We have already emphasized the complex politics of classification, and the difficulties of recognizing and naming 'classes' directly. As we discussed in Chapter 1, the idea of class offends us at the same time that we find it fascinating.

What is therefore interesting is the way that our model differentiates classes in the middle of the hierarchy partly in terms of their relationship to expertise and knowledge itself. Thus, the technical middle class appears different from the established middle class in being culturally disengaged and not partaking of what one might conventionally see as middle class lifestyles. It is, instead, a group with a restricted social range and limited cultural interests, with a tendency to work in technical occupations and which has marked scientific interests.

This technical middle class has attracted increasing interest from historians in recent years and we can see them as an increasingly significant bloc with a different kind of expertise to that of older middle class groups. Mobilized around a range of technical interventions, from new weaponry to research methods, and, of course, information technology, this is a group of scientifically oriented people who have become increasingly significant in British society. In place of the older, more intellectual class oriented towards the humanities, art and 'culture', this is a group which has a more technical expertise. We can increasingly trace the imprint of this class in post-war Britain to the rise of technical and scientific modes of expertise, including within the social sciences, from the 1950s onwards.[8]

In a similar way, we can also see the emerging service workers as defined by having unusually high amounts of 'emerging cultural capital', a kind of ironic, reflexive and self-aware orientation towards knowledge and culture, one which marks them out from the older middle classes, who have a more traditional and canonical orientation. As we have already discussed, this is a younger age group, one which is often highly educated, but which is less steeped in the conventional canon and has a subtly different orientation towards lifestyle. These people champion contemporary cultural forms, relish social media and are actively engaged in keeping fit and playing sport. They are more oriented towards 'screen culture' than their older peers. This kind of expertise also brings with it its own distinctive forms of snobbery which are implicated in the remaking of class today, and which we will go on to talk about more in Chapter 11.

We can understand class as a crystallization of different kinds of capital through examining the interplay between economic, social and cultural capital. At the end of this exercise, our argument is a relatively simple one. The primacy of the dividing line between middle and working class has little purchase today. Although we can still distinguish boundaries in the central reaches of the class structure which allow us to differentiate more 'middle class' from 'working class' groups, this does not seem to be the boundary which we should fixate on. In particular, within the middle reaches of the class structure, age and expertise are major modes of differentiation and contestation, leading to considerable complexity and diversity.

However, at the top and bottom we can see much more distinctive classes which lie at polar opposites to each other. There are virtuous and vicious circuits in place in both of these extremes. And this, we argue, demonstrates why we might focus on the power of class divisions at these extremes. An elite and a precariat class can be differentiated from a more fragmented set of groups in the middle. In particular, we now live in a more polarized world and one where the wealth elite are increasingly distinctive vis-à-vis the rest of the population. This argument, analytically, focuses on how different sorts of capital cross-fertilize each other, and how, in today's highly market-driven, capitalist environment, these modes of accumulation intersect with intense power. In a nutshell, this is the new landscape of social class in the twenty-first century. Having staked out this case, we will now show this imprint manifests in key arenas of social life, social mobility, education and geography, in the rest of this book.

# PART THREE

# Social Mobility, Education and Location

# Climbing Mountains

In 1958 the inspirational social entrepreneur Michael Young, the driving force behind the formation of the Consumers' Association as well as the Open University, and the first chair of the Social Science Research Council, wrote a prescient book, *The Rise of the Meritocracy*.[1] Taking note of the trend towards upward mobility associated with grammar-school children gaining access to university education and then moving into professional and management jobs, he pondered the long-term implications of this shift. On the face of it, this was surely progress. No longer were these elite jobs solely reserved for the sons of the upper-class elite, who had had the right education at private school and Oxbridge or some other hallowed university. Young reflected on the situation: 'The talented have been given the opportunity to rise to the level which accords with their capacities, and the lower classes consequently reserved for those who are also lower in ability.'[2]

But in fact Young's prognosis was not optimistic. He suggested that the rise of meritocracy would actually produce a new superior caste, composed of those with high IQs, ruthlessly separated by a testing regime from the 'lesser' beings who lacked such abilities. He forecast the hardening of class inequalities linked to the rise of these meritocrats, with those lacking requisitely high IQ levels being confined to menial and unrewarding jobs. Young's satire was directed against the grammar-school system with its use of the 11-plus examination to pluck out the wheat of the 10 to 15 per cent of eleven-year-olds, who would be selected for superior academic education, from the chaff, who would be relegated to a second-rate education and a life on the factory floor or in the office. Consequently, his was one of the voices which argued passionately for comprehensive schooling.

Yet, although Young's campaign for comprehensive-school education was largely victorious, in the longer term, perhaps he has been proven right? Young's ironic refrain that '[c]ivilisation does not depend on the stolid mass . . . but upon the creative minority . . . the restless elite' has, in fact, become a policy mantra throughout much of the world.[3] Perhaps those meritocratic processes have actually been implicated in the striking inequalities of different sorts of capital and classes which we have unravelled in this book. In this chapter, we use the metaphor of mountain climbing to unpack this argument. What we have seen in Britain – as in many nations – is an increasingly vertiginous social landscape, with a lot more total economic capital – a lot more rock and earth – and with the highest mountains now rising much further above the valley than they did three decades ago. It follows that those with the most fitness, talent, determination and endeavour are best placed to climb these mountains. Young also pointed to the fact that this intense 'race to the top' generated a mechanical and narrow view of what 'merit' might mean – based on the skill in passing educational tests. In this process, other skills and capacities that mountaineers might have – an ecological awareness of wild-life, a sense of the environment, empathy for other moun-taineers – get stripped out and became redundant. In the competition to get to the top, however, those who join the meritocratic route to the summit from the highest base camps have much better prospects of getting to the top. And, we might also add, their chances are even better if they can mobilize and combine every advantage possible – their eco-nomic, social and cultural capital – so that they have the most effective kit on their arduous adventure.

We should not overstretch this metaphor, but the impli-cations are clear. A more competitive, ruthless and indeed meritocratic system can nonetheless generate high levels of inequality in life chances which go hand-in-hand with very unequal prospects.

## Social mobility in contemporary Britain

In the light of his dystopic arguments about the baneful effects of meritocracy, Young might not be surprised that educational expansion and reform seem to have gone hand-in-hand with a notable consensus which has emerged in poli-tics and the media that social mobility in Britain is in striking decline.[4] This view was first mooted during the New Labour era and was strongly reinforced by the Coalition government elected in 2010. The problem was underlined in 2011 when the government published a cross-departmental strategy with the central slogan 'improving social mobility is the prin-cipal goal of the government's social policy'. This was accompanied by a number of impassioned speeches from the deputy prime minister, Nick Clegg, railing at the enduring shackles of the British class system. 'We must create a more dynamic society,' he said at a major conference on mobility in 2012, 'one where what matters is the person you become, not the person you were born.'

In fact we need to be cautious in thinking that social mobility is in decline. A lot depends on how it is measured. The dominant sociological approach has been derived from the Nuffield mobility study carried out from 1968 to 1971. In this hugely impressive piece of research, John Goldthorpe and his colleagues focused on mobility between the seven occupational classes defined in Chapter 1, and especially between the working, the intermediate and the service classes. Goldthorpe's core argument was that from the middle decades of the twentieth century there was a considerable rise in upward mobility, which was due mainly to the rise of professional and managerial occupations which sucked up children born in lower social classes into higher ones. When comparing the prospects of middle- and working class children, however, little had changed – the relative advantages of those coming from a middle class compared to a working class background proved fairly constant. And he argues that this picture has endured until the present day, with only a slight recent tendency for upward mobility for men (but not for women) to decline.[5]

Goldthorpe's findings are powerful and convincing in their own terms, but they depend on the model of class he deploys, because this defines the parameters between which mobility is measured. We have already suggested in Chapter 2 that these occupational classes may not be discriminating enough at the higher levels of the social hierarchy.[6] They might distinguish between the hills and the plain, but not between the highest mountains of the range. And indeed, if we measure mobility between different groupings other than the 'big classes' used by Goldthorpe, other conclusions can be drawn. Economists, for instance, measure mobility between income groups, an approach more in keeping with our account of economic capital here. The arguments of economists based at the Centre for Economic Performance at the London School of Economics headed by Jo Blanden and Stephen Machin have been especially influential.[7] They found that by examining incomes of people in Britain compared to their parents, first for those born in 1958 and then for those born in 1970, a clear and statistically significant decline in income mobility between these two generations could be found. These economists further argued that this decline could be associated with the fact that children from better-off families had benefited disproportionately from the expansion of higher education and the higher earnings that tend to accompany graduate jobs.

Over the past decade this research has led to arguments between economists and sociologists which have had the unfortunate effect of pitching occupational against income measures of mobility, as if these need to be mutually incompatible. Given our interest in using concepts of economic capital rather than occupational class, we are attracted to the economists' approach, which we think offers a more disaggregated and refined indicator of mobility than 'big' occupational classes.[8] This is especially true when we look at who gets to the mountain tops. Is the relatively small elite class at the top of the social structure relatively impervious to outsiders, or is it possible for new people to negotiate its highest slopes?

In addressing this question, the multifaceted GBCS offers considerable evidence on the relationship between different sorts of capital and mobility which we will bring to bear here.[9] It can provide a more *multidimensional* lens on contemporary mobility rates, and therefore the process of 'class formation'; one that moves beyond the purely economic or occupational and instead considers the additional role that social and cultural capital play in class movement and division (as outlined in Chapter 5).

Table 6.1 shows the rate of mobility into the seven GBCS class categories which we defined in Chapter 5, using a person's class origin as that defined by the occupation of their main parental earner when they were fourteen years old. The figures are from the nationally representative GfK data-set, but in brackets are the corresponding figures from the GBCS. In providing the broad interpretations, we focus on the nationally representative patterns. Table 6.1 identifies four social groups from which respondents may come, those from the highest-status (senior managerial and traditional professional) occupational backgrounds; those from slightly less high-status backgrounds (middle managerial and modern professional), categorized as short-range upwardly mobile; those from intermediate and technical occupational backgrounds, categorized as mid-range upwardly mobile; and finally those from low-status occupational backgrounds (manual workers and those who have never worked), who are categorized as long-range upwardly mobile. Returning to our mountaineering metaphor, we might view the first of these as having a base camp in the lofty mountain passes, the second group as having base camps well up the valley sides, the third as having a base slightly above the valley bottom, and the final group having to start out from the valley floor.

Table 6.1 should be read across the rows. We thus learn that 51 per cent of those in our elite class had parents who were in class 1 (senior managerial and professional) compared to only 11 per cent who had parents who were in the precariat. This is a remarkable difference, with over twelve times as many of the elite coming from the most advantaged backgrounds compared to the precariat. Only 11 per cent of the elite have climbed from the valley floor compared to the majority, who, because of their starting position high up on the mountain, have had to do little or no climbing at all. At the other extreme, the picture is reversed: 65 per cent of the precariat remain where they grew up, on the valley floor (their parents having been in semi-skilled and routine employment). And we can see that only 4 per cent of the precariat come from senior managerial or traditional professional backgrounds: there is not much mobility going from top to bottom of British society either. Few of those on the mountain tops, or even the valley sides, move down. It is actually rather difficult to fall all the way down the mountain slopes!

If we look at the proportion of our seven classes who are recruited from the most humble backgrounds, a clear fourfold division is apparent. The lowest proportion of those from routine and semi-routine occupational backgrounds end up in the elite with the established middle class (19 per cent). All the other classes have approximately the same range (between 38 per cent and 47 per cent) until we get to the precariat, where the proportion rises dramatically to two-thirds. So, the headline is that there are real limits to how much social mobility there is into the higher social classes.

The most striking finding from Table 6.1 is that the small elite class is, in fact, much more exclusive than any of the other classes. This is a powerful indication that our redrawing of class boundaries reveals marked patterns of closure which are less evident when occupational class measures are used. To return to our mountaineering metaphor, whereas numerous types of fit and motivated people are able to reach the top of Snowdon or Ben Nevis, those summiting on Mont Blanc, let alone Everest, are an altogether more select bunch.

Much of the political anxiety concerning declining social mobility has centred on entry into what are often called 'the professions'. In particular, there has long been a perception that Britain's traditionally high-status professional arenas, such as law, medicine and engineering, remain stubbornly elitist and recruit largely those who have been privately educated or who hail from privileged class backgrounds. Particularly influential in bringing this issue to public attention has been the former Labour minister Alan Milburn. Milburn experienced profound upward mobility himself, from his birth on a council estate in County Durham to a role in front-bench Cabinet politics. Yet the obstacles he faced during his own upward journey, particularly in the

**MAIN PARENTAL INCOME-EARNER'S OCCUPATIONAL CLASS[1]**

| GBCS CLASSES | CLASS 1: SENIOR MANAGERIAL OR TRADITIONAL PROFESSIONAL | CLASS 2: MIDDLE MANAGERIAL OR MODERN PROFESSIONAL | CLASSES 3-5: INTERMEDIATE OR TECHNICAL WORKERS | CLASSES 6-7: MANUAL WORKERS OR NEVER WORKED | TOTAL NUMBER OF RESPONDENTS (IN BRACKETS SHOWS FROM GBCS) |
|---|---|---|---|---|---|
| Elite | 51 (55) | 11 (26) | 28 (13) | 11 (7) | 61 (35,288) |
| Established middle class | 39 (35) | 11 (34) | 31 (20) | 19 (11) | 252 (69,917) |
| New affluent workers | 18 (16) | 8 (28) | 33 (31) | 41 (24) | 169 (9,297) |
| Technical middle class | 42 (37) | 6 (33) | 15 (18) | 38 (11) | 57 (15,382) |
| Traditional working class | 16 (23) | 9 (26) | 27 (30) | 47 (22) | 131 (2,622) |
| Emerging service workers | 21 (28) | 9 (33) | 28 (23) | 43 (17) | 205 (27,780) |
| Precariat | 4 (13) | 4 (20) | 27 (28) | 65 (40) | 151 (1,114) |
| Population as a whole (from different backgrounds) | 25 (37) | 8 (31) | 28 (20) | 38 (12) | 1,026 (161,400) |

Table 6.1

Family of Origin and the GBCS' 'Seven Classes'

1. The nationally representative GfK survey is used, but for comparison purposes the GBCS equivalent numbers are in brackets. These give an indication of the way that the GBCS is skewed towards those originating from class 1 and class 2 families. (Percentages may not equal 100% as they are rounded up.) The main parental income-earner's class is derived from an occupational measure linked to the NS-SEC, where class 1 represents senior managerial or traditional professional, class 2, middle managerial or modern professional, classes 3–5 cover intermediate and technical occupations, and classes 6–7 represent manual workers and those who have never worked

select arena of politics, convinced Milburn that working towards equitable access to the professions represented the lynchpin in improving social mobility.[10] In 2009 he authored the damning 'Unleashing Aspiration' report to the Panel on Fair Access to the Professions that came to be known as the 'Milburn Report'. He argued strongly that certain professions, such as the media, law and medicine, remained a 'closed shop' and were not doing enough to 'open themselves up to a wider pool of talent'.[11] He has since continued to apply political pressure in this area, authoring a series of similarly influential reports in his role as Chair of the Social Mobility and Child Poverty Commission.

Yet while Milburn's reports have provided powerful and extensive accounts of access to the British professions, they have relied upon data collected from a variety of disparate sources, some of which are now somewhat dated. The GBCS provides a valuable new resource. Figure 6.1 uses the GBCS to examine mobility into a number of high-status occupations, looking at the highest and lowest proportion of these which have been recruited from the most advantaged parental class – that of senior managers.

Figure 6.1 shows that even among elite occupations, there is a huge variation in how likely it is for those born outside senior manager ranks to gain entry. Ten occupations have over 50 per cent of their members who have originated from these select backgrounds, with barristers and judges at the top, ranging down through medical practitioners, brokers, solicitors and chief executive officers. What is most striking is how many of these occupations are associated with the law or finance – with only medical practitioners being exempted from this.

We can compare these groups with elite occupations which draw a lower proportion of their members from senior managerial backgrounds.[12] Many of these occupations are in information technology, suggesting that this relatively new area of employment may be more open to talent drawn from wider pools. Looking more broadly at the patterns of mobility, the most inclusive high-status groups (in descending order) are: scientists, accountants, engineers, senior IT workers and academics.

These findings point towards an intriguing distinction within the professions between a more traditional, 'gentlemanly' version of the professions in law, medicine and business, which remain defiantly exclusive, and a more technical, but more 'open' stratum of emerging professionals in the form of researchers, IT workers, and IT and telecommunications directors. One explanation for this, supported by previous research,[13] is that the more opaque and hard-to-acquire resources of cultural and social capital that the privileged tend to inherit from their parents continue to be more important for ensuring access into the most traditional professions.

And there is a further twist here. It so happens that those elite occupations that are more likely to recruit people who come from senior-manager families are also more likely to have higher income rewards. This is a 'bees round a honeypot' effect: the more economic capital is associated with a specific job, the more likely it is that it draws to it those from privileged backgrounds. Table 6.2 demonstrates this point

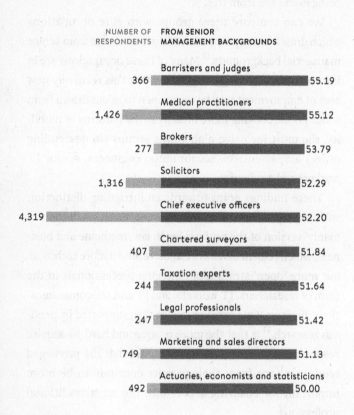

|  | NUMBER OF RESPONDENTS | FROM SENIOR MANAGEMENT BACKGROUNDS |
|---|---|---|
| **Barristers and judges** | 366 | 55.19 |
| **Medical practitioners** | 1,426 | 55.12 |
| **Brokers** | 277 | 53.79 |
| **Solicitors** | 1,316 | 52.29 |
| **Chief executive officers** | 4,319 | 52.20 |
| **Chartered surveyors** | 407 | 51.84 |
| **Taxation experts** | 244 | 51.64 |
| **Legal professionals** | 247 | 51.42 |
| **Marketing and sales directors** | 749 | 51.13 |
| **Actuaries, economists and statisticians** | 492 | 50.00 |

### Figure 6.1a

The ten jobs filled by those with the HIGHEST percentage of senior management (SM) backgrounds (NS–SEC1 occupations only)

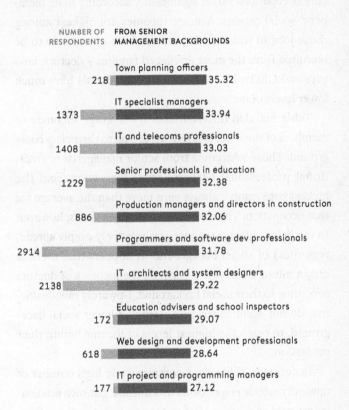

NUMBER OF RESPONDENTS | FROM SENIOR MANAGEMENT BACKGROUNDS

**Town planning officers**
218 — 35.32

**IT specialist managers**
1373 — 33.94

**IT and telecoms professionals**
1408 — 33.03

**Senior professionals in education**
1229 — 32.38

**Production managers and directors in construction**
886 — 32.06

**Programmers and software dev professionals**
2914 — 31.78

**IT architects and system designers**
2138 — 29.22

**Education advisers and school inspectors**
172 — 29.07

**Web design and development professionals**
618 — 28.64

**IT project and programming managers**
177 — 27.12

### Figure 6.1b

The ten jobs filled by those with the LOWEST percentage of senior management (SM) backgrounds (NS–SEC1 occupations only)

clearly. It shows that the distribution of income within these elite occupations varies significantly according to its members' social origins. Average incomes are highest among those jobs in which their personnel are most likely to be recruited from the most privileged families – doctors, lawyers and CEOs. By contrast, IT professionals have much lower levels of income.

Table 6.2 also differentiates the average incomes of members of these occupations according to their class background. Those who come from senior managerial or traditional professional backgrounds – who start from the highest base camp – always earn more than the average for that occupation. The size of this difference varies, however. In medicine, average incomes are relatively evenly spread, regardless of social background. It appears that there is only a minor discrepancy between the incomes of doctors according to their social background. Upwardly mobile doctors do not seem to struggle, despite a lower social background, to reach the highest levels of income within their profession.

In contrast, there are a comparatively high number of upwardly mobile respondents in academia, but such academics are paid an average of up to £13,000 less than those from more privileged backgrounds. Perhaps the upwardly mobile academics are less likely to work at elite universities where pay tends to be higher. More generally, among lawyers, barristers and judges, CEOs and financial intermediaries, income differences by origin are particularly pronounced. Many of these occupations, notably the law, depend on recruiting graduates from higher education, but this does not appear to mute these differences. Meritocratic recruitment does not eradicate the advantages which are enjoyed by those who come into these occupations from privileged backgrounds. Those occupations directly associated with finance see especially marked differences. Financial intermediaries from higher managerial and traditional professional backgrounds earn on average £24,000, nearly 40 per cent, more than those from routine and semi-routine backgrounds.

Let us reflect further on this. We are quite rightly troubled by the existence of a gender pay gap within many occupations, which can be as much as 50 per cent in some managerial occupations. But it also appears that there is a 'social class background pay gap'. Those who are best paid in many elite occupations are those who come from the most advantaged backgrounds. This 'class salary gap' regularly reaches 25 per cent in many of the more affluent occupations, but this has never previously come to light and should also be a cause for concern.

What we are therefore witnessing here is a process of mutual reinforcement of advantage which takes place at the upper levels of the social hierarchy. The more lucrative the occupation, the more likely it is to be composed of people from advantaged backgrounds. And the best-paid members of these occupations tend to also be disproportionately drawn from the most privileged backgrounds. We have a mutually reinforcing process, which, as Pierre Bourdieu would argue, shows how those with capital can convert their advantages in numerous ways.

## FAMILY OF ORIGIN AND CURRENT SALARY

| OCCUPATIONAL GROUP | SENIOR MANAGERS AND TRADITIONAL PROFESSIONS | MIDDLE MANAGERS AND MODERN PROFESSIONS |
|---|---|---|
| Scientists | 50,790 | 45,740 |
| Engineers | 55,066 | 49,678 |
| IT professionals | 61,899 | 53,770 |
| Doctors | 80,226 | 78,925 |
| Other medical professionals | 60,617 | 57,266 |
| Higher-education teachers | 68,264 | 61,534 |
| Education professionals | 60,324 | 57,012 |
| Lawyers, barristers, judges | 86,363 | 75,273 |
| Public sector (outside health) | 57,946 | 50,131 |
| Accountants | 63,848 | 57,237 |
| CEOs, directors, presidents | 101,052 | 87,751 |
| Other senior business people | 68,668 | 61,081 |
| Financial intermediaries | 84,797 | 68,843 |
| Journalists | 53,876 | 48,958 |
| Other NS-SEC 1 occupations | 59,417 | 51,678 |

Table 6.2

Average Income by Occupational Group and Family of Origin
*Source:* GBCS data

| INTERMEDIATE AND TECHNICAL OCCUPATIONS | MANUAL AND NEVER WORKED | AVERAGE FOR ALL IN THESE ELITE OCCUPATIONS |
| --- | --- | --- |
| 46,832 | 44,179 | 47,928 |
| 47,648 | 47,554 | 51,237 |
| 50,301 | 50,462 | 55,296 |
| 68,840 | 74,915 | 78,221 |
| 60,262 | 53,929 | 58,924 |
| 57,553 | 55,000 | 62,640 |
| 56,207 | 56,989 | 57,901 |
| 67,450 | 65,583 | 79,436 |
| 52,810 | 49,341 | 53,163 |
| 52,009 | 52,990 | 59,118 |
| 84,606 | 83,467 | 93,881 |
| 57,437 | 56,678 | 63,233 |
| 60,942 | 60,767 | 74,130 |
| 46,102 | 46,895 | 50,168 |
| 51,306 | 49,411 | 54,738 |

# Social and cultural capital in the mobility process

Those coming from the most advantaged backgrounds tend to be well endowed with all kinds of capital. Figure 6.2 indicates how class of origin affects the possession of economic capital – focusing on those in the elite alone. In every case, those who are from senior managerial and traditional professional backgrounds have more income and savings, and have higher-valued houses. Their houses are worth substantially different sums – the homes of those from senior managerial backgrounds are £34,000 more expensive than those of their incoming counterparts on short-range mobility trajectories and £43,000 more than those of their mid- and long-range counterparts. There is an accumulation of economic advantage here which allows those with inherited assets to outstrip other members of the elite from less privileged backgrounds.

Figure 6.3 also shows that those from senior managerial family backgrounds are more likely to know higher-status people and to participate in highbrow cultural capital than others among their elite peers.

At the apex of the social hierarchy, economic, social and cultural capital intersect and reinforce each other. It is not impossible for those without one or more of these to join the upper reaches, but it is harder for them to do so.[14] This is not because they are formally excluded, but because, in the competitive race to the top, those with the most advantages on all possible scores are the ones who are likely to have that

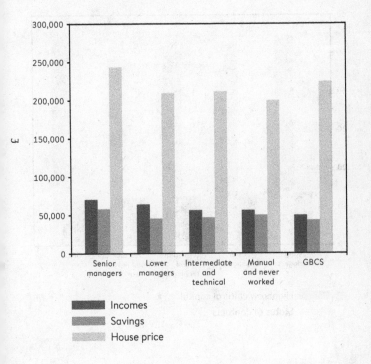

**Figure 6.2**

Economic Capital of the elite by Family of Origin
(average £ of GBCS respondents in NS-SEC 1 according to
the occupational social class background of their family)

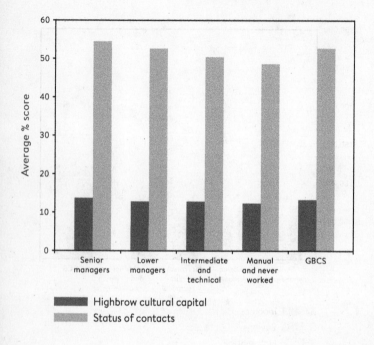

**Figure 6.3**

Cultural and Social Capital of the elite by Family of Origin (average scores (as defined in chapter 5) of GBCS respondents in NS-SEC 1 according to the occupational social class background of family)

extra bit of leverage to do better. And, indeed, this argument chimes with the views of our interviewees very clearly. Louise, a management consultant from south London, had experienced remarkable upward mobility. She was brought up on a council estate by a single mother (who was long-term unemployed for most of her childhood). Yet, despite only gaining modest O-level results, Louise had rapidly worked her way up within the beauty industry, from shop-floor assistant to senior management. Now earning over £250,000 a year, she works as a highly prized consultant and sits on the boards of a number of high-street beauty brands. For Louise, this professional milieu, which she described as being dominated by those from privileged backgrounds, invokes a complex set of emotions. On the one hand, she explained that she doesn't hide her past from her colleagues and, in fact, 'makes a point' of being open about her background: 'Most people know I couldn't read or write at fourteen, couldn't do this, couldn't do that, and actually I think there's a respect there.' But while there may be admiration for Louise's upward trajectory, it also acts as a cultural barrier – particularly in terms of the more informal networking aspects of her work. She describes a culture of informal chatting in the workplace, where talking about the arts, sharing anecdotes about holidays or discussing children's schooling can be an important way of oiling the wheels of business relationships or building rapport with senior colleagues. In this realm, Louise described a strong sense of isolation, a feeling of not having anything in common with those around her. 'I don't really participate, you know, I'm very distant.' In fact, for Louise, there was a clear frustration at the oblique manner in which her colleagues utilized these shared cultural references and lifestyle 'chit-chat' as career resources, or 'for a leg up', as she put it. 'I don't need to play golf with you to get a job,' she said, in exasperation. 'You know, give me the job because I can deliver the business, or don't give it to me at all!'

Louise's experience of the subtle but significant role that cultural and social capital played in her experience of an elite occupational arena was echoed elsewhere. While upwardly mobile respondents rarely felt their tastes or social networks had *directly* inhibited their careers or relationships, they nonetheless sensed that they lacked some of the advantages of those more naturally plugged into a privileged milieu. This feeling of deficit appeared in seemingly banal ways, in the cultural minutiae of Alan being advised on the 'correct' way to have his steak cooked (rare, not well done), or in Jeremy's panic at having to take part in 'intellectual conversation' at the dinner table with his middle class boyfriend's parents. But it also sometimes manifested itself as a more overt and concrete disadvantage, such as when George reflected on the powerful social connections wielded by his public school-educated colleagues in law, or when Samantha explained her difficulties in 'getting ahead' in political lobbying because she couldn't afford to take the unpaid internships that helped propel her colleagues forward in their careers.

To recap, stable members of the elite tend to have higher levels of all three types of capital than those who have recently gained entry into this group. This provides them with advantages in the competitive race to the top of the highest peaks. As Figure 6.2 illustrates, those from more humble backgrounds earn less, have less expensive properties, have fewer influential social contacts, and have less highbrow cultural capital than their more privileged peers, *even when they are in the same job*. Moreover, as interviews showed, these deficits also often carried an emotional dimension, with the upwardly mobile feeling vulnerable and inadequate in elite settings. And in the last part of this chapter we want to show that this psychological dimension is crucial for understanding the meaning of mobility and in shaping how people pursue their ambitions.

## Gearing up for the climb: the experience of upward mobility

What we have shown in this book is that the volume of economic capital has reached unparalleled levels in recent decades, and in addition its possession is extremely skewed, especially at the top. Cultural capital and social capital are also highly unevenly distributed. We have likened this to an icy, mountainous landscape, where those focused only on the climb to the top must be extremely well equipped with the relevant specialist skills. But in Britain today, where hills have given way to mountains, where does this leave the many people who aspire to improve their position but do not necessarily share such highly competitive orientations? It creates emotional challenges and costs which might explain why some people may prefer a less competitive outing, leaving the icy peaks to those most advantaged, in terms of being best equipped with a strong and well-organized climbing party, but also, most crucially of all, starting from the highest possible 'base camp'.

British culture has long delighted in lampooning the travails of the upwardly mobile, from Hardy's *Jude the Obscure* and H. G. Wells's *Kipps* right through to Monty Python's 'Four Yorkshireman'. These fictional portraits highlight how 'errors' of taste and etiquette mark the upwardly mobile out as outsiders continually striving (but ultimately failing) to gain full acceptance at the top of their professions. And in such a way, elite mountaineers accustomed to the highest peaks may indeed look down on the day-trip hikers they see hazardously negotiating the lower slopes beneath. Perhaps the most memorable caricature of the upwardly mobile in recent years is Hyacinth Bucket, the aspirational housewife from the 1990s BBC 1 sitcom *Keeping Up Appearances* (who insisted her surname be pronounced 'Bouquet'). Despite her desperate attempts to embody upper-middle class refinement – in dress, accent and taste – the sitcom parodies Hyacinth's social failure, from the perspective that she can never quite embody the cultural capital she so desires in order to escape her lower-middle class roots. What is at stake here is the social faux pas of being 'above oneself', of appearing to have higher aspirations than are warranted – of not 'knowing one's place'.

In fact, there is ample work showing that those who climb a modest way and can see their position as being markedly better than their parents are likely to feel content and satisfied. John Goldthorpe argued that the upwardly mobile whom he had studied in the early 1970s tended to be overwhelmingly content with the progress of their lives.[15]

Goldthorpe, however, concentrated on mobility broadly into the professions and management, rather than the higher elite level that we have distinguished here. Furthermore, when the boundary between middle and working class was clearly marked, as it was in the 1950s and 1960s through the distinction between a salary and a wage, then it is quite plausible that anyone who feels as if they have crossed this threshold may feel content. And indeed, this sense of satisfaction was evident for a minority of our older upwardly mobile respondents. These older men from the post-war 'baby-boomer' generation were more likely to have experienced upward mobility as a smooth and successful experience and therefore rejected the role that class had played in their own and other people's lives. For respondents like Giles, a retired banker, class identity was therefore often used as a 'convenient excuse' for not working harder or for not achieving upward mobility.

However, when divisions in the middle ranges of the social structure are more opaque and complex – as they are today – then it might also follow that people are uncertain about whether they have been upwardly mobile or not, and may also be more likely to take their cues from those whom they see at the very top of their profession. In this case, we might imagine that a sense of inferiority may be more likely. Our interviews reveal indications of this. The upwardly mobile had certainly faced many external hurdles, but the difficulties they reported were invariably as much about internal self-doubt as the judgements made, or barriers enacted, by others. Many reported a paralysing suspicion that they somehow 'weren't good enough', that they felt like a 'fraud', or that a 'fall' was just around the corner. Jennifer, a fifty-two-year-old writer from the west of Scotland, had been brought up in council housing in Glasgow, but had gone on to become a successful author of fiction. However, she describes the literary world as one which had been hard to navigate because she didn't feel she had the kind of cultural poise of many of those around her, who were from more privileged backgrounds. 'I don't have a lot of confidence when it comes to networking in the writing world,' she told us. 'I suppose I feel a bit gauche and clumsy with a lot of things – when we're talking about eating, or holidays or whatever.' What was significant here and in other instances in which Jennifer talked about her status anxiety was that this wasn't necessarily the result of any snobbishness she had experienced from her literary colleagues, but more of an internal niggle based on comparing herself with those whom she saw at the very top of her new professional world.

A common sentiment among our interviewees, therefore, was a feeling of being 'caught between two worlds' (Fiona), of not 'knowing where I fit in' (Jennifer), or being 'stuck in the middle' (Jeremy). Sarah, for example, seemed acutely aware of the incongruity between her life now – as a successful district nurse married to a middle class engineer – and her upbringing on a 'rough' council estate in northern England. She therefore strongly distanced herself from what she saw as the 'underclass' of her background, but at the same time noted that the permanent imprint of this history prevented her from feeling part of the middle class. Sarah therefore constantly expressed her desire to 'escape' the 'shame' of her past, but at the same time explained how she was continually forced to confront it – through caring for her elderly parents ('Because that's what I should do'), in living near her home town ('I just feel uneasy, I don't want to go back to that'), or via painful recollections of her wedding day ('There was an awful social divide, it was the worst day of my life').

Such a sentiment of being torn between two worlds was common in some manner in many of our interviewees, especially among those who had experienced especially long-range trajectories or had recollections of very sudden moments of mobility, particularly during their childhood. Here there was often a shared sense of feeling somehow 'culturally homeless',[16] and each had their own stories of the exhausting emotional labour required to reconcile such contradictory sources of identity. These were especially marked among immigrant groups, who often narrated complex stories of feeling that they did not belong to British society, even if they had been upwardly mobile into its higher reaches.[17] The interplay between ethnicity, immigration and class caused intense tensions here.

Gita, a graphic designer from London, had first-generation Ugandan Indian parents, who had spent their lives running a newsagent in the East End. Gita had gone to university and had a successful career, but her career had been marked by an exhausting balancing act between the cultural values of her working class ethnic and middle class occupational identities. This manifested itself most prominently when Gita decided to divorce her husband, with whom her parents had arranged the marriage, in her late twenties. For Gita, this decision was intimately connected to ideas of feminist emancipation that had been introduced to her at university and had been informed by advice she had received from white, female middle class colleagues at the time. However, the divorce had caused an irrevocable rift with her parents and the local Indian community. For Gita, the divorce was the source of a multitude of difficult emotions. At once a proud signal of her feminist identity and financial independence, it was also the root of a strong sense of shame – an emotion from which, she noted, it was almost impossible to escape. 'Because my family is linked very much to the Indian community, even if I don't want to be, I'm pushed back . . . y'know, somebody knows someone and so on . . .' For Gita, the result of such social suffering was a profoundly conflicted sense of self, oscillating between the loyalties of family and the opportunities of mobility:

> I've always thought I've never really belonged, but then
> I always thought it was just me, y'know? Because I felt
> I didn't believe totally in the Indian culture, but I didn't
> belong in my English friends' lives because they were a
> lot more free. So I've always drifted, dipped in and out
> of different cultures, always been quite a detached person
> wherever I go.

Our aim in presenting the stories of those like Gita is not to somehow suggest that Britain's upwardly mobile are somehow unhappy people or suffer from psychological disorders. Not only is it far beyond the scope of our study to make such an assertion, but most of our interviewees seemed to be juggling this multitude of emotions valiantly, even perhaps 'successfully'. However, this data illustrates simply the profound *emotional imprint* of social mobility. Whether successfully managed or not, reconciling such an array of difficult emotions clearly demands an exhausting amount of mental work. It also indicates that there are limits to the ambitions of the would-be mobile, who may fear that reaching the summit of British society implies a certain betrayal of class or cultural origins. Either way, the strong retention of a working class identity among many upwardly mobile respondents indicates that the emotional pull of class loyalties can entangle subjects in the affinities of the past, and why – despite prevailing political rhetoric – the constant quest for upward mobility may not be something that all unequivocally aspire to.

There is a very well-known social scientific adage – that equality of opportunity can only be made real when it is associated with equality in general. The less equal societies are, the less easy it is for there to be social mobility between its extremes. Our arguments here are following a well-worn route. However, we also make a bolder claim that meritocratic processes go hand-in-hand with this dynamic. We have followed Michael Young's logic regarding meritocracy through to its conclusion, and provided ample evidence for his dystopic account. And this argument is, on the face of it, highly counter-intuitive. We might expect meritocracy to mark the end of rigid class divisions, that no longer can your friends and family 'pull strings' to find jobs for you, no longer can the Old Boys' club operate. We might, indeed, imagine that meritocracy would allow more mobility and also create a social order where people would feel rewarded for their talents and energies; that anyone would be able to scale the highest mountain peaks.

However, what a more competitive and unequal society

has generated is actually strong class divisions, where a person's class of origin leaves a powerful stamp on her or his life chances. It strongly affects the prospects of moving upwards, and it also has a psychological imprint. This competition for access to the most privileged and best-rewarded positions at the top of the social hierarchy appears skewed in favour of those from the most advantaged backgrounds. Occasionally this might be due to nepotism, or overt discrimination; but more often, this largely reflects the fact that as capital accumulates and the peaks of advantage steepen, those who start higher up don't even need to climb the lower slopes at all and can focus on negotiating the icy paths to the summit. And in order to prevail at these altitudes they are able to draw on the full range of advantages available to them – from their social networks through to their cultural capital – all of which, singly and in combination, play a part.

Let us be clear that we are not saying there is no social mobility, or even that social mobility is declining. This all depends on how mobility is measured, and in the middle ranges of the social hierarchy the chances of making a significant change in life's trajectory are good. Yet, despite the fact that there seems to be a lot of movement into this middle part of the class structure, mobility into the upper echelons and traditionally high-status professions is markedly more difficult. Moreover, even when the upwardly mobile are successful in obtaining a privileged position, they still often fail to amass the very highest levels of economic, cultural and social capital. Those upwardly mobile into the GBCS's elite category, for example, are paid less, are less well-connected and less engaged in traditionally high-status culture than those from the stable elite echelons; and, when the upwardly mobile do participate, it is less likely to be in the traditionally elite arenas, such as the opera house or après-ski. This might explain why a lingering sense of deficit rooted in those from a lower-status background often underpinned the experiences of the upwardly mobile among those who felt they lacked the requisite cultural and social equipment to belong to the very top – even when, in fact, they had been successful.

And this stretching of the peaks of advantage can have marked effects on personal psychologies more broadly. As the respondents featured in this chapter show, individual identities carry – at least in some shape or form – the symbolic baggage of the past. While for some this was worn lightly, as a reminder of how far they had come and how much they had achieved, for the majority this sense of success was tempered by the fact that mobility had, at times, constituted a distinctly bumpy emotional ride. The self-reported class identities often showed a complex set of affinities informed as much by origin as by destination. Many expressed a sense of being caught between two worlds, constantly juggling contradictory sources of identity. Thus, while the contemporary experience of upward mobility in Britain may involve indisputable gains in economic capital and social status, it is important to consider that such benefits can often come with a considerable psychological price tag.

# A Tale of Two Campuses?

UNIVERSITIES AND MERITOCRACY

Michael Young's satire on 'the rise of the meritocracy' focused mainly on the power of the school system to differentiate children on the basis of their IQs and said little about the significance of universities in affecting future careers. He wrote at a time when only 5 per cent of children went to universities. However, in the years since, the university system has expanded dramatically, and in this chapter we will show how universities play a key role in affecting social mobility, especially at the top levels. Our main argument is that going to university matters a great deal for entering the elite, but it is not the only ticket to elite entry, and certainly not the Golden Ticket. It matters too *which* specific university is attended and *where*: the destinations of graduates from different 'types' of university vary widely and there are some striking – and in some cases surprising – outcomes for graduates of particular institutions. We will argue that intense educational competition reinforces a strong pecking order between universities, in which it is the elite institutions which play a vital role in permitting access to the most advantaged positions.[1]

These findings are very important because currently we have little long-term understanding about what happens to

British graduates after they leave university. We know that there are inequalities in access to universities by class, gender and ethnic background and pupils from state and independent schools have different chances of going to university. Such inequalities are especially stark for the most selective 'elite' institutions. We also know that graduates from the most prestigious universities, such as Oxford and Cambridge, are over-represented in privileged walks of British life. A high proportion of the top judges, members of the Cabinet, chief executives – and indeed the upper echelons of the BBC – have graduated from Britain's two most ancient universities. In the 2010 to 2015 British Parliament, for instance, the Prime Minister, the Leader of the Opposition, the Shadow Chancellor, the Foreign Secretary and the Chief Secretary to the Treasury all studied for the exact same degree – Philosophy, Politics and Economics (or PPE) at Oxford. Beyond prominent and highly visible individuals such as politicians and journalists, however, we know very little about how attending particular universities is associated with differences in wealth, success and influence. Here the rich detail of the GBCS helps us to draw a picture of the social and economic position of graduates from different universities.

## More higher education doesn't mean more equality

Britain, like most of the globe, has seen an explosion in rates of participation in university attendance (and in other sorts of higher education). At the turn of the twentieth century, university was an unusual pursuit for the British: less than one in every hundred young people entered university in 1901. Even for the most privileged young people, university remained a minority activity. Whether or not Evelyn Waugh's *Brideshead Revisited*, with its languid portrait of hedonistic aristocrats at Oxford, was an accurate picture of university life in the early twentieth century, it was still an unusual one, even for the elite: only about one in three upper-class young men were in university in 1930.

For those from more humble backgrounds, university was practically unthinkable. Thomas Hardy's novel *Jude the Obscure* (1985) related the letter sent by the Master of Biblioll College to the ambitious stonemason seeking entry to the hallowed university:

> Sir, – I have read your letter with interest; and, judging from your description of yourself as a working-man, I venture to think that you will have a much better chance of success in life by remaining in your own sphere and sticking to your trade than by adopting any other course. That, therefore, is what I advise you to do.

Indeed, there was just *one* student from a 'plebeian' background at Oxford in 1835, and none in 1860, and the higher education participation rate for the 'lower class' in 1870 and 1890 in Britain is estimated to be zero.

But by 1962, on the eve of the Robbins Report, which would accompany a dramatic expansion of the number of both universities and students, one in every twenty-five young people were in higher education. Successive waves of politicians saw the expansion of higher education as essential to the breaking down of old class barriers. For Gordon Brown, Labour Chancellor of the Exchequer in 2000:

> I say it is time to end the old Britain where what mattered was the privilege you were born to not the potential you were born with. Remove the old barriers, open up our universities and let everyone move ahead.

Successive expansion drives have seen student numbers rise rapidly (see Figure 7.1), such that currently just under half of British young people access some form of higher education before the age of thirty, with rates even higher in Scotland. Going to 'uni' has become commonplace and, for many sections of the population, virtually an expectation. Successive increases in the cost of a degree to students in the form of tuition fees and loans for living expenses seem to have had little impact on rates of participation.

Expansion has not, unfortunately, led to greater equality among young people from different backgrounds. Yet it is certainly true that attending university is no longer unthinkable for disadvantaged young people, as it was in the nineteenth century. There are numerous examples of very long-range social mobility through higher education. Prominent individuals from humble backgrounds such as the writer and broadcaster Melvyn Bragg, former attorney general Baroness Scotland, historian David Starkey and actress Julie Walters have achieved their success at least in part due to higher education.

So the absolute number of young people from less well-off homes entering university has increased dramatically since the 1950s. However, the number of young people from more advantaged backgrounds entering university has also increased

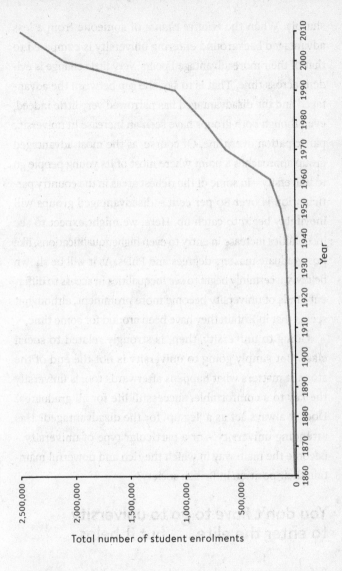

**Figure 7.1**

Higher education enrolments in the UK, 1860–2010

sharply. When the *relative chance* of someone from a less advantaged background entering university is compared to that of their more advantaged peers, very little change is evident across time. That is to say, the *gap* between the advantaged and the disadvantaged has narrowed very little indeed, even though both groups have seen an increase in university participation over time. Of course, as the most advantaged group approaches a point where most of its young people go to university – in some of the richest areas in the country participation is over 80 per cent – disadvantaged groups will inevitably begin to catch up. Here, we might expect to see inequalities increase in entry to even higher qualifications, like postgraduate masters degrees and PhDs. As it will be shown below, we certainly begin to see inequalities in access to different kinds of university become more prominent, although it seems that in Britain they have been around for some time.

Going to university, then, is strongly related to social class. But simply going to university is not the end of the story. It matters what happens afterwards too: is university the key to a comfortable, successful life for all graduates? Does it always act as a 'leg up' for the disadvantaged? Has attending university – or a particular type of university – become the main way in which the rich and powerful maintain their position in British society?

## You don't *have* to go to university to enter the elite . . . but it helps

Before we consider where graduates from different universities end up, it is worth looking at the problem from the opposite direction: what proportion of the elite went to university? And what about those who didn't? Figure 7.2 shows what proportion of our GBCS classes were graduates.

First of all, we should note that our elite group is not entirely dominated by graduates. Just over half of the elite in our nationally representative sample have a degree, although this increases to closer to two-thirds for those between the ages of twenty-five and fifty, so for the younger generation it appears to be increasingly important. A substantial minority of the elite have acquired that status without higher education. There are, of course, many prominent individuals, particularly in the world of business, who did not attend university. Famous entrepreneurs such as the electronics and football magnate and television star Lord Alan Sugar, former managing director of Birmingham City FC Baroness Karren Brady, Virgin magnate Sir Richard Branson and *Dragons' Den*'s Deborah Meaden are not graduates and in this way are not particularly unusual among their peers. Nor does graduate status hold much apparent advantage in the entertainment business or sport.

In politics, however, there has been a decline over time in the proportion of MPs who did not attend university. Only three of the thirteen British prime ministers since 1945 (Churchill, Callaghan and Major) were not graduates. All the others went to the University of Oxford (four of them going there from Eton College), with the exception of Gordon Brown, who graduated from the University of Edinburgh (with a degree and a PhD). Among the twenty-three members of the Cabinet at the outset of the 2010 UK Coalition government, only two were not graduates; nine were Oxford graduates, and a further six had attended Cambridge.[2] This

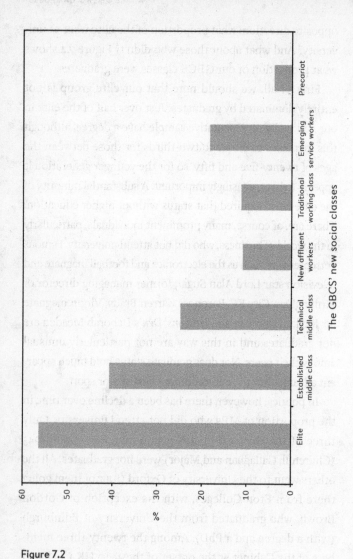

**Figure 7.2**

Percentage of each social class who are graduates

*Source*: The nationally representative data-set from the GBCS (collected by the GfK market-research company)

is not a party political trend either. Labour Party Prime Minister Gordon Brown's first Cabinet in 2008 included twenty-one graduates out of twenty-two members, with seven from Oxford (six of whom were PPE graduates) and three from Cambridge.

So although not all of the elite class are graduates, it is the most 'graduate' of our seven classes. Nevertheless, those in the elite are not guaranteed a place in the sun by the simple fact of going to university, even to the most prestigious and selective 'ancient' universities. Figure 7.3 shows that although graduates are five times more likely to be found in the elite than non-graduates, still only three in every twenty graduates is found in that class. The established middle class has the greatest number of graduates: just under half of graduates are assigned to it. In contrast, graduates are largely absent from the precariat, where the majority have no educational qualifications. Only one in ten of the elite reports the same.

What overall picture of the role of higher education in social mobility do we get from the Great British Class Survey? In some respects, it is a familiar one. Social class differences in entry to university find their echo in the different social class outcomes seen for graduates and non-graduates. The expansion of higher education has not led to greater equality of access to universities; yet there is a tightening association between graduate status and membership of the most advantaged groups in British society.

As we saw with members of the British political elite, simply being a graduate does not seem to be sufficient to access the very highest positions. The university attended is

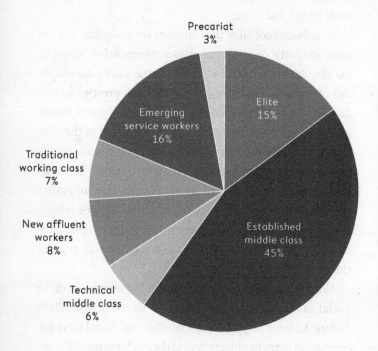

**GRADUATES**

- Precariat 3%
- Elite 15%
- Established middle class 45%
- Technical middle class 6%
- New affluent workers 8%
- Traditional working class 7%
- Emerging service workers 16%

**Figure 7.3**

Social class of graduates and non-graduates compared

*Source:* The nationally representative data-set from the GBCS

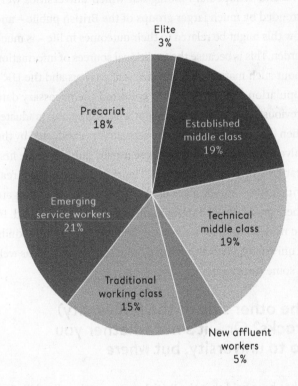

## NON-GRADUATES

Elite
3%

Established
middle class
19%

Technical
middle class
19%

New affluent
workers
5%

Traditional
working class
15%

Emerging
service workers
21%

Precariat
18%

important too. It is one thing to look at the universities attended by very prominent people when such information is publicly available via biographies such as those in *Who's Who* and Wikipedia. Finding out which universities were attended by much larger groups of the British public – and how this might be related to their outcomes in life – is much harder. This is because the traditional sources of information about such matters, like government surveys and the UK's Population Census, have not collected the necessary data previously. We know a little about what happens to graduates when they leave university through surveys conducted by the universities themselves, but these usually only cover the first year or two after graduation. The rich detail of the Great British Class Survey gives us the opportunity to investigate where graduates of different universities are to be found. In the next section, we look at the findings for different kinds of university, uncovering some quite stark contrasts, as well as some surprises.

## The other side of the (university) tracks? Or – it's not whether you go to university, but *where*

It has been said that the British are exceptionally skilled at creating hierarchy from diversity. That seems particularly apt in considering the British higher education system. There are now over 150 universities in the UK, of varying age, size and character. These are often seen as belonging to distinct groups. The ancient universities of Oxford and Cambridge, for instance, are hundreds of years old and based on a system of colleges, with many traditional features, but also strong reputations for their research. 'Redbrick' universities are typically found in major industrial cities and were usually founded in Victorian or Edwardian times. They are so named after the material from which their most iconic buildings are constructed. Birmingham, Manchester and Sheffield are notable examples. With a civic foundation, these universities are also known for their research, but have a more urban, industrial feel, perhaps, than the ancient institutions. 'Plate-glass' universities like Sussex, Warwick and York are also named from their architectural features; they were mostly founded in the 1960s and are often based on out-of-town campuses. The 'new' or 'post-1992' universities are those institutions which were formerly polytechnics and which converted to university status en masse in 1992. Strong integration with their region, a focus on applied and technical subjects and relatively open access characterize them. There is clearly diversity then in the character and purpose of British universities.

However, this diversity coincides with strongly expressed status differences between universities. British higher education is awash with different rankings, both official and unofficial, which sort universities into hierarchies. Universities are assessed on the quality of their research through the Research Excellence Framework and students are asked to express their 'satisfaction' with their education through the National Student Survey. These results and other metrics are combined in different ways in newspaper league tables. Although each such league table is subtly different, the same institutions appear in similar places in each and there is a noticeable relationship between university age and type on the one hand and league table position on the other. The construction of league tables, whilst giving the impression of rigorous processing of statistics and objectivity, is based on subjective judgement about what is counted as 'good'. Different measures, such as counting the proportion of students recruited from deprived backgrounds, would lead to a radical re-ordering of the tables.

The compulsion to rank universities is not unique to Britain, but it has a strong expression here. It is interesting that the appearance of newspaper university league tables tracks the post-1990 take-off in student numbers very closely. International studies in the sociology of education suggest that when access to an educational level expands, differences within that level become more important. For example, it is no longer enough to obtain a degree – getting a good honours classification is now crucial. In the recent past the idea of the 'sportsman's third' was still current – a lowly third-class honours degree obtained by someone who spent most of their time on the sports field and in the bar rather than in the library while at university.[3] Nowadays, the '2.1' or 'upper second-class honours' degree is considered to be a critical threshold to reach to obtain graduate employment. But perhaps more importantly, going to a particular type of university acquires a new significance as an individual's means of distinguishing her/himself from university graduates more generally. Many graduate recruiters target a limited set of universities only, and there is clear evidence that entry to postgraduate higher degrees is strongly associated with attending a small set of older universities.

These university status differences are not new, of course, even if they have acquired additional significance. Status differences are also very fine-grained. Former British Prime Minister and Oxford graduate Clement Attlee's famous, condescending judgement sums this up nicely: 'Thought so. Cambridge man. All statistics. No sense of history.' Even within Oxford or Cambridge there are higher- and lower-status colleges, and league tables which indicate which college has the highest proportion of first-class degrees (and by implication the most intelligent students in Britain) are eagerly perused. In 2013 Lady Margaret Hall was unofficially declared to be 'Oxford's stupidest college'.[4]

But the salience of these status differences has shifted over time. It used to be common to group universities by their type, without assuming they could be placed in a linear league-table format. Thus Oxbridge, the London colleges, the 'civic' universities (such as Birmingham, Leeds, Liverpool or Manchester) of the industrial North and Midlands, the 'technical' universities such as Southampton and Surrey, and the campus 'plate-glass' universities (such as Essex, Lancaster, Sussex, Warwick or York) built in the 1960s all had their particular niches in the ecology of higher education. The humanities and pure sciences were promoted at Oxbridge and London; the modern social sciences were championed at the 'plate-glass' universities; more technically orientated forms of academic education at the civic universities; and so forth. But these kinds of categorizations no longer have much meaning, as universities are increasingly ranked on linear scales using metrics such as the Research Excellence Framework and responses on the National Student Survey.

Insofar as there is a distinctive elite group of universities it is represented by the 'Russell Group', but this is actually an amalgam of previously distinct university types. A senior academic at the University of York (established in 1963) used to recount an anecdote of his meeting a famous politician and former minister with strong Oxford associations at a reception in the Houses of Parliament. On introducing himself to the politician, he was met with the question: '*Is there* a University of York?' Now, York is considered an 'old' university, and is a member of the Russell Group of universities along with Oxford, a club of twenty-four institutions which present themselves as the most academically selective and research-intensive of their kind. The Russell Group is typically held up as an academic elite by both supporters and critics and increasingly frequently within politicians' speeches and policy announcements.

Students recognize these status differences, as the quotations below from students at university in Bristol and Sheffield illustrate. Crucially, though, they also recognize other distinctions which are associated with the differences in university status. A good example comes from the Paired Peers project, which compares the university experiences of matched pairs of students at the University of Bristol and the University of the West of England, Bristol, a former polytechnic:

> This is just generalizing, but mainly you're going to be from different social backgrounds, you're more likely to be working class and go to [the University of the West of England, Bristol] than working class and go to [the University of

Bristol]. That's just, I think, our perception of it. And so if you go out, if there's a group of people, you generally spot by the way they talk, what clothes they're wearing . . . kind of . . . you can spot students anyway, I think, you can generally tell: 'They're Bristol Uni or they're UWE.'[5]

This quotation shows that students associate the two different universities with young people from different social classes who are distinguished by different behaviour, clothes and so on – what Bourdieu would label as different 'habitus'. One university, Bristol, is more 'middle class' or 'posh' than the other. This is relative, since Bristol is sometimes seen as an institution for 'Oxbridge rejects', a branch below the very top of the status tree. Another quotation, from a study of student chants and university rivalries, shows students' knowingness about their university's status position:

*Sheffield Hallam* to *Sheffield*: I'd rather be a poly than a \*\*\*\*!
*Sheffield* [*in reply*]: I'd rather be a \*\*\*\* than unemployed!

The students from Sheffield Hallam, a former polytechnic, recognize the lower status this history conveys, but suggest they have dignity, unlike their upmarket neighbours. The students from Sheffield also show a knowing sense of irony in suggesting that their degrees will have higher labour-market value, at the expense of their personal popularity. As we shall see when examining differences in cultural capital between graduates of different universities, there is a little of the 'cool' versus 'nerdy' in this student 'banter', but at its heart is a recognition of the different outcomes that await graduates from these universities.

A strength of the GBCS is that it allows us to look in detail at these differences between institutions. Are they as stark as these anecdotal examples suggest? After all, we have already seen that having graduate status is associated with a higher social class position.

Figure 7.4 shows the social class of graduates (who undertook the GBCS), aged from thirty-five to fifty, in five pairs of universities in the cities of Bristol, Cambridge, Manchester, Oxford and Sheffield. For each city, we compared the social class of their Russell Group university's graduates with those from their new university/former polytechnic. In all ten universities, between 75 and 80 per cent of graduates are to be found in either the elite or the established middle class. However, in each city, graduates of the older, more traditional university are much more likely to be in the elite than graduates of the neighbouring, newer university. This contrast is particularly stark in Cambridge, where more than half of the University of Cambridge's graduates are in the elite, compared to just one-eighth of those at Anglia Ruskin University. The contrast is smallest in Sheffield, an observation which might provide further ammunition for student chanting! The results also support the observation by students in Bristol, quoted above, about the class differences between the institutions. They help us to understand why students from privileged backgrounds have been reported by the Paired Peers project to say that they are at university '*in* Bristol', giving the impression that they are at the University *of* Bristol, when instead they are actually attending the University of the West of England, Bristol.

We can also see differences in Figure 7.4 between the

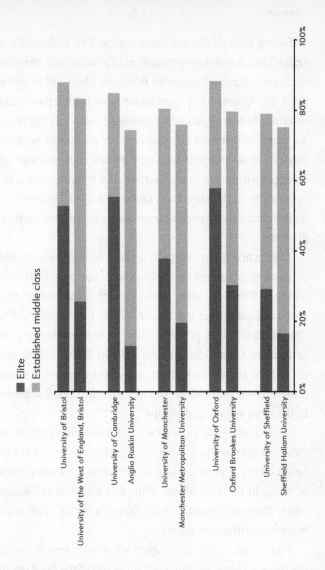

**Figure 7.4**

A tale of two campuses? The social class of graduates
(aged 35 to 50) in selected pairs of universities

different Russell Group universities. The University of Oxford has the highest proportion of graduates in the elite, narrowly eclipsing Cambridge in second place and Bristol in third. The University of Manchester has a smaller proportion of elite graduates, ahead of Sheffield. So while there are apparent differences in outcomes for graduates between Russell Group and post-1992 universities, there are also differences within the Russell Group. But notice too that the proportion in the elite from Oxford Brookes University is higher than that recorded for graduates of the University of Sheffield.

Care is needed in interpreting these figures because graduates of higher-status universities were more likely to complete the GBCS, so there are more of them to analyse than there are post-1992 graduates. As we have explained in Chapter 1, this bias is itself telling. In fact, graduates from Oxford and Cambridge are over twice as likely to have done the GBCS as graduates from any other university, which attests to our point about the way that the GBCS appealed to the most advantaged groups.[6]

Which universities produce the most elite graduates? Table 7.1 shows the top fifty institutions from the GBCS based on the percentage of graduates who were categorized as being in the elite group. This, in a sense, is our league table. There are several notable features of this table, some more surprising than others.

First of all, universities which are usually seen as having the highest status are clustered at the top of the list. Oxford, Cambridge and the University of London colleges dominate the table. Higher education researchers often talk about a

'Golden Triangle' of universities. The 'triangle' describes an imaginary three-sided shape with points in Oxford, Cambridge and London. The exact composition of the London 'corner' can vary, but typically it includes the London School of Economics, King's College London, University College London and Imperial College London. All six of these 'golden' universities are indeed in the top ten for the highest percentage of graduates in the elite.

Together they take a sizeable proportion of resources, such as research income. The close association between being in the elite and attending an elite university is not unexpected, but it is the first time that this has been captured on such a large scale. And what is also striking is the extent of the lead enjoyed by this group over other Russell Group universities. Oxford has nearly twice as many graduates who are in the elite group compared to graduates from highly prestigious and highly ranked universities such as Edinburgh, St Andrews, Warwick and Essex. We seem to be able to detect a clear threshold, with ten universities having 35 per cent or more of their graduates in the elite, a proportion which then falls away sharply below this.[7]

Second, almost one-third of graduates of universities outside of the UK in the GBCS were to be found in the elite. There were many graduates of North American universities in this group, although individual institutions did not stand out among them. It is not possible to tell, from the GBCS, whether this set of graduates were born in Britain and had studied abroad, or instead were foreign-born graduates who had moved to the UK to work after completing their education. Given what we know about British students' reluctance

| INSTITUTION | ELITE |
| --- | --- |
| University of London[2] | 47 |
| City University London[3] | 47 |
| University of Oxford | 44 |
| London School of Economics | 41 |
| University of Cambridge | 40 |
| King's College, University of London | 39 |
| Imperial College London | 39 |
| London South Bank University | 38 |
| University of Bristol | 36 |
| University College, University of London | 35 |
| Queen Mary University of London | 31 |
| University of Exeter | 31 |
| Non-UK institution[4] | 31 |
| University of Westminster | 31 |
| Aston University | 31 |
| University of Surrey | 30 |
| Non-university institution | 29 |
| University of Durham | 29 |
| University of Manchester | 29 |
| University of Reading | 28 |
| University of Sussex | 28 |
| Heriot-Watt University | 28 |
| University of Southampton | 28 |
| University of Birmingham | 27 |
| University of Nottingham | 27 |

## Table 7.1

Percentage of University Graduates (Aged 25 to 65)
Who Are in the Elite Group[1]

1. Only institutions with 200 graduates or more who did the GBCS are included
2. Graduated from a constituent college of the federal university (insufficient information from respondent to determine which one)

| INSTITUTION | ELITE |
| --- | --- |
| University of Edinburgh | 27 |
| University of St Andrews | 27 |
| Kingston University | 26 |
| University of Wales | 26 |
| Royal Holloway, University of London | 26 |
| Newcastle University | 26 |
| London Metropolitan University | 26 |
| University of Liverpool | 25 |
| Oxford Brookes University | 25 |
| Brunel University | 25 |
| University of Aberdeen | 25 |
| University of Warwick | 25 |
| University of Greenwich | 24 |
| University of Essex | 24 |
| Loughborough University | 24 |
| University of Leeds | 24 |
| University of Brighton | 23 |
| University of East Anglia | 23 |
| University of Bath | 23 |
| University of Dundee | 23 |
| Open University | 22 |
| University of Kent | 22 |
| University of Leicester | 22 |
| Coventry University | 22 |
| Middlesex University | 22 |

3. There was a much lower response rate from City University than from other universities at the top levels of this table, which may unduly bias the results, making City University respondents seem to be relatively more elite than those from other universities. For a full discussion of this issue, see Paul Wakeling and Mike Savage, 'Entry to Elite Positions and the Stratification of Higher Education in Britain', *Sociological Review*, 63(2), 2015, 290–320
4. Higher education institution outside of the UK

to study overseas, we can infer that these are graduates from abroad who have moved to the UK for work and so perhaps it is not that surprising that so many are in the elite. Over half of these elite graduates of non-UK universities are based in London, suggesting that they may be part of the globally mobile transnational elite which is characteristic of the city.

That concentration around London-based universities is a third striking feature of Table 7.1. Fifteen of the top fifty-ranked universities are in London and in fact only a few London-based universities are not on the list (ignoring small specialist institutions, only the universities of West London, East London, Roehampton and Goldsmiths College London are missing). Some of the universities which *do* make the list are former polytechnics. London South Bank University and the University of Westminster both have a high proportion of their graduates in the elite. London Metropolitan University, which has high numbers of ethnic minority and disadvantaged students, often appears near the bottom of newspaper university league tables. Yet it is thirty-second on our list, above many higher-status universities outside London, including one-third of the members of the Russell Group. This is a remarkable demonstration of the apparent power of the London institutions over those outside the south-east.[8]

We have an emerging picture here of the transmission of advantage through higher education. We know that there are social class differences in entry to different kinds of universities. Higher-status universities recruit a greater proportion of their students from among the most advantaged groups. Higher education in general gives graduates an advantage in the class structure. The elite class is made up disproportion- ately of those from the most prestigious universities. This is not a black-and-white picture: many of those in the elite are not graduates. Some lower-status universities, especially those based in London, also have many elite graduates. As we have already seen, London has a concentration of power and advantage which may spill over into its universities more generally. But the overall conclusion must be that different universities provide different pathways into the class struc- ture. Graduates from a small group of the most prestigious universities are disproportionately represented in the elite. Expansion of higher education is not sufficient to break this pattern and to some extent may have reinforced it.

We can provide a more refined picture of how these elite universities seem to be especially important in affecting chances of entry into the elite. Table 7.2 shows the effect of having different educational pathways. We separate out Oxford, as the most 'elite' institution identified above; the other Golden Triangle universities; the remaining Russell Group universities; other higher education institutions and non-graduates. The majority of those from senior managerial or traditional professional backgrounds who attended inde- pendent school and a Golden Triangle university in the GBCS sample are found in our elite class. Indeed, almost two-thirds of those taking the 'royal road' – coming from a senior managerial or traditional professional home, and going to an independent school and then Oxford – reach the elite.[9] At the opposite extreme, only one in fourteen of those from a working class background who went to comprehen- sive school and did not attend higher education attained an

| UNIVERSITY ATTENDED | SENIOR MANAGER OR TRADITIONAL PROFESSIONAL ELITE MEMBERSHIP IN % | | SEMI-ROUTINE/ROUTINE ELITE MEMBERSHIP IN % | |
|---|---|---|---|---|
| | INDEPENDENT SCHOOL | COMPREHENSIVE SCHOOL | INDEPENDENT SCHOOL | COMPREHENSIVE SCHOOL |
| Oxford | 63.9 | 49.4 | 35.7 | 39.3 |
| Other Golden Triangle | 53.9 | 37.0 | 29.4 | 31.7 |
| Other Russell Group | 48.7 | 29.0 | 35.0 | 15.7 |
| Other | 40.7 | 23.0 | 17.5 | 11.5 |
| None | 39.2 | 9.4 | 9.1 | 7.2 |

Table 7.2

Elite Membership by Social / Educational Pathway for GBCS Respondents (Aged 30 to 49)

elite destination. It also shows that for any combination of social class background and secondary schooling, attending Oxford (and to a lesser extent another Golden Triangle university) confers advantage. These effects are clearly different from attending a Russell Group university. However, an independent education is particularly effective in social reproduction, because those with senior managerial or traditional professional parents, but with no degree, are as likely to enter the elite, at least among our respondents, as working class, comprehensive-educated Oxford graduates. It may be that those from these backgrounds attend the more prestigious independent schools and just as with universities we should also distinguish the most elite private schools from the rest.

## Universities and different sorts of capital

How do we explain these class differences? We can see these universities facilitating prospects for the accumulation of the different sorts of capital. In short, we are not claiming necessarily that there is an overt class effect, in which graduates from King's College London (for instance) are intrinsically seen as more worthy of elite entry than those from the University of Middlesex (for instance). Rather, by seeing the different patterns around attending specific universities and the acquisition of different kinds of capital, we can see the underpinnings of class divisions today.

It is clear that university attendance is associated with one's economic capital (see Figure 7.5). Ranked by the mean earnings of their graduates, the top ten places are taken by

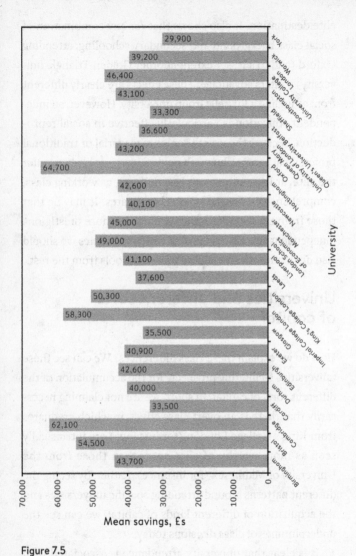

**Figure 7.5**

The economic capital of graduates, by university attended[1]

1. For more details, see Paul Wakeling and Mike Savage, 'Entry to Elite Positions and the Stratification of Higher Education in Britain', *Sociological Review*, 63(2), 2015, 290–320

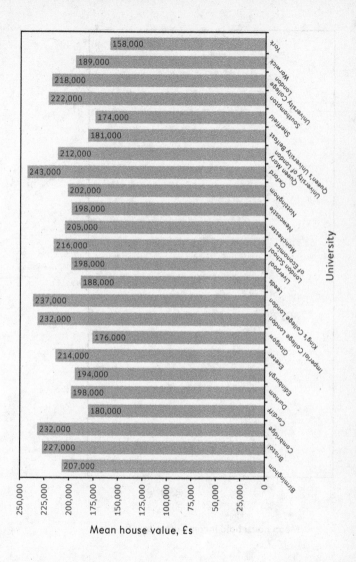

Mean house value, £s

University

| University | Mean house value, £s |
|---|---|
| York | 158,000 |
| Warwick | 189,000 |
| University College London | 218,000 |
| Southampton | 222,000 |
| Sheffield | 174,000 |
| Queen's University Belfast | 181,000 |
| Queen Mary University of London | 212,000 |
| Oxford | 243,000 |
| Nottingham | 202,000 |
| Newcastle | 198,000 |
| Manchester | 205,000 |
| London School of Economics | 216,000 |
| Liverpool | 198,000 |
| Leeds | 188,000 |
| King's College London | 237,000 |
| Imperial College London | 232,000 |
| Glasgow | 176,000 |
| Exeter | 214,000 |
| Edinburgh | 194,000 |
| Durham | 198,000 |
| Cardiff | 180,000 |
| Cambridge | 232,000 |
| Bristol | 227,000 |
| Birmingham | 207,000 |

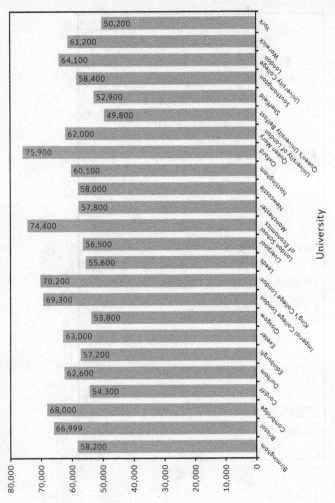

Mean household income after tax, £s

University

| University | Value |
|---|---|
| York | 50,200 |
| Warwick | 61,200 |
| University College London | 64,100 |
| Southampton | 58,400 |
| Sheffield | 52,900 |
| Queen's University Belfast | 49,800 |
| Queen Mary University of London | 62,000 |
| Oxford | 75,900 |
| Nottingham | 60,100 |
| Newcastle | 58,000 |
| Manchester | 57,800 |
| London School of Economics | 74,400 |
| Liverpool | 56,500 |
| Leeds | 55,600 |
| King's College London | 70,200 |
| Imperial College London | 69,300 |
| Glasgow | 53,800 |
| Exeter | 63,000 |
| Edinburgh | 57,200 |
| Durham | 62,600 |
| Cardiff | 54,300 |
| Cambridge | 68,000 |
| Bristol | 66,999 |
| Birmingham | 58,200 |

the Golden Triangle universities, City University, the University of Bristol and non-UK institutions.[10] Oxford graduates' average household incomes are £75,900, coming out higher than those for Cambridge graduates' households at £68,000. Since many graduates meet their future partners while studying at university any university-specific (dis)advantage in salary could be doubled. It has been suggested that educational 'homogamy' – people forming intimate partnerships with those qualified to a similar level – is increasing and is adding to class inequalities.

Sheffield Hallam students may be heartened somewhat to hear that their nearby rival graduates' annual household income is 'only' £5,000 higher. For Cambridge, the equivalent gap with Anglia Ruskin graduates in our data is over £20,000. We also see inequalities in household savings between graduates of different universities. Those who were at the highest-status institutions have savings equivalent to almost one whole year's household income. Graduates of lower-status institutions tend to have lower savings. Most fall in a range of around £25,000 to £45,000 in savings, as opposed to £60,000-plus for Oxbridge graduates.[11]

We can also compare graduates from different universities in terms of their cultural capital, linked into the analysis we have presented in this book of its two forms: 'highbrow' and 'emerging'.[12] This shows some clear contrasts in the types and amounts of cultural capital across different universities. Those where graduates score highest on highbrow cultural capital are the elite academic institutions. The Golden Triangle universities feature prominently, as do those institutions which specialize in the fine and performing arts

(Goldsmiths and the University of the Arts London, for instance). Again there is a strong London flavour to this grouping. This is the university equivalent of what we might call Establishment British (or indeed English) culture – the Proms, Shakespeare, literature festivals, art galleries and the like. There are exceptions, but the stock of universities' highbrow cultural capital is generally related to their academic status. Most of those where graduates have, on average, a lower highbrow cultural capital score are post-1992 universities.

Emerging cultural capital also appears as a distinct dimension. Many of the universities where graduates tend to be lacking in highbrow cultural capital fare much better when it comes to 'cool' capital, and vice versa. Post-1992 universities and those in major student cities are to the fore in emerging cultural capital, suggesting a strong urban and popular component: Leeds Metropolitan University, Manchester Metropolitan University, both universities in Newcastle and in Nottingham, together with several coastal cities – Bournemouth, Bristol, Plymouth and Southampton. This geography points to an alternative cultural axis: English, but provincial. Very few universities' graduates scored low on both kinds of cultural capital (Bradford, Hertfordshire and Hull were the exceptions).

Table 7.3 groups universities by their graduates' average stocks of economic and cultural capital. The table suggests that the economic and cultural endowments of graduates in the UK do not fit straightforwardly on to a single axis and that our approach, which decomposes the effects of different kinds of capital power here, reveals significant variation in the resources conveyed by institutions. Although there is some connection with graduates' levels of cultural and economic capital for each university, not all institutions can be fitted on to the diagonal line of cells running from top left to bottom right. For sure, the most elite universities identified earlier are clustered in the top-left cell; their graduates are high in both economic and highbrow cultural capital, which we would expect given their over-representation in the elite class. In the opposite corner are a group of new universities, mainly in the English provinces, where graduates are low in both economic and cultural capital. The largest group of institutions is in the middle cell, where graduates have medium levels of cultural and economic capital. There are some differences within this group which would emerge in a more detailed table. The graduates of these universities are perhaps the equivalent of the established middle class.

But it is the contents of the other cells that are the most interesting. Three of the cells contain only two universities in total. Goldsmiths graduates have plentiful highbrow cultural capital, but little economic capital, likely a result of the strong arts emphasis of the college and its London location. Aston University, associated with the West Midlands' manufacturing-based economy and specializing in science, engineering and business, has graduates rich in economic capital but with far less cultural capital. No university's graduates combine high emerging cultural capital with high economic capital. Of the other, more populous combinations in the table, it is noticeable that it is those universities which fuse strengths in economic and highbrow cultural capital which seem to have disproportionate numbers of their graduates in

|  | HIGH HIGHBROW CULTURAL CAPITAL | HIGH EMERGING CULTURAL CAPITAL |
|---|---|---|
| HIGH ECONOMIC CAPITAL | Cambridge<br>Durham<br>King's College (UL)[2]<br>London<br>London School of Economics<br>Oxford<br>Non-UK institution<br>University College (UL) | |
| MEDIUM ECONOMIC CAPITAL | University of the Arts London<br>Edinburgh<br>London Metropolitan<br>Loughborough<br>Middlesex<br>Open<br>Royal Holloway (UL)<br>St Andrews<br>Wales | Bath<br>Newcastle<br>Nottingham<br>Nottingham Trent |
| LOW ECONOMIC CAPITAL | Goldsmiths (UL) | Bournemouth<br>Derby<br>Lincoln<br>Northumbria Newcastle<br>Sheffield Hallam<br>Southampton Solent |

Table 7.3
Distribution of Different Kinds of Capital across Universities[1]

| MEDIUM CULTURAL CAPITAL | | LOW CULTURAL CAPITAL |
|---|---|---|
| Bristo | | Aston |
| City London | | |
| Exeter | | |
| Heriot-Watt Edinburgh | | |
| Imperial College (UL) | | |
| London South Bank | | |
| Manchester | | |
| Queen Mary (UL) | | |
| Aberdeen | Lancaster | Bradford |
| Birmingham | Leeds | East London |
| Brighton | Leicester | Hertfordshire |
| Brunel | Liverpool | Portsmouth |
| Cardiff | Oxford Brookes | Robert Gordon Aberdeen |
| Coventry | Queen's Belfast | Strathclyde |
| De Montfort | Reading | Sunderland |
| Dundee | Salford | |
| East Anglia | Sheffield | |
| Edinburgh Napier | Southampton | |
| Essex | Surrey | |
| Glasgow | Sussex | |
| Greenwich | Swansea | |
| Hull | Warwick | |
| Keele | West of England | |
| Kent | Westminster | |
| Kingston | York | |
| Aberystwyth | | Central Lancashire |
| Anglia Ruskin | | Gloucestershire |
| Bangor | | Huddersfield |
| Birmingham City | | Leeds Metropolitan |
| Canterbury Christ Church | | Liverpool John Moores |
| Manchester Metropolitan | | Staffordshire |
| Northampton | | Teesside |
| Plymouth | | Ulster |
| South Wales | | West of Scotland |
| Stirling | | Wolverhampton |

1. Only institutions with 200 graduates or more who participated in the GBCS are included
2. UL = A constituent college of the federal University of London

the elite. Emerging cultural capital appears less powerful than highbrow cultural capital, but nevertheless still confers some advantage.

We have seen that universities are a feature of life in twenty-first century Britain to an extent almost unimaginable a century ago. They are no longer the preserve of a tiny section of the population; in fact attending university is now a normal and expected part of the life course for many young people. While there is still much scope for improvement, universities now admit more women than men and students come from all ethnic and social class backgrounds. For some, higher education is a means for achieving social mobility, since, as we have seen, graduates are heavily concentrated in the elite and established middle class categories. Not everyone in the elite is a graduate, nor are most graduates in the elite, but very few graduates are found in the more disadvantaged social classes.

Fundamentally, however, simply expanding the higher education system and making it easier for young people to go to university does not unsettle social hierarchies. It might have been the case in the past that going to university provided in and of itself a certain badge of status, a marker that a respectable qualification had been achieved. However, this no longer seems to be the case because of extensive internal differentiation within the university sector.

In fact, this differentiation of universities goes hand-in-hand with the institutionalization of our elite class. The spread of meritocratic routes, allowing vast numbers of schoolchildren to gain access to higher education, does not, in itself, produce a more level playing field or spell the end of class divisions. Far from it. Within a highly competitive educational market-place, it is access to the elite institutions which conveys the glittering prizes. But it is not just a story about the old universities continuing to dominate. We can also see that those universities located in the south-east of England and especially in London also seem to 'punch above their weight' in terms of the access to resources which they can bring to their graduates. And it is to the geographical aspects of class that we now turn.

# Class and Spatial Inequality in the UK

Class is geographical. Capital is accumulated, stored, transmitted and traded in, and across, specific locations. We associate particular places with certain class stereotypes, even if those stereotypes are tired or too restrictive to register the socio-economic complexity of our towns and cities. Harry Enfield's 1990s 'George Whitebread' character was a manifestation of a regional archetype *in extremis*: a boorish, racist, plain-speaking Yorkshireman, who 'says what he likes and bloody well likes what he says'. Of course Enfield's regional stereotype is not a literal representation of 'Yorkshire folk'. When George retorts, 'Sophistication!? Sophistication!? Don't talk to me about sophistication, love . . . I've been to Leeds,' the viewer is meant to know that Leeds is actually far less sophisticated than London or one of the great capitals. Yet the quotation also riffs into even more complex associations. If taken simply as a supposedly laughable metropolitan expression of the parochial pretensions of a mere provincial city, it ignores the way that Leeds is also a city which has thrown off its tattered textile mantle for the affluent gown of financial services; a city now at least as well known in the UK's cognitive geography for Harvey Nichols as it is for Harry Ramsden's.[1] In this subtle way, the interplay of associations between classes, people and places sets off powerful, and contested, resonances within the popular imagination.

In recent times classifications of class and space have become more loaded. The view from the educated media-dominating metropolis – quintessentially London – has more power in defining the deficiencies of other locations. London has become a magical and aestheticized city, its quality etched into its innovative-high-rise corporate blocks, such as the Gherkin, but with its aura extending to its murkier territories of the Hackney psycho-geography of Ian Sinclair or J. G. Ballard's west London suburban dystopia.[2] This is the mirror for rendering non-metropolitan space as grey, dull and disreputable.[3] Here the 'Crap Town' rendering (see www.craptownsreturns.co.uk) of the ex-mining village of Easington in the former Durham coalfield gives an ironic, and also deeply offensive, example of where this politics of class leads to:

> Easington has the highest proportion of white people out of any town in the UK, not a reason to shame it outright, but one has to think that anybody with different-coloured skin, a 'funny accent' or who simply hasn't had endured a coal-mining related respiratory disease might run the risk of being eaten, or worse still, made to endure the many, many stories from jaded townsfolk about how Easington 'hasn't been the same since fucking Thatcher shut the pit' and that 'nobody can find work 'round here now'.

Here the line between 'humour' and spatio-class hatred is hard to define. Deprivation is not simply lamentable: the portrait of social decline presented here suggests a degree of inherency – that is, the conditions which pertain to a place are not only the outcome of the UK's industrial collapse and its concentrated effect on specific areas, but are also a result of integral weaknesses within communities like Easington and their seeming inability, or unwillingness, to adapt to the new economic world order. Places are moralized through the lens of the dominant London worldview.

Recently, the journalist Owen Jones has highlighted this polarization in sensibilities in his influential book *Chavs*. In his view not only are the working class more generally becoming an object of scorn in the public imagination, but also by extension the places that they inhabit.[4] Such classifications are accentuated in the surge in digital geodemographic information available on the activities, preferences and locations of millions of people in this country. People are increasingly using mapping technologies because of the direct implications neighbourhood has not only for their house value and insurance premiums, but also for their healthcare and educational implications. The impetus behind these developments has come, not from the academic sector, but from commercial actors like Experian, who see the gains to be made from harvesting this sort of data as a sort of postcode sociology.[5] So, in a very direct way, anyone who uses a loyalty card in a supermarket, searches Rightmove or uses an online credit calculator is part of the dynamic and ongoing process of constructing, mapping and understanding social class in this country. Socio-spatial classifications thus proliferate. Just as we have argued that the dynamics of emerging cultural capital involve the skill and capacity to play with genre labels, so spatial referents become ripe arenas for the educated middle classes to display their emerging cultural capital. Places and locations become subjects for aesthetic, social and cultural refinement'. Benedict thus talks us through his life history of being brought up in a 'conventional' family in Devon, before 'I got kind of seduced, you know, this is really pathetic, but I got kind of seduced by what London had to offer really.' Moving between bohemian circles of squatting and radical politics is 'kind of what you expect when you go to London, and I was kind of punky and whatever at that point anyway'. In Bourdieu's terms this is cultural capital, the capacity to stand back from specific locations and pass judgement. This 'elective belonging' is a mode of middle class relationship to place which recognizes the possibility of leaving and moving somewhere else.[6]

The distinctive geography of Britain needs to be understood therefore in terms of the new approach to class we have championed here. Not only the economic, but also the social and cultural aspects of class all point to fundamental geographical inequities and differences – though in somewhat different ways. Classes themselves are crystallized in distinctive ways in particular locations, with a wealth elite located in London at the apex of the social hierarchy. The power of the boundary between middle and working class which has been the focus of much academic thinking in the past was symbolically and also economically associated with a north–south divide. An educated, middle class southern metropolis with a strong service, financial and trading economy stood in opposition to the industrial north, Scotland and Wales, with powerful trade unions and working class traditions. Of course, the geographical reality was always more complex than this: there was a strong working class presence in parts of London and the south-east, and powerful middle class and elite clusters in the north. But nonetheless, this north–south divide constituted a force field in which the two classes recognized themselves and each other through a range of powerful reference points.

However, just as we have argued that the fundamental class boundaries lie at the top of the social hierarchy, so the power of this regional divide has now broken down. It has been replaced by two other dynamics: firstly, the power of highly segregated urban cores as elite zones. The process of intense elite segregation can be detected in all major British cities – and that new urban investment has generated more powerful manifestations of this. Secondly the dominance of central London is now paramount and overwhelms that of the north–south divide. These two shifts generate a more powerful urban–rural division than used to be the case. Cities (especially London, but the process extends to other cities) are the centres of accumulation. The countryside is defined in terms of the repose – the rest and recuperation – it offers in the context of these voracious urban driving belts.

## The dominance of London

Let us begin simply by underscoring the economic power of London, though this is hardly in doubt. Figure 8.1 shows the GVA (gross value added: a measure of the value of goods and services produced in an area, industry or sector of an economy) of different urban locations within the UK. It

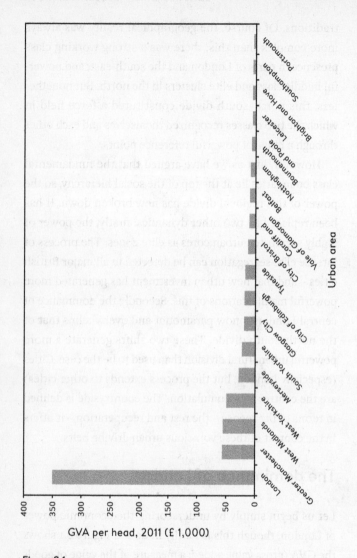

**Figure 8.1**

Gross value added (GVA) per head by urban area, 2011

*Source:* Eurostat: Gross value added at basic prices by NUTS 3 regions

reveals, starkly enough, the astonishing dominance of the English capital.

London's contribution to the nation's economic value is almost seven times that of its closest 'rival' in Greater Manchester, if such a moniker can seriously be applied to such an unequal relationship. Indeed, the gross value of all the seventeen other urban areas in Figure 8.1 combined only just matches London's. This is an economic imbalance that has rarely existed in other nations or at other times in history.

Not only this, but the financial crash of recent years has caused the rest of the country to fall further behind London. Figure 8.2 shows the percentage change in GVA between 2007 and 2011 relative to London, showing a pronounced decline in all major provincial urban centres. Every city lost ground to the capital during this period.

Nascent nationalist identities in Northern Ireland, Wales and Scotland are partly a response to this urban centrality. Within England, Evan Davis has argued that northern cities needed to overcome their parochial cultural differences for the greater good in the formation of a mega-city which could truly rival London in economic terms. This has fed into arguments about the need for a 'northern powerhouse'. In fact, adding the value of Liverpool, Manchester, Leeds, and Sheffield together (by, for example, running high-speed trains between them) would create an urban core with only half the power of London – hardly a major rival.[7]

With such developments it is little wonder that *The Economist* argued that 'economically, socially and politically, the north is becoming another country'.[8] But in fact, it would

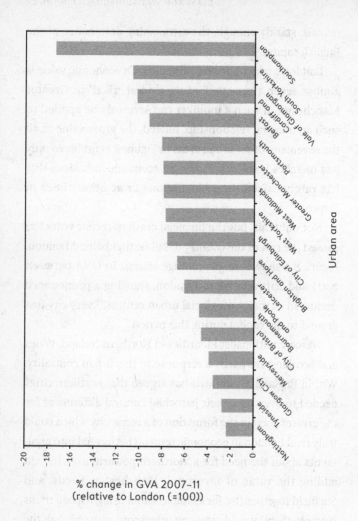

**Figure 8.2**
Percentage change in GVA (2007–11) for 17 major British urban areas in relation to London

*Source:* Eurostat: Gross value added at basic prices by NUTS 3 regions.

be erroneous to see this as predominantly a north–south divide. If we dig down deeper through the spatial scales, the evidence suggests that while the rest of the UK may be way behind London in terms of economic power, in terms of inequality within cities, provincial centres bear a much closer relationship to the capital. Figure 8.3 shows income polarization at local levels: the higher this figure is, the greater the variation of income compared to the average income found in that city. Here we can see that London is more unequal in terms of what its different kinds of workers are paid than other cities, but its lead over the rest of the country is far more modest. All cities, it appears, have marked internal differentiation in the economic fortunes of their residents. It is this intra-urban difference that we want to explore now.

The GBCS, with its unusually granular data, allows us a powerful lens here. Figure 8.4 shows mean household income radiating out from the Bank of England located right in the heart of the City of London.[9] Through this technique we can track the changes in mean income against the distance from the pulsing financial heart of the British economy. As we can see, there is a highly pronounced geography to the spatial distribution of incomes within London. The highest levels of income are of those who live in the band at the core (within the City of London itself, and within a very small collection of extremely affluent neighbourhoods immediately surrounding it on either side of the Thames). It includes also perhaps the very earliest and best-known example of post-industrial gentrification in London in St Katherine's Dock, a very exclusive set of converted warehouses around what is now a marina),[10] and would also extend to the exclusive

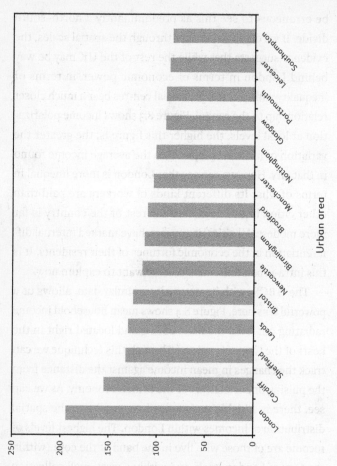

Level of income polarization by unitary
authority (standard deviation from the
mean (£s) 2007–8)

**Figure 8.3**

Income Polarization (2007–8) for 14 Major British Cities

*Sources:* Office for National Statistics: Income: Model-Based Estimates at Middle-layer Super
Output Area (MSOA) Level, 2007–8, and Scottish National Statistics (SNS): Income and
Poverty – Modelled Estimates, 2013

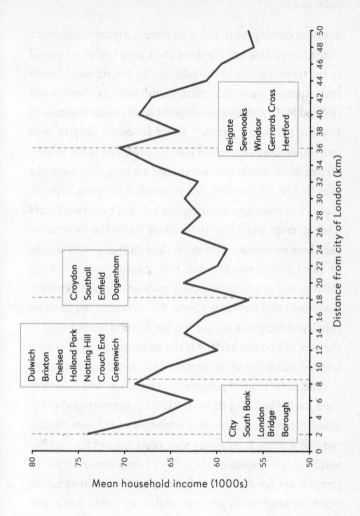

**Figure 8.4**

Mean household income aggregated to 2-kilometre-widths band radiating out from the Bank of England in the City of London
*Source:* GBCS data

Barbican development. But then there is a sharp decline into King's Cross, Bow and Elephant and Castle before we ascend to the respectability of the 8-kilometre-distant band, which encompasses areas of historic wealth such as Chelsea and Holland Park, with long-established areas of gentrification in Notting Hill and Brixton.[11] There follows a drop of over £10,000 in mean incomes in just 10 kilometres, at the 18-kilometres mark, which embraces outer, working class boroughs such as Enfield, Southall, Dagenham and Croydon, another place, interestingly, fighting back in 2013 on two fronts against 'crap' and 'chav' town labels. From the proletarian periphery we ascend again to the rural and semi-rural arcadia of the London stockbroker belt, encompassing solidly middle- and upper-middle class stalwarts such as Windsor, Sevenoaks and Gerrards Cross. Yet income levels in these privileged locations do not top the income levels found in the core of London itself. It is the throbbing heart of central London which lies at the centre of economic accumulation.

The same kind of geography is apparent when we map class itself. Figure 8.5 shows the spatial concentration of the elite – the most advantaged of our new social classes – within our major cities. It measures what proportion of the elite live within only one quarter of the city's postal sectors. It shows that it is not London that leads here, but Greater Manchester, where as much as 82 per cent of the city's elite live in just one quarter of the whole built-up area's postal sectors. So in fact, London is not unusually exclusive in the extent to which the elite are physically segregated from other social classes. More broadly, economic and social divisions do not conform to a neat cleavage between the north and south; they bisect

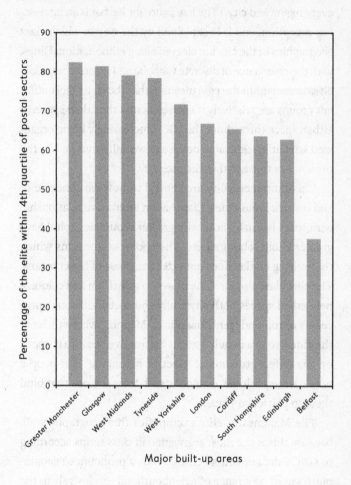

**Figure 8.5**

Percentage shares of the elite within just one quartile
of postal sectors in 10 major built-up areas in Britain

*Source:* GBCS data

every region and city. (The low figure for Belfast is an interesting exception, and it is explained by the way in which class geographies in the city are cleaved along ethno-national lines, with the emergence of discrete Catholic and Protestant middle class areas within the city, meaning that the city's most affluent groups are relatively dispersed across the urban space.)[12] Urban space throughout the UK is increasingly being organized so that its central zones are powerfully stamped by the presence of those in the elite category.

Class and inequality are central to how we conceive of and construct our cities. Class has an interactive relationship with space because those with greater economic capital have greater choice about where. They possess freedoms which the housing market does not extend to those of lesser means. The elite class also have the power to transform and colonize new urban spaces both physically and socially, through processes of top-end 'gentrification'.[13] Mapping where those in the elite live in a detailed way is instructive because it opens up the different forms of 'elective belonging' that people hold – the emotional, economic and other reasons that bind them to particular places.[14]

The Manchester elite exemplifies this geography well, because this is the most segregated in class terms according to GBCS data of British cities. It has a pronounced geography focused on a range of neighbourhoods exclusively to the south of the city centre. Firstly, there is a huge north–south divide within the city. High-end suburbs are located predominantly in the south of the city, where their feeder roads and rail networks lead to the university and hospital complexes of the Oxford Road corridor. At their outer extremes, these roads lead to the Victorian elite suburbs of Altrincham and Bramhall, on the metropolitan boundary with Cheshire. The inner suburbs of Didsbury, Cheadle and Chorlton-cum-Hardy have also undergone major revival in recent years. While Didsbury and Cheadle constitute solidly middle class suburbs and have had high status for many decades, Chorlton has undergone massive gentrification, which has seen it transformed from a predominantly working class area with a sizeable Irish migrant population in the 1960s to its current bohemian social formation of coffee shops and pricey restaurants.[15] It is interesting to note the emergence of a new centre of gentrification around multi-cultural Levenshulme, immediately to the east of the eschewed Moss Side. This is another area of modest Victorian terraces and larger Edwardian semis, traditionally a working class area, but it is now in a similar process of class transition as young professionals with families who cannot afford the cost of housing in established areas like Chorlton move in. However, secondly, what is of particular interest is the distinctive zone of elite concentration focused squarely on the city centre and on the city's 'Northern Quarter', which has been mooted by the city council as an alternative cultural neighbourhood, with an ever-increasing concentration of trendy bars and vintage-clothing shops. Hardly anyone lived there twenty-five years ago: in the 1980s central Manchester was a largely derelict and uninhabited space, with run-down warehouses.

Now revamped industrial buildings provide a new appealing aesthetic for young, affluent singletons looking for a taste of the loft lifestyle in north-west England and the area has become a hub for those working in the creative economy.[16]

We can only understand the regeneration of central Manchester which has taken place over the past twenty years as specifically linked into its positioning as an elite space. This is a process which has happened to a greater or lesser extent throughout the UK.

So, the new elite has a distinctive geography, one which seeks out and defines urban cores, not only in London, but in all the cities. It is a central urban class. The broader regional division between north and south, which used to define the fundamental contrast between working and middle class, industry and services, has now paled in the face of this metropolitan remaking of elites.

## Class, politics and the socio-cultural landscape

The social class geography of the UK is too complex to reduce to simplistic north–south dichotomies. This much is clear from the patterns of intra-regional and intra-urban inequality that have been explored and discussed in the previous sections. Yet the 'north–south divide' remains an incredibly powerful trope in both political and public discourse. The notion of the southern 'softie' versus the 'tough' northerner endures: a 2014 article in the *Sunday Times* entitled 'Life's Really Not So Bad, You Soft Southerners', reported that levels of long-term mental illness tended to be higher in northern towns and cities than in southern ones.[17] This was reported without any reference to the socio-economic context of towns at the top of its associated list, such as Middlesbrough and Blackpool, which have far higher levels of relative deprivation than areas at the bottom of its list, such as Harrow or East Berkshire, shifting the emphasis from economic explanations of these variants to something more inherent about these places.

The roots of the north–south discussion can be traced back to long before the Industrial Revolution, from where so many of our preconceptions of distinctions between the satanic mill towns of the north and the pastoral idyll of the south emerge.[18] Ron Martin argues that it was during the twentieth century that these regional caricatures gained a coherently classed, and by extension, politicized identity:

> The archetypal northern working class family was headed by a semi-skilled or unskilled manual worker, living in a council house, and who was both a staunch trade unionist and a fervent Labour voter. The archetypal southern middle class household was headed by a blue-collar or white-collar worker, who was more likely to be an owner-occupier, less inclined to be a union member and much more disposed to vote Conservative.[19]

Of course this vision of the north was associated with a divergence of disparate and necessarily antithetical constituent identities: Yorkshire Tykes, Scousers, Geordies and Mancs.[20] Liverpool and Manchester are physically separated by only 30 miles of tarmac across boggy Chat Moss, but in cultural terms they are much, much further apart. These different local identities played into very distinctive cultural identities, all of them highlighting different kinds of working class culture, ranging from the trade unionist and socialist culture of Sheffield, through to the cosmopolitan and respectable ethos in Manchester and the maritime and trading culture of Liverpool.

From the 1960s, these distinctive northern geographies were increasingly subordinated to the growing power of London and the south-east. Doreen Massey, writing in the mid-1980s, identified that 'in the new geography of jobs, most of the high-level, high-status and well-paid research, technical and development functions are located in the South and East of England'.[21] The older history of a northern Randstad, with its distinctive urban cultures, was increasingly stripped away, by what Martin has called our northern 'nineteenth-century city states', leaving a collection of conurbations.[22]

The contemporary hold of these regional images remains important. Consider John's account of how his regional identity was deployed both by him and by his employers as a tool in the workplace:

John: I think part of my success has been I've worked consciously at being a professional Yorkshireman, erm, and that's a certain class element to it, I think, you know . . . and brusque, sort of, but I mean I don't think they'd ever doubt that, you know, no silver spoon was in this mouth [*laughs*].

Questioner: So it's a regional identity, as well, that is as, or more important, to you than . . .

John: It – the regional identity, was to my advantage in certain situations, which I used to play to because they used to put my pointed questions down to Yorkshire brusqueness. One guy who always had me – and I mean I used to sit in the top executive committees on some of

the things in the bank, and I know why I was there – I
mean, he used to say I was the man on the Clapham
omnibus, but no, it was to ask the awkward question,
and then they could go out of the meeting and say, 'Well,
it's just John being obnoxious' to the guys.

Thirty years on, those stereotypes still hold some relevance
when glimpsed through the lens of the GBCS, but it has now
been overlain by a more nuanced geography. Figures 8.6(a)–
(e) uses a statistical mapping technique called a Local
Indicators of Spatial Association (LISA) to show the geographical distribution of the elite group at the top of the new
class model.[23] The method returns four types of significant
cluster: high areas of capital surrounded by other high areas
('high-high'); conversely, low areas of capital surrounded by
other low areas ('low-low'); outlying areas of high capital surrounded by areas with low values ('high-low'); and vice versa.
Figure 8.6(a) shows that the elite are clustered heavily in and
around London and the south-east of England more generally, while much of northern England constitutes an opposite
cluster, where elite populations are lower than might be
expected, particularly across wide areas of Lancashire and
Yorkshire. Yet as we have argued above, even here there are
pockets of high elite populations in Cheshire, the Ribble
Valley and in Yorkshire's own 'Golden Triangle', which lies
between York, Leeds and Harrogate. It is important to realize
that the skewed distribution of the elite in the UK represents
not just an economic divide, but embodies social and cultural
cleavages also.

This is clearly evident in Figures 8.6(b)–(e), which map

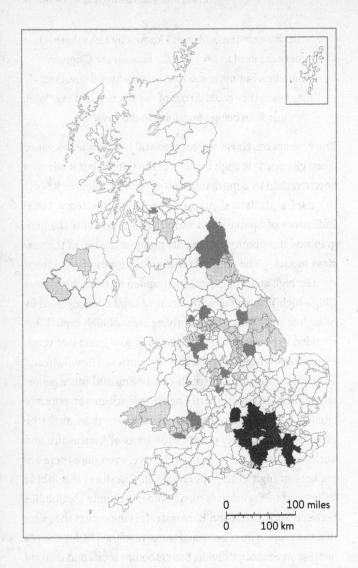

**Figure 8.6a**
Elite Clusters

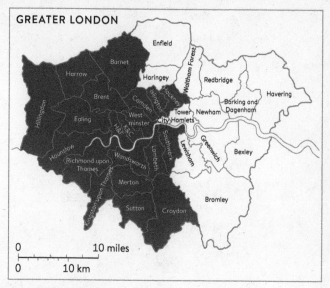

GREATER LONDON

Enfield
Barnet
Harrow
Haringey
Waltham Forest
Redbridge
Havering
Brent
Camden
Islington
Hackney
Ealing
Hillingdon
Westminster
K&C
City
Tower Hamlets
Newham
Barking and Dagenham
H&F
Hounslow
Richmond upon Thames
Wandsworth
Southwark
Lambeth
Lewisham
Greenwich
Bexley
Kingston upon Thames
Merton
Sutton
Croydon
Bromley

0                    10 miles
0          10 km

K&C    Kensington and Chelsea
H&F    Hammersmith and Fulham

LISA: Elite, cluster description

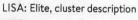

high–high
high–low
low–high
low–low
not significant

**Figure 8.6b**
Social Capital: Status

GREATER LONDON

Enfield
Barnet
Harrow
Haringey
Redbridge
Havering
Brent
Camden
Islington
Hackney
Waltham Forest
Hillingdon
Ealing
Westminster
K&C
H&F
Tower
Hamlets
City
Newham
Barking and
Dagenham
Hounslow
Wandsworth
Southwark
Lewisham
Greenwich
Bexley
Richmond upon
Thames
Lambeth
Kingston upon Thames
Merton
Sutton
Croydon
Bromley

0          10 miles
0        10 km

K&C    Kensington and Chelsea
H&F    Hammersmith and Fulham

LISA: Social capital: Status, cluster description

high–high
high–low
low–high
low–low
not significant

| 0 | | 100 miles |
| 0 | 100 km | |

Figure 8.6c

Social Capital: Range

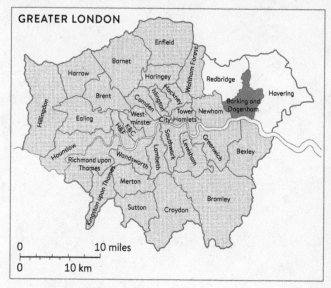

GREATER LONDON

Enfield

Barnet

Harrow

Haringey

Waltham Forest

Redbridge

Havering

Hillingdon

Brent

Camden

Islington

Hackney

Barking and Dagenham

Ealing

West-
minster

K&C

City

Tower
Hamlets

Newham

H&F

Hounslow

Southwark

Lewisham

Greenwich

Bexley

Richmond upon
Thames

Wandsworth

Lambeth

Kingston upon Thames

Merton

Sutton

Croydon

Bromley

| 0 | | 10 miles |
| 0 | | 10 km |

K&C    Kensington and Chelsea
H&F    Hammersmith and Fulham

LISA: Social capital: Range, cluster description

■ high–high
■ high–low
■ low–high
▓ low–low
□ not significant

Figure 8.6d
Social Capital: Highbrow

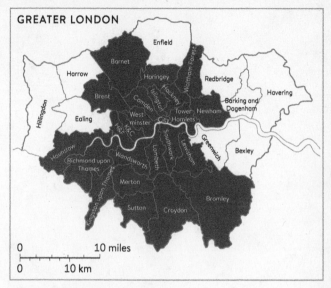

**GREATER LONDON**

Enfield

Barnet

Harrow

Haringey

Redbridge

Havering

Brent

Camden

Islington

Hackney

Waltham Forest

Barking and Dagenham

Hillingdon

Westminster

Ealing

K&C

H&F

City Hamlets

Tower

Newham

Greenwich

Bexley

Hounslow

Wandsworth

Southwark

Lewisham

Richmond upon Thames

Lambeth

Kingston upon Thames

Merton

Bromley

Sutton

Croydon

| 0 | 10 miles |
| 0 | 10 km |

K&C   Kensington and Chelsea
H&F   Hammersmith and Fulham

LISA: Cultural capital: Highbrow, cluster description

- high–high
- high–low
- low–high
- low–low
- not significant

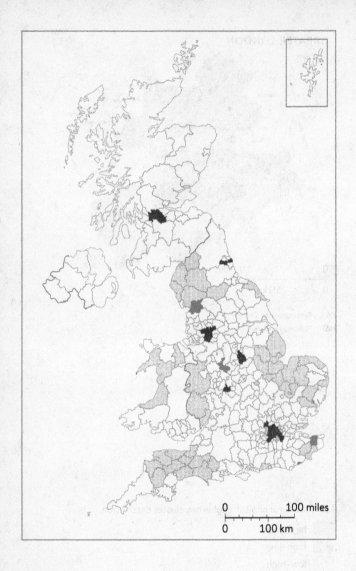

Figure 8.6e
Social Capital: Emerging

GREATER LONDON

Enfield
Barnet
Harrow
Haringey
Waltham Forest
Redbridge
Havering
Brent
Camden
Hackney
Islington
Barking and
Dagenham
Hillingdon
Ealing
West minster
Tower Hamlets
City
Newham
Hounslow
K&C
H&F
Southwark
Lewisham
Greenwich
Bexley
Richmond upon
Thames
Wandsworth
Lambeth
Kingston upon Thames
Merton
Bromley
Sutton
Croydon

0        10 miles
0     10 km

K&C    Kensington and Chelsea
H&F    Hammersmith and Fulham

LISA: Cultural capital: Emerging, cluster description

▪ high–high
▪ high–low
▪ low–high
▪ low–low
▫ not significant

the key indicators of social and cultural capital using the same technique. Turning to social capital first, Figure 8.6(b) shows the mean status of the GBCS respondents' social networks. This is the measure which effectively quantifies the popular notion that it is 'who you know, rather than what you know' that counts. If there is any truth in that adage, it presents an astonishing portrait of the intersection between social and economic geographies in this country, with those with the highest-status contacts heavily clustered in London and the south-east once again, while once again in Wales and the north of England, clusters of low-status networks are to be found.

However, if we turn to the range of people that respondents report knowing, we find a completely different picture. It is overwhelmingly in the peripheral regions that the breadth of people's networks is greatest. Living in London may convey access to higher-status friendship groups and associations, but within much narrower networks. What is also distinctive here is that the pattern is reflected more broadly in an urban–rural divide. People in cities generally know fewer people, who tend to be of higher status. Those living in rural areas generally know a much wider range of people.

Finally, in terms of cultural capital, there is once more a south-eastern bias in terms of the possession of highbrow cultural capital (which includes activities such as attending classical dance and opera performances). This is perhaps understandable, given the concentration of the UK's highbrow cultural arts establishments in the capital, although pockets of provincial concentration are evident too.

Meanwhile, the distribution of emerging cultural capital presents a different and more dispersed picture, pointing not just to London, but to a number of British cities as repositories and breeding grounds for new forms of cultural engagement. Emerging cultural capital, with its association with young people, is predominantly an urban form, and once again, the power of the urban–rural divide is clear here.

The maps in Figures 8.6(a)–(e) steer us away from simplistic north–south binaries in understanding spatial inequalities in the UK, with 'onshore islands' of economic, social and cultural accumulation located outside the south-east of England. However, if we focus specifically on three indicators which provide the most powerful indices of advantage in British society today (household income, status of social contacts and high cultural capital), the dominance of London and the south-east becomes absolutely undeniable. Table 8.1 ranks the top twenty unitary authorities in terms of these three indicators and presents a startling view of how social, cultural and economic geographies intersect in this country and, moreover, just how concentrated such resources are in and around our capital city. Of the sixty places available in the table, forty-one are taken up by areas which are represented more than once across the columns showing the three indicators, while seven areas (Kensington and Chelsea, Westminster, the City, Camden, Richmond upon Thames, Hammersmith and Fulham and Chiltern) are in the top twenty across all three measures. Only seven of the thirty-six entries lie outside London and the south-east region.

This matters because it has become one of the most tired tropes in mainstream public discourse in this country that

## SOCIAL CAPITAL

| RANK | | STATUS SCORE |
|---|---|---|
| 1 | Kensington and Chelsea LB[1] | 56.91 |
| 2 | City of Westminster LB | 56.53 |
| 3 | City of London | 56.45 |
| 4 | Camden LB | 55.81 |
| 5 | Richmond upon Thames LB | 55.81 |
| 6 | Wandsworth LB | 55.74 |
| 7 | Hammersmith and Fulham LB | 55.70 |
| 8 | South Buckinghamshire | 55.37 |
| 9 | Islington LB | 55.27 |
| 10 | Elmbridge | 55.22 |
| 11 | St Albans | 54.90 |
| 12 | Oxford | 54.83 |
| 13 | Cambridge | 54.78 |
| 14 | Southwark LB | 54.74 |
| 15 | Lambeth LB | 54.57 |
| 16 | Merton LB | 54.51 |
| 17 | Windsor and Maidenhead | 54.24 |
| 18 | Barnet LB | 54.06 |
| 19 | Tower Hamlets LB | 53.97 |
| 20 | Chiltern | 53.87 |

**Table 8.1**

Top Twenty UK Unitary Authorities, Ranked by Social, Cultural and Economic Capital

*Source*: GBCS data
1. LB = London borough.
Authorities lying outside London and south-east England are highlighted

# CULTURAL CAPITAL

| RANK | | STATUS SCORE |
|------|--|---:|
| 1 | Kensington and Chelsea LB | 16.32 |
| 2 | City of Westminster LB | 15.44 |
| 3 | City of London | 15.36 |
| 4 | Camden LB | 15.20 |
| 5 | Hammersmith and Fulham LB | 14.86 |
| 6 | Islington LB | 14.84 |
| 7 | Hackney LB | 14.57 |
| 8 | Lambeth LB | 14.49 |
| 9 | Chiltern | 14.48 |
| 10 | Richmond upon Thames LB | 14.48 |
| 11 | Chichester | 14.47 |
| 12 | Lewisham LB | 14.45 |
| 13 | Oxford | 14.45 |
| 14 | West Devon | 14.41 |
| 15 | Ryedale | 14.38 |
| 16 | Southwark LB | 14.37 |
| 17 | Winchester | 14.33 |
| 18 | Greenwich LB | 14.30 |
| 19 | South Oxfordshire LB | 14.28 |
| 20 | Harrogate | 14.27 |

## ECONOMIC CAPITAL

| RANK | | INCOME (£) |
|---|---|---|
| 1 | Kensington and Chelsea LB | 94,593 |
| 2 | City of London | 93,907 |
| 3 | South Buckinghamshire | 91,961 |
| 4 | Elmbridge | 84,678 |
| 5 | City of Westminster LB | 83,050 |
| 6 | Sevenoaks | 79,845 |
| 7 | Windsor and Maidenhead | 77,925 |
| 8 | Richmond upon Thames LB | 77,644 |
| 9 | Camden LB | 74,353 |
| 10 | Wandsworth LB | 73,872 |
| 11 | Chiltern | 73,657 |
| 12 | St Albans | 72,117 |
| 13 | Hammersmith and Fulham LB | 71,768 |
| 14 | Mole Valley | 71,302 |
| 15 | Tandridge | 71,235 |
| 16 | Brentwood | 70,748 |
| 17 | Hertsmere | 70,726 |
| 18 | Woking | 70,390 |
| 19 | Waverley | 70,239 |
| 20 | Merton LB | 69,140 |

power is disproportionately concentrated in the south-east region, yet metrics to highlight the intersection between these complex circuits of influence and interaction have remained elusive. In this example, we can see explicitly, for the first time, the concentration of resources across what have previously been considered nebulous or hidden domains. And these concentrations of resources have a highly pronounced and imbalanced geographical distribution.

What comes out of our analysis therefore is a complex geography which operates across several dimensions: urban–rural; north–south; and the metropolitan capital of London versus the rest. All these divisions ultimately articulate the central power of London itself. We might, crudely, characterize earlier periods as having contrasted different spatial imaginaries in which London might have been dominant, but in ways which were contested. The power of provincial, county and regional identities was strong. However, London now operates as the unquestioned centre of elite geography.

It follows from this argument that subjective notions of class identity are bound up with place and location. And indeed, the GBCS supports such an interpretation. Our analysis of its data shows a statistically significant relationship between distance from London and all of the measures of class identity. As distance from London increases, there is a decline in the number of people who identify themselves as 'middle class', while this is matched by a rise in the share of people who call themselves 'working class'. If the same analysis is conducted solely on those people who are members of the elite, we find almost identical patterns: with a positive relationship between distance from the capital and working class self-identification matched by a commensurate decline in those identifying as middle class. So regardless of the social, cultural and economic capital available to an individual, the relationship between distance from the capital and subjective class identity remains strikingly constant.

We live in a highly inegalitarian society, where macrolevel policies are either inadequate or unable to counter the wide and widening disparities between rich and poor. It is little wonder, then, that those inequalities are reflected at lower spatial scales as we peel back the layers of the onion and dig down through the geographies. Our country is economically dominated by one city, the economic power of which far outweighs even its massive demographic supremacy. Yet, spatial inequalities exist within all our cities, and the geographies of affluence and deprivation are too multifaceted to be explained by simple north–south binaries. Intersecting all these is the significance of class divisions.

There is therefore an unequal geography in the cultural and social domains as well as in the economic. These overlap, but imperfectly, showing that the wider identities of places cannot be read from their economic capital and prosperity alone. A powerful urban–rural divide, as much as a regional one between north and south, is marked in terms of the way urban centres operate as foci of cultural capital (especially emerging cultural capital) and social capital.

And marking out these new urban spaces, we see the power of the elite as having a profound geographical imprint, as this is fundamentally an urban class. The old aristocratic class with roots in the land, at the apex of the class structure, has given way to a more fundamentally urbanized class – though one quite possibly with second homes tucked away in areas of repose. This, as Piketty has demonstrated, is an aspect of the profound shift in the organization of capital towards residential property and away from agricultural land.[24]

Underscoring all this is London itself. London's dominance can be seen in multiple dimensions. London is where all three capitals converge and intersect. And London also defines other places in its shadow, in a kind of relational embrace in which other places gain their identity in terms of their difference from, or more occasionally the way they may ape, the English capital. In making this argument, there is a clear overlap with our findings in Chapter 7 regarding the power of elite universities, all of which are located close to London. London is now a vortex – a voracious and intense space, in which an elite class finds its home.

# PART FOUR

# The Class Divide in 21$^{st}$ Century Britain

# The View at the Top

## BRITAIN'S NEW 'ORDINARY' ELITE

In the early twenty-first century, the very wealthy are subject to increasing attention. The remarkable reception of Thomas Piketty's *Capital in the Twenty-first Century*, allied to increasing concern about spiralling remuneration at the top, has made the sociological analysis of the elite essential. But we need to guard against the view that this new, wealth-elite marks a return to the aristocratic, landed and gentlemanly class which held sway in Britain until the later twentieth century. It is easy to be confused here by the prominence of old idioms and the relics of aristocracy which abound. The success of the National Trust and the 'exhibitionary complex' which places stately homes at the heart of British leisure habits exemplifies this ongoing fascination with the landed classes. Television shows from *Brideshead Revisited* to *Downton Abbey* continue to deploy a 'gentry' aesthetic, which circulates through brands such as Laura Ashley, Burberry, Hunter, Barbour and Jack Wills, which are still able to command a distinctive presence. The traditional private school and stately home continue to serve as default sites for so much English novel writing (recent examples being by J. K. Rowling, Sarah Waters and Ian McEwan).

Yet, in fact, such idioms no longer give us a handle on the organization of privilege in Britain. The staggering decline of the aristocratic class in the years after the Second World War has been emphatically demonstrated by David Cannadine.[1] In 2013 only a small minority of the wealthiest people in Britain were from landed and titled backgrounds – a far cry from the 1980s.[2] Even the Duke of Westminster, whose fortune is buttressed by huge swathes of central London real estate, struggles to get into the top ten.

In retrospect, the 1980s marked the last blast of this old aristocratic culture. It was the last moment when sociologists such as John Scott could still write about the 'upper class' as a kind of closed, landed elite.[3] Margaret Thatcher's Conservative government, elected in 1979, presided over the de-industrialization of the old manufacturing heartlands, and this ushered in a new kind of cultural confidence from those with money to spend. This marked a sharp change from previous decades when the wealthy kept their heads down in a period when equality was seen as a good thing. In the 1970s levels of inequality reached their nadir and tax rates on high-income earners reached their peak. In the 1980s, however, the flaunting of wealth started to take on a new legitimacy. The central cultural motif of the 1980s was the 'Sloane Ranger', a phrase coined by the marketing consultant Peter York to recognize the revival of a 'posh' landed-gentry aesthetic at the heart of a new consumer culture. But tellingly, as York makes clear, this idiom appealed to an aspirant class who sought to identify with the aristocracy: it was not the revival of the landed class itself.

> The Sloane culture we described then was a rather secret
> garden, neither the grandest toffs, nor the aspirant
> commercial middle-middles, but something else in
> between . . . the newspaper and TV coverage, of course,
> was overwhelmingly about champagne flutes, luxury
> brands, Ascot and smart celebrity polo. Increasingly, it
> became an identity people tried on for size; an identity with
> proxies in brands and behaviour, rather than beliefs.[4]

In retrospect, the Sloane Ranger idiom actually looked forward to a consumerist era in which the trappings of 'posh'
could be identified and attained by upwardly mobile outsiders. It represented the commodification of the posh 'brand',
and its hiving off from the old landed elite itself. The archetype was Lady Diana Spencer, married into royalty through
her unhappy union with Prince Charles in 1981. Although
from an aristocratic background, she defined a new 'ladylike'
aesthetic which positioned itself against the heart of the
Establishment. The outpouring of public grief at her prema-
ture death in 1997 was a telling marker of the symbolic shift
in which 'posh' was now democratized.

We can understand the sea change represented by this
new posh aesthetic by comparing it to the furore which took
place in 1954 when the popular writer Nancy Mitford published an obscure article about the speech patterns of the
English aristocracy in *Encounter*, a new monthly journal
which set out the stall for the literary elite who illuminated
the bleak years of post-war austerity Britain. Mitford coined
the distinction between 'U' (upper class) and 'non-U' accents,
revealing a distinctive social code which separated out the

truly posh from those who merely aspired to be so. This decoding caused a sensation – rather like the Sloane Ranger idea thirty years later. Whether one used the term 'loo' (U) or 'toilet' (non-U) became a major bone of contention and fed middle class dinner party conversation for years to come. However, the focus of this debate was about the impossibility of fundamentally being 'U' unless you were born into the linguistic community itself. And it remained impolite for ladies or gentlemen to draw attention to this implicit apartheid. Mitford's friend, the novelist Evelyn Waugh, whose *Brideshead Revisited* lamented the declining world of the aristocracy, chided her lack of taste for drawing attention to the difference between 'U' and 'non-U':

> Were you surprised that your article on the English aristocracy caused such a to-do? [. . .] Class distinctions in England have always been the matter for higher feeling than national honour, the matter of feverish but very private debate. So, when you brought them into the open, of course everyone talked, of course the columnists quoted you and corrected you. [. . .] Should delicacy have restrained you? your friends anxiously ask. There are subjects too intimate for print. Surely class is one?[5]

In 1954 really polite people were not meant to talk about class. Nancy Mitford was the progeny of the aristocracy. If she had been an upstart sociologist, or a socialist agitator, then ranting about class might be understandable, if not excusable. It would just be a sign of 'a chip on the shoulder' (to use another favourite expression of the time). But surely a lady should know better?

In the 1980s, however, no one turned against marketing consultants for whipping up versions of 'posh' for popular consumption. The genie was out of the bottle. The aristocratic formation knew that its innate superiority was no longer assertive or powerful enough to make a stand against the vulgarization of poshness. For Grayson Perry, in his 2012 BAFTA-winning documentary series 'The Vanity of Small Differences', the symbolic decline was all too visible:

> In the light of the sunset they watch the old aristocratic
> stag with its tattered tweed hide being hunted down by the
> dogs of tax, social change, upkeep and fuel bills. The old
> land-owning breed is dying out.

And by the 1990s, as Peter York writes in 2015, noted that 'the Sloane style couldn't have been more unfashionable. The accent, the language, the dress code, the "miniature stately home" interior styles were all wrong, wrong, wrong . . . Sloane seemed archaic and unprofessional – only for the magic world of Richard Curtis rom-coms – in the new high-maintenance world of Big Money London.'[6]

In the early twenty-first century, the old aristocratic, landed, upper class is a thing of the past. We need to insist on this, given the unfortunate tendency to revert to the idea of the 'Establishment' as a central feature of British society and governance.[7] This term was coined by the historian A. J. P. Taylor and taken up by journalist Henry Fairlie in 1955 to capture the idea that rule was exercised 'socially' through upper-class connections – such as those made in elite schools, clubs and institutions. It became popular over the following decade, especially among left-wing critics, who emphasized that the failure to 'modernize' Britain was due to the hold of the old aristocratic elite.[8] The idea of the 'Establishment', however, has always acted less as a sociological concept and more as a means for upwardly mobile critical intellectuals to define their credentials by railing against it. Its recent revival is unfortunate.

We believe that a better sociological understanding of today's wealth-elite needs to depart from older concepts of the aristocratic upper class and the 'Establishment'. As we have shown in previous chapters, this approach also involves contesting the contrasting simplistic media stereotypes which champion the success of the 'working rich', the upwardly mobile and 'dynamic' business-elite class. Access to the most affluent positions is far from being a level playing field and is indeed marked by inequalities which intensify as capital accumulates. Therefore, the stereotypes of self-made, thrusting businessmen, such as Richard Branson, Alan Sugar and Philip Green, who, through skilful and energetic business leadership, succeed in acquiring and selling businesses at the forefront of consumer demand, also need to be treated as somewhat mythical creatures. Even though the provenance of these figures is amplified through this vision now being paraded on our television screen courtesy of *The Apprentice*, *Dragons' Den* and suchlike, it is a far from accurate picture of the social inequality which exists at the top of British society.

It follows, therefore, that we need a more subtle approach than to simply critique the vicarious fortunes of bankers and financiers, who command huge bonuses and dividends, deploy tax breaks or earn windfalls from public-sector privatization or deregulation. The moral panic about bonuses, the culture of takeovers and corporate raiding, and the significance of the 'non-domiciled' rich, lured to London by the tax breaks that successive governments have made available, all plays into this populist sentiment. There is a danger that our attention is thus distracted, turned away from the 'ordinarily wealthy' who extend well beyond the top '1 per cent'. Of course, we don't doubt for one moment that it is the 'super-wealthy' who have been the prime beneficiaries of economic change in recent decades, and who need extensive public scrutiny. Nonetheless, sociologically, we need to extend our gaze. Chapter 5 suggested that the top 6 per cent, for instance, all have levels of economic capital which set them well apart from any other social group, and whilst we should not fixate on this as an exact figure, it is nonetheless indicative that a larger group of extremely affluent households should command our attention.

In taking this path, we draw on two other perspectives. Firstly, Pierre Bourdieu elaborates the idea of 'the field of power'. Rather than see the upper layers of society as composed of a coherent and cohesive group along the lines of the 'Establishment', Bourdieu identifies it as a scene of internal contestation and dispute between the most powerful and well-resourced agents from different sectors and professions, such as the financial, political, legal and journalistic elements. This emphasizes, importantly, how powerful groups do not necessarily see themselves as a united or cohesive force, but may be more aware of their internal differences as they jostle for influence.[9] This usefully directs us towards registering the fractures, as well as the solidarity, between those at the top.

A second influence is Thomas Piketty, who argues that economic trends are leading to the resurgence of a wealth elite which echoes that found in the aristocratic age of the nineteenth-century Belle Époque. As we have seen in Chapter 2, the very wealthy have reaped the rewards of the steady accumulation of their assets, especially in the British context (through the accumulation of housing assets and savings). He is especially interested in the potential of *rentier* income, in the way that the moderately well-off, as well as the very wealthy, can expect to accumulate economic capital steadily, often in unspectacular ways. The rise of second homes, as well as buying properties for rent, are all part of this process. Therefore, even though Piketty is concerned with the super-wealthy, he also brings out the importance of those who have done extremely well, even if they are not positioned at the very summit of wealth.

Drawing upon these arguments, our analysis points towards the significance of an 'ordinary' wealth elite which now comprises a sizeable group within the population – if we see it as around 6 per cent of the population, over a million people. Even this relatively large elite group enjoys massive advantages over others. As we saw in Chapter 5, their mean household income – after tax and other deductions – is £89k, almost double that of the next highest class, and the average value of their homes – £325k – is also much higher than that of any other class. Their average savings, at £142k, are also exceptionally high and well over double those of any other class. Fundamentally, then, this is a wealthy class, set apart from the other six classes on the basis of striking economic advantages. This is a class which basks in the sun, with very high levels of economic affluence. But it also has distinctive social and cultural characteristics.

## The strange GBCS sample skew

The imprint of this ordinary wealth elite takes strange and surprising forms. We can return to reflect on the strange GBCS sample skew which we first discussed in the Introduction. There is a fascinating and hugely revealing finding here. The more that people belonged to some kind of 'elite' category, in any of the dimensions we might measure – e.g. earning very high incomes, attending elite universities, living in the most wealthy areas – the more likely they were to do the GBCS. Furthermore, this is not an incremental addition, but an exponential one. The most elite were *much* more likely to do the GBCS compared to those who were simply moderately wealthy. For instance, graduates from Oxbridge were twice as likely to do the GBCS as graduates from any other university.[10] CEOs were twice as likely to do the GBCS compared to any other professional or managerial group (though we can also see another striking spike among journalists and some cultural professions). Geographically, it is those in the most affluent and privileged locations, and especially those in the City of London, Oxford and Cambridge, who were massively more likely to have done the GBCS than would have been expected, even given the class make-up of these locations. The exclusive London Barbican estate was the epicentre of the GBCS.

This is an arresting finding in its own terms, given the general view that elite classes are difficult to research and generally don't wish to expose their own practices to scrutiny.[11] One indirect lesson from the GBCS is that 'class research', just like 'class talk', appears to have become a 'really upmarket' practice, and the very advantaged seem to have been attracted to the GBCS in disproportionate numbers.

There are four possible reasons for this upmarket elite sample skew. It might reflect errors in the web survey itself. Respondents might jokingly have claimed to be Oxbridge graduates or CEOs to have deliberately 'spiked' the survey. If true, this is telling testimony to the way that our research was tied into the very processes of irony and knowingness which we have referred to in this book as being part of 'emergent cultural capital'. However, whilst there might be a few cases where this kind of ironic 'spoiling' took place, we do not think that this was a major factor. The responses from Oxbridge graduates and CEOs do not, generally, appear as jumbled, or as diversionary, as one might expect if respondents had been merely pretending. We might have expected more spoof references to occupations which were in the public eye, such as 'bankers', rather than CEOs, which is a term which is not such a wide point of reference.[12]

A second possibility is that, given that the GBCS was launched by the BBC alongside programmes about social exclusiveness,[13] some Oxbridge graduates and CEOs might have felt the need to do the GBCS to emphasize their relatively meritocratic credentials. They might have wanted to demonstrate that they did not fit the 'posh' or 'exclusive' stereotypes which were being peddled by the BBC or that still operate in the public imagination. Rushing to their iPads to do the GBCS might have been an attempt to insist that the old stereotypes did not actually apply – not in their case, at least. However, if this was the case, then these respondents were ineffective in making this point. On most measures, they are exclusive. A high proportion of the very wealthy were prepared to admit to an upper-middle class identity – one which is generally eschewed among a wider population.

There are other reasons which do explain the sample skew – and also testify to central characteristics of the elite class itself. It is actually testimony to a kind of technocratic confidence. The ordinary elite have the intellectual confidence and interest to take part in a BBC research project about class. They are interested in themselves, in comparison to other social groups, especially when this can be represented as a 'scientific' project which extends public understanding. Rather than possessing the 'gentlemanly' identity of a group which thinks it is superior but finds it vulgar to openly broadcast this view, this elite group now displays itself, albeit within a scientific framing.

Furthermore, doing the GBCS was a chance for an individual to obtain the private gratification that they had, indeed, made it to the top. It was a way of privately learning that you had done well, even without publicly owning up to being part of the 'elite' category. Indeed, the BBC tried to play into this sensibility by designing the GBCS so that respondents were given a 'coat of arms', which produced scores on their economic, social and cultural capital when they completed the quiz. People who thought to themselves that they were doing 'pretty well' may have been attracted to the GBCS to privately test out whether this was backed up sociologically. This would explain the sample skew towards the wealthy and well educated.

At the end of our interviews we asked people to fill in the BBC Class Calculator and asked for their reflections on the class position the quiz had identified for them. Those identified as being in the elite were uniformly uncomfortable with the label.

*Henry*: The word 'elite' just kind of grates, it sounds like the best of the best and assumes that a different class is better than another one.

*Benedict*: Partly it's the idea that if you're elite, you're cut-off from a lot of people who aren't.

*Georgia*: I definitely don't perceive myself as upper class, because to me that just goes into snob territory and that's a terrible thing.

*Louise*: To me it wasn't right. I don't feel elite . . . because it comes with the assumption that you think your shit don't stink. I don't think I'm a superior being at all. I've never forgotten where I've come from. And that's what fuels me to do better, be more . . .

*Anthony*: There's a danger of feeling smug about it and I would hate that.

Further evidence for this interpretation comes from reflecting on the tweets from those who had been told they were in the 'elite' category according to the BBC's Class Calculator. When respondents were told that they were in that category, they characteristically engaged in modest, self-depreciating dis-identification from the 'elite' label, yet at the same time displayed a certain vicarious pleasure, albeit laced with humour and irony:[14]

> According to the new #bbcclass survey I am elite. Nice to see a long-obvious reality reflected in hard data at last. Kneel! Bow! And so on . . .

> According to the great british class survey [sic], my parents fit into the 'elite' class. Where the hell is my Range Rover?!

> I'm offended that I wasn't involved in this 'Great British Class Survey' . . . They would have added a class above 'elite' if I was, though.

> Doing the British Class System test and @xxxxxx comes out as elite? I think it's broken . . .

> Me too. So embarrassed I'm not telling anyone: MT @xxxxx. According to the new #bbcclass survey I am elite . . .

The GBCS elite skew therefore showed the existence of a subtly confident elite group, which did not wish to publicly announce its 'eliteness' in the form of a direct claim to public recognition – as with the old aristocracy – but which instead liked to frame its own role through a scientific discourse which offered personal reassurance about status. This is testimony to a new kind of elite class, which is aware of how different it is from other social classes, which seeks to avoid overtly 'snobby' and public manifestations of such 'elite-ness', but which nonetheless recognizes its own importance.

Our interviews with people in this category revealed in telling ways how respondents classified as elite had a complex and often uneasy relationship with their economic advantage. Conversations about money were often sensitive ones. When we asked people to tell us how much they earned and also about the value of their property and assets, questions were rarely answered matter-of-factly, giving a figure and nothing else. Instead, respondents were keen to explain, even justify, their wealth. Meritocratic justification ran deep. Many were somewhat defensive, emphasizing that their assets reflected 'hard work' and significant achievements. They were 'just deserts'. Georgia recalled the time when her mother had questioned her expensive taste in shoes: 'What, am I supposed to feel bad for that? I've worked hard to get that.'

Others played down their wealth by positioning themselves in a comparative sense. In a similar manner to that described in Chapter 2, respondents frequently steered conversations about money towards friends or family even more fortunate than themselves. As George noted: 'We always feel we're not that well-off, because, you know, we know people who are partners in law firms, bankers, people who live in much bigger houses closer to central London. So we're always conscious of someone better off than us.' There is a general tendency to find someone better-off to compare yourself with.

For others, unease about money was more rooted in a sense that the accumulation of wealth had been serendipitous, even accidental. These respondents were invariably those living in London or the south-east and who had seen the value of their homes rocket. Stuart explained that he and his wife had seen their terraced, three-bedroom house rise in value 900 per cent since they had bought it twenty-two years earlier. 'It's embarrassing to be this well-off,' Stuart told us. 'It's pure chance, because we just happen to be fifty-five minutes from London. Similarly, Fiona, an IT consultant who lived in south London, had also seen her home increase in value by 550 per cent in thirteen years. What was interesting was that, outwardly at least, Stuart and Fiona seemed somewhat uncomfortable with the way their properties had unwittingly catapulted them upwards economically. While, of course, they were happy to be financially secure, there was a sense of guilt about a windfall that Stuart described as 'bonkers' and 'random'.

## An elite 'constellation'

The contemporary elite class defies traditional 'upper-class' presumptions. It is a differentiated and hetereogeneous formation, which is nicely captured by the idea that it is a *constellation*, which lacks a unitary defining feature, but the definition of which arises from the interplay between its different stars. Thus, its cultural motifs vary and it does not conform to a simple highbrow norm. To be sure, in the GBCS those in this category score highest on 'highbrow' cultural capital, meaning that they are more likely than any other class to participate in, and have taste preferences for, prestigious forms of culture, such as opera, classical music and theatre. Certainly, for older elite-class members, these kinds of cultural activities had been significant. Anthony, a professor of biology, had managed to ensure himself a place at university to do a PhD because he shared a keen interest in rugby with his supervisor, and he relates how talking about these shared interests at his interview (and beyond) was key to their relationship. However, this cultural competence and confidence is not just confined to those possessing highbrow interests. While traditional elite classes in the past marked their distinction by selectively consuming *only* this visibly prestigious kind of culture, members of today's elite class are also in tune with contemporary and popular culture, with younger members in particular also enjoying video games, contemporary music and so forth.

Occupational diversity within the elite category also makes up part of this constellation. For all the talk of bankers and finance, there is no unitary group to be found among the wealth elite class. Different fields (business, media, law, academia, etc.) compete with each other for the ultimate goal of defining their authority in the public domain. These elite-class occupational blocs may have distinctive cultures of their own, so that they form distinctive niches within a broader formation. This is especially true for some of the older professions, which may tend to recruit from their own ranks. Architects are much more likely to be recruited from families with parents from professional backgrounds (presumably, often from families of architects) than are the 'creative core' of professionals as a whole (32 per cent versus

22 per cent). The same applies to lawyers (37 per cent of whom come from families with professional backgrounds against 22 per cent with that kind of background for the creative professions as a whole). On the other hand, managers and directors are much more likely to be recruited from those with parents with a senior managerial background (31 per cent compared to 24 per cent for creative professionals in general).

The concept of the elite as a constellation brings us back, once more, to the centrality of London, which acts as the spatial arena in which different kinds of elite members start to orbit, circulate and jostle. The dominance of London takes on new forms from those which have existed in the past. Admittedly, from the eighteenth to the mid-twentieth century, London was at the centre of the aristocratic practice of attending the court and displaying its debutantes during the 'Season', but, during the nineteenth and twentieth centuries, distinctive county, urban and regional elites could meaningfully contest London's hegemony in various ways until the later twentieth century (for instance, via the Anti-Corn Law League or through Chamberlain's municipal Conservatism). This kind of regional or non-London-urban elite group is, we would suggest on the basis of our data, now much weaker – if it exists at all. Having a relationship with London venues and its 'scene' is now fundamental to the new elite-class practices. For instance, two similar individuals, making their way in the professions, would have very different prospects according to whether they were based in London or the north of England.

However, gaining entrance to the 'elite' category is also a

matter of achievement. Being willing and prepared to work in London or the south-east seems very important to this, and the capital acts as a vortex which sucks up the energies of those drawn into it. There is no evidence that native Londoners are advantaged over those who migrate to the city. Some of our interviewees saw this process very clearly. George explained how his ability to enter his profession had hinged largely on a pivotal period after graduation, when he was able to work in a number of unpaid internships whilst living at home with his parents (just outside London). While George obviously worked hard to establish himself during this period, his ability to get a foothold up in his career was dependent on both the financial support and geographical positioning of his parents. In the case of John, a retired IT director, the pull of London was also intimately connected to how he narrated his career success. A self-confessed, 'proud Yorkshire man', John had a strong connection to a rural life-style and had strongly resisted moving his family to London. But he described how, as he ascended the managerial ladder at a large high-street bank, his work demanded his presence in the capital and he found himself commuting there from Cheshire four days a week. While John admitted this 'took a heavy toll' on him personally and physically, he was also un-equivocal that he 'had to do it', that his career progression had depended on such sacrifices.

London is not just the single incubator for the elite, a uni-tary zone which cultivates and nurtures people on their way to the top. It also contains distinctive zones in which differ-ent members of the elite constellation find their residence – testifying again to a degree of geographical concentration of this class. London's elite chief executive officers make up the most affluent of the elite-class sectors. They are clearly located in the central heartland of London, where property prices are especially high. One large contour circles around Kensington and Chelsea, and a second is based around the City, Westminster and into Islington. There are a few more peripheral zones which go from Greenwich to Battersea – though they evade Wandsworth – and then loop towards Putney in the west and Balham to the south.

If we turn to consider London's cultural elite, rather different patterns can be found. This class of people is not located in central London, and instead they are to be found in the conventional intellectual and bohemian centre of Hampstead, then, more recently, throughout the more recently established zones of Crouch End and Hackney. A further concentration of members of this class live in Camden and Notting Hill, and, south of the river, in Clapham, Balham and Tooting.

London's legal elite is different again. This has a number of very crisply defined locations: in the heart of the City of London (close to the Law Courts), Hampstead, Camden Town (both of which give ready access to the Law Courts), as well some domiciles dotted about in a few suburban areas close to Waterloo Station (which also gives ready access to the courts).

The complex geography of London itself marks the constellation of different elite sectors, which give a stamp to certain areas and which also represent the cultural differences between the different categories of the elite class itself. From the truly pricy and lavish surroundings of Chelsea and

Knightsbridge, to the intellectual heartlands of Crouch End and Hackney, these areas represent subtly different versions of elite practices, and help to define the geographical and social characteristics of this elite constellation.

Within this elite constellation, it is ultimately the star of the corporate elite of senior managers which shines the brightest. Other elite sectors, located in more disparate places within the metropolis, and with lesser amounts of economic capital, glow more dimly. CEOs are the most over-represented occupation among our 'elite' class. So, to be part of the 'ordinary' wealth-elite, you don't necessarily have to have been brought up in a traditional upper-class way. It is important, however, to partake of certain kinds of cultural and social activities. Living in and around London, knowing your way around highbrow cultural capital, having a relation-ship with elite higher education and working at the top end of professional and corporate hierarchies now constitutes a pervasive elite constellation which extends well beyond a small 'Establishment' to define a central arena in which privi-lege is performed.

## Taking advantage of meritocracy

For all their seductive appeal, images of a persistent 'landed gentry' should not be taken as realistic representations of the contemporary elite class. Notwithstanding the languor of the Oxbridge college, the late-summer glory of country estates and the proliferation of 'gentry' brands, the symbolic power of these icons needs to be understood as a foil against which an 'ordinary' wealth-elite can define itself in more meritocratic

ways. The fact that this aristocratic class is so routinely cari-
catured and lampooned is now central to its ongoing significance. By classifying this supposed stereotypical group as
cohesive, socially inward, even inbred, and by characterizing
the upper class as a nepotistic 'old boys' network' where
informal contacts developed at school and university often
act as pivotal lubricants of prestigious professional trajectories, a wider, ordinarily wealthy elite class can emphasize its
distance from those wellsprings of old elitedom and claim a
more modest place for themselves.

The 'ordinary' elite class is fundamentally marked by meritocratic motifs – but in ways which should not be taken at
face value, but which instead mark today's performance of
privilege. Sociologists often distinguish cultures of 'ascrip-
tion' separately from 'achievement'. In the former case,
people are born into their social class and have little active
control over changing it, whilst, in the latter case, people
have the capacity to achieve a distinctive social position on
the basis of their endeavours. It is widely thought that contemporary societies have moved towards a 'meritocratic' culture of achievement, and in some respects this is true, but
with important caveats. Our 'elite' class has often achieved
its advantaged economic position through performing well
in the education system and then succeeding in the cut-
throat world of high-level professional and managerial
employment. This is a meritocratic culture which is honed
around particular, competitive versions of what it is that sig-
nifies merit and which, increasingly, informs the vision of
elite schools and universities. We have pursued this point in
Chapter 6 through the metaphor of mountain climbing, in

that those who start from the highest base camps are better able to succeed in the competitive and gruelling struggle to the top.

We cannot usefully understand the role of elite education through seeing it as simply a funnel into the Establishment. We follow in the footsteps of Shamus Khan, who emphasizes how elite private education is no longer concerned with schooling a predefined aristocratic elite, but instead imparts meritocratic skills and practices which are required to get ahead in competitive corporate and professional environments. We have shown that we need to move beyond a focus on private schooling alone towards the recognition of the power of elite universities. In the traditional model, attendance at a private school, or, in a contrasting way, a grammar school (for the upwardly mobile), was important in conferring potential membership of the elite class. However, whilst private schooling continues to bestow major advantages, there nonetheless is considerable recruitment into elite class from those without such education. Thus, for the London business elite – probably the most economically privileged group in Britain – there are nearly as many members in our GBCS sample who came from comprehensive schools as private schools (25 per cent versus 30 per cent).

Even controlling for other factors, such as parental class background, age, ethnicity, gender, university attended and the choice of subject studied, it is clear that attending independent schools will in the longer run affect future household income considerably, and also, to some extent, later on, becoming a member of the elite class. However, this same analysis shows that elite university education plays an additional role in recruitment to that same class. We have demonstrated the very striking gradient in economic capital between the most exclusive universities and other Russell Group universities, which appears to indicate that a key boundary separates out Oxbridge and the elite London colleges from all other universities, with Bristol, Exeter and Durham being on the coat-tails of this group.[15] Therefore, the terms of the sociological distinction between 'meritocratic' and 'ascribed' positions are no longer very useful for us in understanding the contemporary elite. These are morally loaded terms which allow 'self-made' men (or women) to pat themselves on the back, because they have not simply been born into privilege. However, our data shows that these contrasts are too stark. It is the more privileged who are best placed to get on the meritocratic ladder.

A strong belief in the culture of meritocracy was evident in interviews with our respondents in the elite class. Although many came from advantaged professional backgrounds, most chose to frame their success more in terms of hard work and merit than privilege. This often involved positioning themselves in opposition to those who might be seen as 'posh', 'upper class' or, in fact, part of an elite, and who might, therefore, be associated with inherited and undeserving privilege. As Georgia, a communications director, told us:

> I've always felt kind of privileged, not in a sense of I . . . you
> know, some of my friends went to private schools and
> know nobility and they've mixed in some very, in my mind,
> weird and wonderful circles, and when you use the term
> 'privileged' it's often referenced in that kind of old-school

sense. Whereas I suppose I know it's me that's got me to where I am, so . . .

Giles, a banking IT director, spoke similarly about those around him in banking whom he saw as being 'born with a silver spoon in their mouth[s]':

I do worry that we're creating not a class but a band of people that are cocooned from cradle to grave, almost a ghetto mentality. And it's somewhere in the middle class upper end there, where, you know, the poor little things are going to nursery, then they're going to the next school with the same strata of people surrounding them, and then they go to university and it's the same strata. I mean, we go to Portugal, and you can see them, they never go outside the complex, they don't go into the local restaurants, they don't go to the local villages to see what's happening. And I'm thinking: what experience have these people got? And then they think they're leading a superior life.

Even when respondents were more critical about their own advantage, it was interesting that they still ultimately reverted to notions of meritocracy. George, for example, noted:

We are acutely aware of our significant privilege. But also, to a degree, we have worked hard for it as well, with not the easiest starts. Easy in some ways, but not compared to many people.

Nigel, a highly successful upwardly mobile academic turned businessman, very thoughtful and considered, only became irate when discussing private schooling, which he insisted did not aid an individual's chances of getting on:

> People say going to a private school [improves your chances of social mobility], but I've known some people go to private school and do nothing with their life, you know, in fact, my cousin – he's split up with his wife and his wife married a GP and the GP sent him [the cousin's son] to a private school in Edinburgh and so he went to a private school, George Watson's, one of the top ones in Edinburgh and whatever that cost per year, and he then . . . after two years, gave it up, and is now a policeman, joined the police force 'cause he wanted to be a policeman.

This chapter has therefore developed our arguments about the significance of the elite in Britain today. In fact, we think the 'ordinary' elite is not always very glamorous, nor is it a glittering, self-recruited group. This wealth-elite is not socially 'closed', and its members normally have to work hard and 'perform' in order to join it. As Khan has argued with respect to American elite schooling, it is thus a group which is committed to a culture of 'achievement'. However, it is also clear that the prospects of becoming part of this class are very different, according to social background, and it thus reproduces forms of privilege.

This elite is not a cohesive formation. It is internally differentiated along occupational-sector lines. Although we have no evidence about inheritance, it is likely that membership of this class is based less upon dynastic wealth, and that it has a considerable proportion of the self-made. However, it is not fractured upon geographical lines. The geographical concentration in London and the south-east is vital in giving it a coherence and solidarity which would otherwise be lacking. We can understand London as a fundamental seat and site of the new 'ordinary' elite. London is important also as a site of major international interests and influence, and one where elite groups with offshore wealth and those who are non-British born and educated are prepared to find a base – which they would largely avoid in any other British location in any but exceptional circumstances.

Thirdly, within this differentiated and fractured elite, senior corporate managers dominate, having eclipsed those within the previous gentlemanly professional formation (who still enjoy a 'rump' presence in certain respects). This differentiated 'ordinary' elite is not an ascribed status group, but is more fluid and exhibits certain meritocratic motifs. These meritocratic motifs can be associated with the evident significance of certain universities in facilitating access to senior positions. These lines of entry are important in providing modes of legitimacy, even though, as our analyses showed, these are predominantly highly exclusive channels of recruitment. The meritocratic elite succeeds by not appearing to be exclusive, even though it is the product of highly unequal processes.

Finally, we have argued that it is useful to recognize the role of 'elite practices' in giving shared reference points to this internally differentiated elite. These elite practices include a shared metropolitan geography, a very particular educational profile, and the deployment of certain modes of highbrow and emerging cultural capital. 'Eliteness' is performed not by simply copying ascribed 'highbrow' habits and practices, but by demonstrating individual originality and 'knowingness'. It is hard work being one of the 'ordinary' elite. But let us now turn to another very hard-working group, who do not have these economic advantages – the group we have called the 'precariat'.

# The Precarious Precariat

THE VISIBLE INVISIBLE PEOPLE

We now move to a very different world from that of the elite. This is the 'precariat' class, who are positioned at the bottom of the social hierarchy. They are a group who have very low amounts of all the kinds of capital which we have analysed, with incomes of only a few thousand pounds a year, little savings and wealth. They also – unlike our 'ordinary' wealth-elite – were not attracted to being part of the GBCS. Although around 15 per cent of the population fit into the precariat class, fewer than 1 per cent of the GBCS respondents fitted the precariat profile – and those small number who did do the GBCS were rather atypical, being more likely to be down-wardly mobile into this class than born into it.

The precariat are the GBCS's 'missing people'. Whereas the elite and well educated found the Class Calculator on the BBC website fun to engage with, the precariat did not. This is hardly surprising, because the GBCS was used by those with cultural capital as a way of expressing their cultural knowledge and their confidence. The precariat are placed at the bottom, and no one wants to come last, so it was expected that this group would not be as visible in the GBCS as other groups. Rendering their invisibility more visible is vital to bringing contemporary class relationships to light.

The complicity between receptiveness to particular research methods and social inequality is itself an issue to be challenged.[1] Whereas the elite now command attention and interest, lying at the centre of media attention and social research, the precariat recedes from view, and this limits our awareness of social inequality and class divisions today.

We addressed the absence of the precariat in the GBCS by conducting additional research with those who seemed to fall into the precariat class. Lisa Mckenzie, one of Britain's leading researchers on the precariat, joined the project to lend her ethnographic skills to this vital task. Her job was to try to understand more deeply why this group had not engaged in the original survey, but also what they thought about the survey and how they were positioned within it. She was brought into the GBCS team because of her previous research on mothers who lived on a council estate in Nottingham, as well as her later work undertaken with a group of young men who were unemployed and living on the same council estate.[2]

The style of this chapter is deliberately different from the others. We have had to find resources outside the GBCS to unravel the lives and experiences of some people of the precariat class, and this therefore might grate with the book's style elsewhere. But this discrepancy, of course, precisely underscores our fundamental point regarding the salience and depth of class divisions today. There is no one style of analysis or presentation which can bring such classes together.

# Worlds of shame and stigma

Despite increasingly popular support for liberal attitudes across a range of issues today, there is a hardening of stigmatization of those at the bottom reaches of society. Discriminatory terms such as 'scum' and 'chavs' circulate extensively, in social media, in school playgrounds, and in streets, shops and pubs across the land. This is not a new phenomenon. Stephanie Lawler and Les Back have both argued that working class people are rarely taken seriously, and it is often assumed that they are easily 'readable' to middle class observers. It is rarely considered by the general public when observing working class people and neighbourhoods, that working class people, and especially the poor working class, the precariat, can know or understand themselves and their situation, and that they can articulate their understandings, perceptions and feelings extremely well.[3]

Unfair, patronizing and mean representations of poor, working class people, and the places where they live, are everywhere in the UK. They have been documented in the work of Skeggs Beverley and Diane Reay as well as by Lawler.[4] Lawler argues that working class people are rarely named as members of a specific class, but are often known and reproduced as 'disgusting subjects', usually through targeting disparaging descriptions of their bodies and clothing, shell-suits and large gold earrings, which are used as shorthand identifiers of working class people.[5] On the social networking site Facebook there is a facility where you can send 'council estate gifts' to your friends. The most popular council estate gift is an image of a group of young people in sportswear titled 'mob of chav scum': 824,000 people have sent this 'gift' to their friends on the site, and this is followed by images such as 'a piss-stained phone box', and a 'rundown community centre'. There are other 'council-estate gifts' such as 'over-the-top Christmas lights', and 'balcony draped with washing'. Lawler argues that these cultural references invoke signifiers which do a great deal of work in encoding a valueless and repulsive way of life.

Bodies, their appearance, their bearing and their adornment, are central to encoding the poor, and when those codes are joined up with images of particular kinds of living space, and especially with the term 'council estate', it leaves the reader to 'join up the dots of pathologization' in order to see and understand the picture: that certain ways of dressing and speaking and certain habitations indicate not only a despised 'class position, but also an underlying pathology'.[6] This underlying pathology that Lawler and Skeggs uncover is also about taste, or the lack of it. Once more, the work of Pierre Bourdieu provides insights into this, in his emphasis that those with the most power get to decide which cultural resources are tasteful, with regard to ways of dressing, personal style, music, art, language and social pursuits. However, as we saw in Chapter 3, Bourdieu argues that whilst the culture of the middle class is deemed legitimate and tasteful, it is the culture of the working class which is considered illegitimate and lacking in 'taste'. Lawler and Skeggs transport this argument further by exclaiming that the cultural practices of the working class are not only descried as 'tasteless', but are also pathologized, encoded as immoral, wrong and criminal. This leads to a situation where the working class in general, and the precariat in particular, are defined as 'lacking' culture, as not measuring up to 'respectable' standards.

Beverley Skeggs has argued that the consequences of stigmatization, and rebranding the poor working class as valueless, have become even more central in creating new ways of exploitation through the fields of culture and the media inventing new forms of class differentiation which are being produced through processes which Bourdieu would describe as ones of of 'symbolic violence'. Such is the power of this discourse that the identification of the lowest social classes runs the risk of becoming implicated in the stigmatization of such groups. Certainly, the GBCS was itself implicated in this powerful politics of stigma and shame. Some of the parodies of the Class Calculator showed how this work could be turned into an abusive repertoire. See, for instance, the example shown in Figure 10.1, which 'amusingly' suggests that if you know people from all of the occupations which were asked about in the GBCS you are part of a 'drug dealer' class. Or even more tellingly, in another example, the Class Calculator has been wittily Photoshopped to reveal the existence of a 'total fucking scumbag' class. The fact that the GBCS was sucked up into the vortex of hate is itself highly telling about the power of stigmatizing motifs when they are allied to forms of classification.

Cultural capital operates through the organization of cultural hierarchies which operate differentially across social classes. We saw in the previous chapter how today's elite class revels in its own significance and that this is shown through that class's attraction to the GBCS. The precariat,

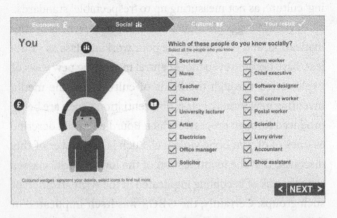

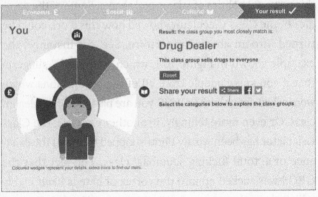

**Figure 10.1**

A parody of the class calculator

however, being on the receiving end of extensive stigmatizing, seeks to hide from view. This cultural gulf is one of the most telling features of today's class divide.

## Precariat worlds

Let us begin then with a revealing exchange which took place when a group of Nottingham workers were asked about which class they imagined they were in. Despite their grim circumstances, the responses were ambivalent. Richard replied initially, 'Probably middle class, I'd probably say . . . I go to work, I've got a car, all right, quite decent money. That's what I think, six hundred pounds a week.' After this defensive reaction, his friend Joe responded with, 'I think I'm working class.' At this point, Richard changed his mind and said, 'Oh yeah, working class . . . yeah, working class, that's the one.' Joe elaborated further: 'I'm educated working class.'

Neither Richard nor Joe felt a clear class identity, but, rather, wanted to give the 'right kind' of answer. This went alongside a desire not to be positioned at the bottom of the heap. There was also, clearly, defensiveness. Richard felt the need to justify saying that he was middle class by noting that he had a car and earned six hundred pounds a week. More educated middle class people we talked to, by contrast, did not feel the need to explain themselves in this way. Joe, meanwhile, insisted that he was 'educated' working class, presumably to differentiate himself from the less educated. These men were all too aware that in identifying themselves they needed to counter powerful views about how others would position them – at the bottom of the pile.

These are the considerable numbers of people stuck in the valley bottoms who can only gaze up at the mountain tops above them. The GBCS was taken (in paper form) to women connected to a drop-in centre for street prostitutes in Nottingham and to cleaners and beauticians in London. These encounters present a striking picture of those at the sharp end of exclusion and inequality in contemporary Britain.

The women in Nottingham also displayed a sophisticated understanding of how classification worked. When they were handed the GBCS, and shown pictures of differing kinds of streets and residents and asked which they lived in, they quickly spotted the omissions. 'Why is it all white people? . . . Yeah, and there's not even no Asians, no blacks, no whites, no Pakis, they're a mixture. They're not like fucking . . . That [picture] looks like the dentures advert, that one looks like insurance. Did you copy that or something?' On the defensive, Lisa Mckenzie insisted she had not manipulated the pictures,[7] before the women began making fun by pretending that they lived in other kinds of streets altogether: 'I've got mansions, with a gate. With security.'

These are worlds characterized by strong awareness of how stereotyping works and how this is a selective and morally loaded process. There was a very sophisticated awareness as to how the questions were framed, what they were designed to elicit, and how to use parody to challenge that. When asked about 'your tastes and interests, so how often do you watch television?' Lesley immediately understood the implications of the question and replied that she watched television, 'From when I get up in the morning, from six in the morning until six at night. And then it's sex every night every week.' When told to 'be serious', Lesley defended her tongue-in-cheek response. Then she replied: 'No, in the morning I watch an hour of *Frasier* and then I watch *Housewives*, and then I watch the cooking channel, and then I watch the baking channel, and then I watch Nigella Lawson . . . I do all the baking channels, really, and then I cook.' When asked what she cooked, she replied, with a laugh – 'Beans on toast!' We see here a characteristic ironic reaction, in which the focus is on how Lesley plays with the stereotypes which might be formed from different responses, whilst ultimately aware that others will see her in stigmatizing tones. It is in this way that these kinds of response are subtly different to the replies of those with cultural capital who had confidence in the legitimacy of their judgements.

To characterize such worlds as ignorant or un-reflexive would therefore be a great mistake. Lesley went on to display her knowledge of the visual arts: 'Yeah, I like the black-and-white pictures, but I also like new artists, some good painters as well, but I also like the photographers. I tell you what I'm not really into, you know, artists like Damien Hirst and Tracey . . . I like Tracey Emin, her first work, I like Damien Hirst, but I didn't like the sheep, I didn't like that. But I like Tracey Emin's, you know, the bedroom? [. . .] Because it was real, you just went, "Oh my God, that is like my kid's room!" Do you know, like when you went and saw it, you went, "No way!" I went, "Oh my God!" Do you know what I mean? Could you imagine that? But if she wasn't an artist that bedroom would not have made nothing, do you know what I mean?' Here again, Lesley shows her awareness of the subtle boundaries between what is, and what is not, counted as legitimate art – though in her case this takes the form of reclaiming Emin's unmade bed for an aesthetic taste which is outside of that of the legitimate art world.

The precariat world is therefore one in which people are 'knowing', but it is nonetheless also one which recognizes how people are placed on the receiving end of other people's definitions and initiatives. Such perspectives colour the everyday experiences of urban life which confront those without economic capital. When Lisa undertook sociological studies in east London, one of the best places to meet the local people with whom she wanted to engage was the local pub. There was a heavy, brooding, atmosphere there. The local people did not understand the humour of using their former job centre and community advisory offices as kitsch or interestingly themed places for cafes. The changes happening in their neighbourhood made them feel uncomfortable. They didn't see where they could 'fit in' any more. They talked about other changes that make them feel 'unsafe'. The rise in rents in the neighbourhood caused them great anxiety. Owning a home there was not something they could even dare to imagine. The devastating impact the bedroom tax, benefit caps and austerity cuts to local community services have had on their families and themselves were and are felt sharply and painfully. They raise their voices and shout and swear; they are angry with – and frightened by – these precarious times.

Consequently, the precariousness here is about the pace of change, and the lack of security families have in finding and staying in work that will pay the ever-increasing rents. They do not know how long they have left in their community as the rents rise: the council is putting more and more pressure upon local people to move out of this part of London and further east into Essex, or even to move north, as far away as Birmingham or Manchester. Their talk is about what will happen to them. Will they be allowed to stay in this neighbourhood, and if not, what will happen to their relatives, particularly the elderly, who have more secure social housing and are more difficult to move? There is constant anxiety about what will happen to their friends and neighbours, whom they fear will become stranded in the middle of east London among the sea of hipsters, the middle class media types and the workers from the City, people whom the East-Enders in this pub have very little in common with. People whom they don't know, and people who don't want to know them.

The talk is full of fear, and anxiety, but also a certain amount of ambivalence, with a touch of hedonism: 'Let's make hay while the sun shines'; 'Fuck it, we might not be here tomorrow'. The people in this pub are precarious workers, men who work on building sites in London, who are now sub-contractors (effectively they are self-employed). Their work situation is precarious; when there is work, they work, and when there is not, they don't. The men who drink in this pub rely upon 'word of mouth' in order to get 'regular and good jobs'; their chances of getting work are clearly patterned by geographical and trade clusters, which are intrinsic to the informal mechanisms of the building industry, and have been revealed by sociological research ever since Paul Willis's landmark study *Learning to Labour* was first published in 1977.[8] The women also work part-time; in the local pubs, or cleaning in the offices of the financial district on their doorstep, often relying on the welfare system to top up their ever-increasing rents through housing benefit, and then on tax credits to top up their hourly rate of pay (which is ever-decreasing in real terms). Their positions are equally unstable: not knowing whether they will be in work, not knowing where they might be living in a year's time and not knowing whether the next round of welfare benefit cuts linked to the government's austerity measures will finally 'finish them off'.

Examples of these precarious lives can be seen all over the UK. In Nottingham, poor women and children live on housing estates that are decaying, have few resources, and where closures of libraries, Sure Start centres and community centres are common. There are few and limited places to shop and meet; if there are any, these are usually small concrete precincts with a post office and a corner shop selling alongside the usual groceries lottery tickets and cheap, strong alcohol. The narratives in the housing estates of the towns and cities in the Midlands and the north of the United Kingdom are of devastation. However, within London, the narratives are different; rather than devastation and decline, there is insecurity and injury. There are many cases, all over London, of poorer families having to leave the city, being forced out by rising rents, and the inability to make work pay. There are families who are struggling to find adequate accommodation which meets their needs in their neighbourhoods, and that they can afford. Social housing is very hard to find, with waiting times on official lists of anything between six and ten years, which, for families with children, is unrealistic. Consequently, the rent demanded by the private sector in London has now gone beyond the income range of anyone earning a low or average wage. This growing precariousness affects women and children differently from men. Men need to stay in London in order to keep their networks and connections (which allow them to work). However, part-time and low-paid work is not enough to keep women and their children in London. Consequently, the precariousness of low-paid workers is becoming increasingly apparent.

Within this bleak context, when introduced into the conversation, the subject of the GBCS lightened the air. This was associated in part with the sophistication and complexity of working class attitudes which we mentioned above. The use of the GBCS as a tool in a more qualitative ethnographic way allowed people who did not do the GBCS on the web to joke about it and to put their lives in a different context. It proved to be a great facilitator, and opened up many hours of discussion and laughter about 'us' and what 'we like to do', and 'them' and why 'they' like to do what 'they do'.

The women from Nottingham – Janice, Lesley and Rosie – were undoubtedly in a highly precarious situation: their lives were filled with insecurities, from where they might get their next meal to where they would be living next week. However, some of the women had a degree of security: they had council tenancies, so they knew at least for the present they were 'safe'. However, none of the women ever doubted for one minute where they might be placed within this survey. When asked which class they thought they might be in, in unison they shouted, 'At the bottom!' But when Lisa introduced the

GBCS to a group of men in their local pub in east London, their reactions to the questions which asked directly about 'class' were very different. Initially, they thought Lisa was 'out of order' for suggesting they were in any social class: they knew what she was 'getting at'; however, they relented from this stance to say that although they hadn't really thought about it, and didn't really care, they were probably 'somewhere in the middle'. There was a clear difference between the men and the women; the women had no doubts or illusions about where in society they were situated (at the bottom). However, the men were more ambivalent about the idea of social class and more resistant to any consideration of it.

It is in this context that we can return to Richard's account, which we mentioned at the start of this chapter. He reported that he had only been in paid work during the last year and was a building sub-contractor, self-employed and doing whatever work came his way, either, as he said, through 'word of mouth', or through an agency. He estimated his earnings at over fifty thousand pounds a year. When asked to qualify this, he said that during one week he had earned almost seven hundred pounds, so he had multiplied this by fifty-two. Although he recognized that this was 'a very good week', he was adamant that 'potentially' that was what he could earn. He also did the Class Calculator with Lisa, which showed that Richard knew a wide range of people, from DJs (whom he considered to be 'artists'), to lawyers (who had represented him in court in the past), and university lecturers – namely, Lisa. Richard quickly realized how his responses had led to his being categorized in a particular way, as the following extract from an interview with him shows:

*Richard*: Can we write 'exercise', go[ing] to the gym?

*Lisa*: No, you can't, 'cause you don't do it. Well, you can do what you want, 'cause this is the interesting thing, would you say that you . . .

*Richard*: Go to the opera, listen to jazz, listen to rock or indie, I listen to indie, go to gigs, play video games, watch sports, no, go to the theatre, I'm going to say, yeah. Use Facebook, socialize at home.

*Lisa*: Do you?

*Richard*: Go to museums or galleries, no, listen to classical music, listen to hip-hop or rap? I'm going to say no, I'm going to say listen to rock or indie, go to the theatre. [*On seeing his result*] . . . Established middle class.

*Lisa*: Established middle class, is that what you've got? [*Laughs.*]

*Richard*: That's wrong, though, isn't it? . . . I don't think that's me, do you? But is it because I was able to say yes to most of those people? That's what it was. I was able to say yes to knowing most of those people . . . But culturally, I said I don't do fuck-all.

It is clear that to characterize Richard as ignorant or unsophisticated would be completely wrong. He was, in fact, highly skilled in his knowledge of how classifications operate in order to produce results, but these were ones in which he was being positioned and had limited power to contest. This self-interpretation and analysis of the classification methods used by the GBCS among those in the precariat category was therefore very revealing; they gave thoughtful and interesting answers to the questions and enjoyed thinking about the things they liked, and the things they should perhaps do more of. Respondents gave wide-ranging examples of activities they took part in, which showed that they were neither passive nor inactive, yet also indicated how such activities did not form part of their everyday repertoire. When asked about visiting stately homes and museums and going to the theatre, the respondents interpreted those questions in terms of what they liked to do – even though they might rarely have the opportunity. When Laura, Barbara and Claire talked about these cultural pursuits, the way they spoke showed that they were clearly extremely engaged in the activities which interested them. They talked about visiting Madame Tussauds waxworks museum in London, taking their children to the Doctor Who museum in Blackpool, and going to see the live comedy shows of *Mrs Brown's Boys*, a popular BBC programme about a working class Irish family. As they talked about these activities which they enjoyed, it was evidently important to them to place them within a social context, in which they associated these cultural events with experiences with family or friends, rather than the more individualized forms of cultural engagement characteristic of the educated middle classes.[9] They talked about going to 'real' museums as children when they were at school, they reminisced about their school trips to stately homes and local museums. However, these were not activities that they continued with as adults, these were childhood memories of 'the school trip'. This is a good example of how survey instruments (such as the GBCS itself), which seek to define activities in bounded ways, can miss out key arenas of social life which happen at the boundaries of interaction.

The GBCS shows that while some groups feel entirely confident to proudly tweet, trumpet or criticize their GBCS status, others know already where they will be placed and so keep away from it. Perhaps this piece of cultural politics is the most striking indication of the depth of class divisions among any which we have produced in this book. But this unwillingness to confirm their class status does not mean that this group of people are not proud of their communities and families. They recognize the adversities they have encountered through their position in society, and list enduring hardships as personal achievements.

When these respondents engaged with this section of the GBCS, they knew that they might be 'getting it wrong' from the point of view of educated observers. They knew they were really being asked these questions within the loaded framework of class, culture and value. However, they explained that humour, community, collectivism and, most of all, fun were what was really important to them. Going on day trips with their families, or on coach trips from the pub to the Kent coast (in the east London group) was what these respondents valued. They knew these would not be seen as 'legitimate' cultural pursuits, and couldn't really understand why liking the opera 'got you more points' than liking *Mrs Brown's Boys*. To them one was funny and the other was boring. Although many of the respondents had seen opera on television, or heard operatic music, it didn't seem like anything they might want to do after a hard day at work. As one young mother from Nottingham reported – 'It seems like hard work to me'. There were also access issues – most respondents didn't know where they could go to the opera (although they also weren't interested in trying to find out). Asking this question about going to the opera was always embarrassing for everyone, interviewers and interviewees alike, since everyone knew what was really being asked: whether they could claim to be middle or upper class. Going through this part of the GBCS with respondents, therefore, was very difficult. This became even more embarrassing when the next question on the survey was about bingo, known to be culturally pigeon-holed as working class and plebeian. This is how cultural capital works within people's lives: cultures of classification and hierarchization proliferate, and thereby can be used to create and reproduce elitism and stigma. If you are answering questions in a survey like the GBCS, or thinking about what you do in your life, there are no problems with questions about stately homes, going to the opera and visiting museums when these are 'your' pursuits and these activities are known as those which display 'good taste' and enable you to move through society easily. However, if your interests and activities include playing bingo, going to the pub or watching television, these are not neutral pursuits; they count against you and show you up as lacking and deficient.

The responses among the precariat to these investigations in the GBCS had many echoes elsewhere. Lisa had been asked many times, over the years, by people in her community, her friends and neighbours, who suspected that she might know something about these matters, why were some things more valued than others? And why are other things devalued even though they are enjoyed? One of the questions most frequently asked by women was about the way that they themselves dressed and why it was criticized. Why are women on television shows were always presented in a particular way – with their hair in ponytails, wearing tracksuits and lots of gold jewellery – when the storyline wanted to show that the character was 'common' [vulgar]? And so it is that class hierarchy is vividly delineated within the supposedly mundane arenas of lifestyle and appearance.

## Who are the precariat?

The term 'precariat' was introduced by Guy Standing, who argues that neo-liberal policies and institutional changes across the globe are producing growing numbers of people with common enough experiences to be called an emerging class.[10] The precariat, according to Standing, are people living and working precariously, usually in a series of short-term jobs, without recourse to stable occupational identities or careers, social protection or relevant protective regulation. They include migrants, but also locals. Standing explains that this class of people are producing new instabilities in society. They are increasingly frustrated and angry, but also dangerous because they have no voice, and hence they are vulnerable to the siren calls of extreme political parties. At the same time, they are becoming loathed and laughed at because of their methods of managing their fear, and the precariousness of their lives. The precariat may arrive at their management of fear through close identification with that which is local, tightening their notions of identity, 'Who we are', via an identification of whom they are not and through complicated and voracious notions of belonging, which may manifest in distinct cultural forms: what they like, what they wear, how they speak and their strong connection to community belonging and values. As a consequence they are seen and known as old-fashioned, rigid and unable to bend to the wishes of a changing globalized market. The ways in which those in the precariat class dress, speak and walk, and how they raise their families, come under scrutiny and are devalued. When Britain needs a low-paid working class – people to serve coffee, clean hotel rooms and look after their children – there are 'better' working class people from Italy, Poland, Nigeria or Brazil who can be enlisted instead. Clearly, as Standing argues, this causes globalized precariousness and a global precariat.

This concept of the precariat is preferable to that of the 'underclass', which has been widely used in the past to designate a group of people 'underneath' the class system who have been excluded from the social mainstream. Although in the hands of American sociologists such as William Julius Wilson the underclass concept has been used sympathetically to explore the plight of vulnerable black people locked out of the labour market,[11] the idea has also been deployed to define a group who are responsible for their own misfortunes because of their pathological behaviour. The term is sometimes also negatively associated with long-term benefit claimants. This kind of categorization can be put in the context of the long history of stigmatization of the poor, which can be traced back for many centuries, and the nineteenth-century preoccupation with the differentiation of the deserving and undeserving poor which we saw in Chapter 1 (when Charles Booth designated the lowest classes as 'vicious and semi-criminal' on his famous map).[12] The naming of the poorest has always been problematic, with the danger that defining them at all might stigmatize their inequality and add to the rhetoric about them as a 'dangerous class'.

Given this difficult politics of naming and classification, we think the precariat concept is preferable to that of an underclass because Standing's term draws direct attention to the way that the vulnerability of these groups is linked to their structural location in society. It also avoids the clichéd stereotypes. The precariat are not passive, culturally disengaged or morally limited. Although the term 'precariat' runs the risk of giving an over-rigid definition of this group, it captures the structural instability of a global market, and a group of people at the mercy of that structure. The precariat concept also recognizes that there is mobility into and out of its ranks, because it situates this group within the wider processes of contemporary labour markets rather than fixing on them as being outside employment altogether.

At the time when the GBCS was taking place there was a plethora of what has been termed 'poverty porn' throughout British media and television. 'Poverty porn' is the prurient fascination with just how badly behaved some of the poor may have become, with its lens focused upon those claiming state benefits, in aptly titled programmes such as *We All Pay Your Benefits* and the now notorious *Benefits Street*. Tracey Jensen a sociologist from the University of East London has argued that there is a clear symbolic division between the 'worker' and the 'shirker', or, in the current manifestation, the 'striver' and the 'skiver', which is embedded in the narrative about Britain's working class population in recent media and political rhetoric.[13] It has become popular opinion, and almost the default understanding, that those who use the welfare state for either all or part of their income are overly dependent upon welfare benefits because of their own 'lifestyle choices', and that as a result they use taxpayers' hard-earned money in order to live the life of Riley, which often includes taking drugs, drinking alcohol and generally having a great time (if we are to believe the poverty porn narrative).

However, recent research from Tracy Shildrick and her colleagues provides clear evidence that this view of those who live the most precarious lives (i.e. the working class poor) is false.[14] They describe the cycle that these people find themselves in as a 'longitudinal pattern of employment instability and movement between low-paid jobs and employment, usually accompanied by claiming of welfare benefits'. Far from being 'lazy' or 'workshy', many people claiming unemployment benefits do so over short spells of time, in between periods of low-paid, poor-quality, precarious, short-term or zero-hours-contracted work. This kind of work is increasing in neo-liberal Britain at a faster rate than permanent, full-time, living-wage work. Importantly, it is no longer confined to entry-level work, which has been seen in the past as a stepping stone into better paid and more stable employment. Rather it constitutes a 'sticky state' of work, a cycle of entrapment which, moreover, has a powerful stigmatizing effect in terms of future job opportunities. It is important to bring these structural arguments into the way we think and talk about the poorest groups in Britain today. There is a direct counterpart here to our reflections on the 'ordinary' elite in the previous chapter. There, following Piketty's work, we reflected upon whether we were seeing the return of a cohesive and visible elite (given the greater accumulation of wealth at the highest levels of society). Should we also reflect upon whether this same trend is involved in the revival of the stigmatization of paupers? Is there a return to the language which spoke of the 'deserving and undeserving poor' that characterized Victorian policy on poverty and emphasized that the poor were largely to blame for their own misfortunes?

If the arguments of our book are correct, there is a further argument to be made about the growing intensity of stigmatization directed at the most disadvantaged. Insofar as the established cultural and social boundaries between upper, middle and working classes which provided a sense of identity in the past have broken down, this might explain why there is a renewed intensity of disapprobation directed at the most disadvantaged. It seems as if the ambivalences and complexities of class identification today generate a strong reaction against those at the bottom, as if a common and shared negative discourse directed against the poor is the main way in which otherwise disparate groups can claim common feelings.

This targeting of the poor has also been a constant policy refrain over recent decades. The Conservative government led by Margaret Thatcher during the 1980s deployed the thinking of the American neo-liberal and right-wing social commentator Charles Murray to promote the 'underclass' theory, alongside the 'cycle of deprivation' theory – the supposed perverse effects of welfare dependency – in order to implement neo-liberal policies such as rolling back the provision of welfare and state benefits and focusing upon the family as a supportive unit rather than addressing structural or societal causes of inequality. This was a reworking and rereading of the early work of the famous anthropologist Oscar Lewis in 1961, who, through his research conducted in Mexico City, showed how the practices of the poor can be renamed as 'deficient' when all they are doing is trying to cope with the everyday stresses that being poor can bring. Lewis noted that some of the poorest people in Mexico City at the time had regular work, but many survived from day to day through a miscellany of activities: working in unskilled occupations, children labouring, pawning personal goods and borrowing from local moneylenders at exorbitant rates of interest. According to Lewis, first and foremost, the very poorest survived because of their strong local social networks among their families, neighbours and friends. Lewis described the social and psychological characteristics of what he called the 'culture of poverty'. He also described other characteristics of the people in this poor neighbourhood, which he described as '[being] distrustful of the basic institutions of the dominant classes, hatred of the police, and they are aware of middle class values ... but do not live by them'.[15]

Lewis's theory of the 'culture of poverty' was used for political ends by Margaret Thatcher's Conservative government to perpetuate the notion that the poor are responsible for their own poverty. This narrative was taken up again during the 1990s, and has strengthened under the recent Coalition (and largely Conservative) government led by David Cameron, with their 'Broken Britain' narrative which focused upon particular behaviour within specific 'troubled families'. Much has been written about the assumed moral values of the educated middle classes in contemporary politics, at the same time as the very different perspectives of those outside these middle class worlds are seen as deficient and limited.[16] What Lewis was attempting with his 'culture of poverty' discourse in the 1960s was to examine the value systems that the poorest live within; thus he was attempting to make sense of and contextualize the everyday actions of people with limited choices (because of the structure and the inequalities within their society), rather than scrutinizing the behaviour of the poor and blaming them for their situation.

The poorest people and the neighbourhoods in which they live in the UK have been shown through many modalities, and the definitions of these people and their places constantly shift. And although the picture seems grim for the precariat, who experience low pay or no pay, insecure housing and being known as 'dangerous', the truth is, it can always get bleaker. This is because disadvantage and inequality do not only show themselves through the lack of material and economic means. Disadvantage may also be pitched through a cultural medium: when a group is denied the other resources necessary to live a life with dignity. This is about respect, and being valued, and what happens to a group of people who have over at least the last thirty years become identified and named as those who *have* little value, and are *of* little value.

The precariat know they are looked down on and ridiculed, which is why they say they would rather stay among 'their own'. It was always more important to this group of people to be liked and respected within their own community than outside it. This makes the instability and the precariousness of the precariat more cruel. Their resilience and resistance in difficult circumstances are misrecognized as crassness; their protection of their preferences is known as 'bad taste', and that, coupled with their sense of community, is viewed as part of their bad judgement and rigidity. Although the precariat are highly visible, and their 'bad taste' the rationale behind the practice of vilifying them, the *value* they have remains invisible. Today's class culture is too loaded towards the privileged to allow them a place.

# Class Consciousness and the New Snobbery

Elizabeth had lived a varied, cosmopolitan life. Now happily settled and semi-retired in Yorkshire, she had spent a lot of time abroad and in different parts of the UK, working in social services, as a teacher and in the arts. She had an interesting reflection on the significance of class today. Whilst emphatic that 'I don't give a toss actually' about which class she was in, she nonetheless ruminated at length about how many people seemed 'excluded' and said that 'people tend to use it [the term "class"] as a weapon really . . . the upper class to keep people at bay, "You're not one of us." And I think, sadly, there is a sort of battle going on.'

Warming to her theme, she related a story recently told by her husband:

But Fred had an interesting experience 'cause he popped over . . . there's the local pub here, which has all sorts of people going in, and he said [that] it was last year, he was sitting in the beer garden and somebody turned round and said to their mate, 'Oh, look at that snob over there.' You know [*laughter*] . . . Poor man, he'd only gone for a beer. So I think it's almost, yes, it's, yeah . . . 'Cause I was quite interested in your class survey, it doesn't seem so

> hierarchical, it seems to be less . . . Whereas the old
> one was, you sort of worked your way up from the
> bottom to the top, didn't you . . . And now I tend to
> think it's more, it's used to keep people out, rather than
> hierarchical . . . I would see it more as exclusion, yes, yes.

Elizabeth's reflections touch on many of the themes of this book. Class does not seem to fit into nice hierarchical layers. But this does not mean that class has ended, far from it, and its traces are evident in casual pub conversation. Class is used to exclude people. But, most tellingly of all, the idea of class is itself at play in defining hierarchies.

Chapters 9 and 10 revealed the power of expertise, knowledge and confidence in orchestrating the class divide today. At one extreme, we identified an 'ordinary' wealth-elite attracted to the GBCS in their droves. They had rich cultural capital, were brimful of confidence and were attracted to engaging with a 'scientific' experiment such as the GBCS. At the other extreme, the precariat hardly did the GBCS at all. This was not because they were ignorant or unaware: it was because they were highly sensitive to the loaded classifications which they might be subject to in its name, and well-schooled in being on the receiving end of negative judgements. A key argument of this book is that expertise itself is not a neutral tool which unravels the social structure, but in fact is bound up with the very construction of class categories and the 'symbolic violence' which is done in their name.

This point returns us to the vexed issue of class cultures today, because there is a very complex etiquette about how and when class may be talked about. This goes to the heart of the new snobbery which is implicated in today's class talk. The etiquette begins with the fact that the public 'naming' of classes is hotly contested and uncomfortable. Just as in Nancy Mitford's day, it is unsettling to publicly bring class to light. Consider the comfy sofas of ITV's *This Morning* – which are not normally known as a battleground of class warfare. But on 4 July 2013 the appearance of *The Apprentice* star Katie Hopkins changed all that. Invited to take part in a seemingly benign discussion about baby names, Hopkins immediately caused chaos when she unassumingly dropped class into the debate. 'I think you can tell a great deal from a name,' she said calmly. 'For me, a name is a shortcut of finding out what class that child comes from and makes me ask: "Do I want my children to play with them?" [ . . . ] It's the Tylers, the Charmain[e]s, the Chantelles, the Chardonnays. There's a whole set of things that go with children like that, quite a disruptive influence in school.'

The normally unflappable presenter Holly Willoughby was visibly shocked. 'That's terrible, listen to what you're saying,' she blurted out desperately. Hopkins knew exactly what she was saying. She continued readily: 'I tend to think that children who have intelligent names tend to have fairly intelligent parents and they make much better play[m]ates for my children.' Now it was the turn of author Anna May Mangan, also a guest on the programme, to round on Hopkins: 'I can't believe that you're such an insufferable snob. Working class children are doing incredibly well at school. For you to categorize them by their names – which they didn't even choose – is cruel, snooty, unkind and so old-fashioned.' Hopkins smiled back and began to respond. But an increasingly irate Willoughby had had quite enough – 'Oh, stop. Stop right there.'[1]

Beyond the studio, public outrage at Hopkins' comments soon picked up a head of steam. Within two days her performance had clocked up three million views on YouTube and thousands of angry viewers flocked to social media to register their disgust. It seemed that if there was one contemporary issue that everyone in Britain could finally agree on, it was class snobbery. Mangan seemed to sum up the mood: snobbery just seemed 'old-fashioned', an unsavoury relic of Britain's class-ridden past. But, in fact, as we have shown in this book, there is a new snobbery at work which demonstrates all too powerfully the imprint of class – but it takes an underground route which does not draw attention to itself as an overt marker of elitism.

## From 'class consciousness' to the 'emotional politics' of class

Generations of social scientists from Marx onwards predicted that capitalism would cause the exploited working class ('proletariat') to feel a sense of loyalty towards their own class, leading them to organize politically in order to advance their class interests, and ultimately overthrow the system. This idea – that people generally identify with the class in which they are positioned – has become part of the sociological mainstream. The socialist historian E. P. Thompson's best-known book, *The Making of the English Working Class*, argued in this vein that during the early nineteenth century, as Britain industrialized, working class people came to be aware of their class identity, which led them to campaign for their interests. The rise of the Labour movement from the later nineteenth century onwards has widely been seen as associated with a strong collective class consciousness on the part of working class people determined to improve their position in society.[2] In this spirit, classic sociological studies of the working classes focused on how they formed tight-knit communities, united by poverty, but also by shared values and culture. The solidarity generated from everyone being in the 'same boat' meant that the working classes had a very strong collective identity.

However, in the twenty-first century, a more muted, individualized and complex set of class identities is to be found. Studies from the 1960s onwards have doubted that most people do feel strong collective class identities and deny that there is much common feeling based on a shared class location. A landmark study by Beverley Skeggs in the mid-1990s explored how young working class women distanced themselves from an over-identification with the working class, despite the fact that class inequalities had profoundly shaped their lives.[3] This was because, on the one hand, the label 'working class' carried such negative connotations, 'used to certify all that is dirty, dangerous and without value', but, on the other hand, being middle class was seen as pretentious. Also, as women, they did not have access to the more workplace-based identities that were tied up with men's roles (through their jobs in manufacturing). In response, Skeggs's young women invested in femininity and respectability in response to the (real and imagined) judgement of others – *judgements based on the values and morals associated with the dominant class*. Yet they did not possess the required sorts of capital – economic, cultural or social – to be anything other than working class women. Skeggs powerfully highlighted the 'emotional politics' at work there, which was associated with their feelings of 'fear, desire, resentment and humiliation'. It also reminds us that class identities are also shaped by gender (along with race and sexuality).

Other qualitative studies, including those conducted by ourselves, make similar arguments. Most people are now ambivalent and hesitant about which class they belong to, and when quizzed about it often prefer to reflect on the way that they straddle different classes.[4] Class is important not so much as an overt badge (when people feel proud to belong to a class), but more in the way that it prompts moral and emotional reactions, especially negative ones. It matters more which class you do not belong to, rather than which one you think you do belong to. It is precisely these sentiments which played into the public interest in the GBCS. And, when people notice social mobility and accept meritocratic values, these emotional effects of class inequality are recast as problems that are to do with individual responsibility. You feel responsible when you fail to succeed and you internalize the shame associated with it, according to US sociologists Richard Sennett and Jonathan Cobb in their book *The Hidden Injuries of Class*.[5] We like to think we are responsible for our own destinies and blame ourselves when we can't or won't climb the mountain.

It follows that class identities operate in a complex and contradictory way. They hold out images and values, often unattainable, remote, or locked in the past. In contemporary popular culture, for example, a romanticization of working class life could see it as more 'authentic' or 'cool', on the one hand, or, on the other, it might be derided and devalued (such as through invoking ideas of the 'chav'). Similarly, dominant middle class culture may also be mocked, as with the social media meme #middleclassproblems. Class labels proliferate, even if only to prompt negative reactions to them.

Our new model of class offers some insights into the meaning of class today. Table 11.1 shows that less than a third of respondents from our nationally representative sample – 32 per cent – actually think of themselves as belonging to a social class. By contrast, more than two-thirds of people resist class identification. Interestingly, the proportion of those thinking they do belong to a class rises to 51 per cent when we consider the replies of the GBCS respondents (shown in brackets), for the obvious reason that those who were more interested in class were drawn towards doing the GBCS.

But there is also a telling pattern in that the proportion of respondents who do not think they belong to a class rises as the class hierarchy descends. Nearly half of the elite think they belong to a class, but only a quarter of the precariat. This is a fascinating inversion of what Marx might have thought, that class consciousness intensifies among the proletarianized, who 'have nothing to lose but their chains'. In fact, those at the bottom of the pile are the least likely to think of themselves as belonging to a class, whilst those with the most advantages are considerably more likely to do so.

## Table 11.1

**Percentage Who Thought of Themselves as Belonging to a Social Class, Differentiated by GBCS Class Categories**

| | ELITE | ESTABLISHED MIDDLE CLASS | TECHNICAL MIDDLE CLASS | NEW AFFLUENT WORKERS | TRADITIONAL WORKING CLASS | EMERGING SERVICE WORKERS | PRECARIAT | TOTAL |
|---|---|---|---|---|---|---|---|---|
| No | 55 (42) | 64 (50) | 63 (45) | 67 (55) | 69 (46) | 75 (54) | 75 (50) | 68 (49) |
| Yes | 45 (58) | 36 (50) | 37 (55) | 33 (45) | 31 (54) | 25 (46) | 25 (50) | 32 (51) |

*Sources: GfK (for the nationally representative sample) and GBCS data: responses to the question in the GBCS: 'Do you think of yourself as belonging to a social class?'*

People in the two classes with the lowest mean age (the new affluent workers and the emerging service workers) were also unlikely to positively identify themselves with a social class. This supports other research[6] that suggests that class identities may be (very gradually) becoming less powerful over time and that younger cohorts are especially resistant to them.

We can unpack these answers further by looking at where people placed themselves in the class structure. Respondents were asked to consider which class they were in, even if they didn't normally think of themselves as belonging to a class. Table 11.2 dramatically demonstrates the continued appeal of working class identities. The single most common response was 'middle working class', which accounted for 41 per cent of all the responses. A staggering 62 per cent gave themselves some kind of working class identity. Less than a quarter see themselves as either upper middle or middle middle class. British people continue to shy away from claiming a more privileged class identity.

Table 11.2 also indicates that wherever people are *objectively* situated in the class structure, they tend most to identify *subjectively* with being somewhere 'in the middle'. The three most privileged groups, for example, the elite, the established middle class and the technical middle class, all locate their class position predominantly in the 'middle' of the middle classes. And this was also the most popular answer for all the classes. People prefer not to identify themselves as privileged, but to steer towards a less noticeable identity. However, the discrepancies between the GfK and the GBCS sample are large, indicating once more how those

## Table 11.2

**Percentage Who Thought of Themselves in Different Classes, Differentiated by GBCS Class Categories**

|  | ELITE | ESTABLISHED MIDDLE CLASS | NEW AFFLUENT WORKERS | TECHNICAL MIDDLE CLASS | TRADITIONAL WORKING CLASS | EMERGING SERVICE WORKERS | PRECARIAT | TOTAL |
|---|---|---|---|---|---|---|---|---|
| Upper/upper middle class | 10 (33) | 2 (7) | 4 (1) | 4 (1) | 3 (4) | 3 (4) | 1 (1) | 3 (12) |
| Middle middle class | 42 (47) | 29 (35) | 29 (9) | 15 (43) | 20 (22) | 11 (21) | 9 (7) | 20 (34) |
| Lower middle class | 18 (10) | 18 (28) | 22 (22) | 9 (24) | 13 (26) | 15 (28) | 11 (14) | 15 (23) |
| Upper working class | 8 (5) | 18 (15) | 2 (27) | 8 (11) | 12 (15) | 9 (18) | 5 (11) | 10 (14) |
| Middle working class | 22 (5) | 29 (14) | 41 (36) | 54 (10) | 43 (26) | 45 (23) | 51 (32) | 41 (15) |
| Lower working class | 0 (1>) | 3 (1) | 3 (5) | 3 (1) | 9 (5) | 17 (6) | 23 (35) | 11 (2) |

Sources: GfK (for the nationally representative sample) and GBCS data: responses to the question in the GBCS: 'If you had to choose one from this list, which social class would you say you belonged to?'

doing the GBCS were often attracted to it for aspirational reasons (as a means of confirming their view that they were middle or upper class). The exception here is among the precariat, where those who undertook the GBCS were more likely to identify themselves as lower working class. (Those who did the GBCS have their response shown in brackets, as before.)

There are intriguing patterns among some of our different social classes. Firstly, the elite are far more likely to recognize themselves as being in the upper or upper middle class than any of the others. Ten per cent of the nationally representative survey and 33 per cent of the GBCS respondents use this relatively exclusive label, far more than any other class. Once more, this is evidence of how members of the elite class are more likely to have a distinctive sense of their own privileged class identity. Secondly, the precariat are much more prone to see themselves as lower working class and very few see themselves as middle class. They recognize their position at the bottom of the social order. Thirdly, the youthful, emerging service workers are also likely to position themselves towards the bottom. Even though they have considerable cultural capital, significant numbers of their members see themselves as excluded from the middle and upper reaches of the class hierarchy.

## A common people?

How can we explain the fact that two-thirds of the UK population don't feel like they belong to a social class? Why are people ambivalent and doubtful about which class they belong to? Our interviews offer valuable clues. When we asked the same question about class belonging, we found that many people deliberately ducked a direct answer and instead immediately shifted the discussion towards the *idea* of class, and, more specifically, why they didn't like it. 'I don't really think about it, to be honest, because it sort of implies a sort of predetermination, doesn't it?' Paul, an accountant, told us. Christopher, a retired railway signalman, was even more dismissive: 'I think of people as people,' he insisted.

This kind of defensive reaction has a long history. It reflects an awareness of how classifications are used as powerful agents, and how people understandably want to draw attention to the ways in which they don't fit the labels which are used. But there is a deeper unease too. Key to this is the perception that the very notion of class poses a fundamental threat to one's sense of self, one's *individuality*.[7] By implying that people were simply the products of their social background, class is seen as a challenge to individual agency, and admitting too readily to membership of a social class is therefore akin to condoning class as a concept, to be complicit in what Paul called 'predetermination'. Batting away questions of class, then, respondents invariably countered that where you ended up in life should be a product of what you have *done* – your hard work, your effort – in other words your individual *merit*. As Alan, a chemicals salesman, summed up: 'I think it's difficult to pigeonhole people [in terms of class] because I always think it doesn't really matter where you come from – life's what you make of it, you know what I mean?'

So even though respondents invariably acknowledged the

importance of class, this often led to an objection to class as a concept. There was also an interesting moral dimension to this. Respondents seemed particularly conscious of the enduring connection between class and snobbery and were keen to guard against any suggestion that they made judgements based on other people's social position. Roberta, a teacher, explained how she navigates this ethical minefield:

> You just have to be really careful because it's almost like the higher up you are the better you are – and that's not it, is it? Well, that's not how it should be, but that's how it's perceived and if you're not careful it ends up as if you're looking down [on others] . . . I think that's why people tend not to talk about it.

Here, then, there were close parallels with the public reaction to Katie Hopkins' comments. People strongly distanced themselves from notions of snobbery and smugness, and instead were eager to stress that they regard everyone in the same way irrespective of their social position. Anthony, a fifty-seven-year-old professor, was particularly forthright. Continually reasserting values of openness and tolerance throughout his interview, he finished by neatly distilling his objection to the issue of class: 'I suppose the basic problem is that I would rather think of people for their inherent value rather than their class.' In this way, in public at least, people placed a strong moral premium on deliberately refraining from drawing class-based boundaries.

There was a concomitant desire to assert 'ordinariness' which was strongly connected to this self-distancing from snobbery. Those in both traditionally working class and middle class positions thus frequently described themselves as 'average', 'normal', 'regular' or 'in the middle'. Tina was a care worker, who earned £20,800 a year and owned a house worth £200,000. From a self-described traditional working class background, Tina had been a factory worker for most of her life, and it was on this basis that she identified as 'middle-of-the-road' working class. But she also stressed that she was both financially more comfortable than others (at fifty, she had been able to pay off her mortgage and take a career change) and, compared to her parents, she was more culturally sophisticated (she had interests in ballet, theatre and classical music). In relative terms to those around her, then, Louise clearly saw herself as more secure, more cultivated and more towards 'the middle' of British society.

This assertion of ordinariness, as we outlined in Chapter 9, even extended to our elite respondents. Rather than playing up the idea that they were associated with privilege through family connections – as the old aristocratic class might have done – their insistence was upon individual meritocratic criteria. This belief was often rooted in reflections upon their social trajectory and in an awareness that they might be in a lower social position than where they had started from. Benedict, for example, had come from a comfortable middle class background, but had spent much of his twenties unemployed and squatting in various properties in south London. The memory of this period clearly loomed large and very much informed his sense of identity even into the present day. He explained:

I'm fairly insistent about this idea of living as close to the street as possible. So whatever happens, I will walk out of that door, I'll step on to the dog shit [*laughs*], I get run over by a boy racer, you know, and kind of that's part of the way things are. And so my connection is deliberate and sustained. I've forced it on myself because I do want to retain that connection and it's an anti-elite move, an anti-elite position.

Benedict's story illustrates this pervasive quest to be 'normal' – to be somehow outside the class system even though the markers of class all around are easy to recognize. Although he and other elite respondents might have accumulated vast economic, cultural and social resources, they instinctively played up their ordinariness. For them, as for all our respondents, class was a highly loaded moral signifier, one that contaminated cherished notions of meritocracy, openness and individuality which they held dear. By being 'ordinary' they could assert their autonomy, their control over the way their lives had developed, and in the process ward off any suspicion that they were socially fixed vessels within an unbending class system.

## Class is under your skin

Writing in the mid-1990s, the British academic Annette Kuhn argued that, '*Class* is something *beneath* your clothes, *under* your *skin*, in your reflexes, in your psyche, at the very core of your being [our italics]'.[8] Kuhn's point was that to really get at how class is hardwired into people's identities you need to go further than just asking a tick-box question about which class label you might identify with, such as we did in the GBCS. People may well outwardly distance themselves from such labels, as we have just shown, but it might actually matter deep down, in ways which can be hard to deal with and recognize. We have seen extensive elements of this already in this book, notably our discussion of the precariat in Chapter 10. Claiming an ordinary, unclassed existence is a response to the high stakes and sharp realities of class division, and notably the gulf between those at the top and bottom of the social hierarchy. And it wasn't so much during explicit discussions about class when this was revealed, but instead in the minutiae of discussions about everyday life (about family, taste, neighbourhoods and politics), when people were drawing boundaries between different neighbourhoods (based on whether they contained 'big houses' or council estates), between people sitting down to eat dinner in front of a television rather than round a table, or on class being literally 'under the skin' through piercings or tattoos.

When conversation focused upon these class anxieties, it was often the lowest class, the group we have called the precariat, which became the brunt of negative identification. Having tattoos is a good example; these were still frequently associated with a particular type of classed person: someone who was unrespectable or uncouth. The ink of a tattoo was seen to render visible what was below the skin's surface, an illustrative representation of a person's character. Similar views circulated around smoking, excessive drinking and obesity – the embodied characteristics of damaged bodies and pathologized identities. For example, Monica, a retired teacher, thought that those with bad taste could be identified in her town through those she saw walking around 'in tattoos and shorts'. During the interview, she very nearly told the interviewer *exactly* what she thought, but then stopped herself because she knew she shouldn't 'judge'. Monica's distaste for those unruly bodies was contained within the context of a more general anxiety she expressed about her seaside town and 'a particular type of person', who was changing her neighbourhood. A drug rehabilitation centre had resulted in users of the service staying in the town, and this, along with her own work as a volunteer in a food bank, had added to her awareness of and her concern about the closing of local shops and her town's economic decline. Poverty and addiction were having a transformative effect, and were personified for her through this disorderly figure, marked by tattoos.

People are very much aware of such markers when thinking about their own place in the world. When we asked Lorraine, a fork-lift truck driver, about her neighbourhood, she immediately compared herself to the other people on the street and said what she imagined they thought of her. She had recently divorced and moved into a much smaller home with her two teenage sons, and spontaneously brought up feeling inferior to other people in their 'nice, beautiful houses': "Cause I just kind of think, no, 'cause I'm at the bottom really here, aren't I? 'Cause it's a rented accommodation, single mum, two boys, you know, that all sort of is a bit of alarm bells for a lot of people.' Lorraine was acutely aware of the identifiers that marked her social position and recognized the hierarchies in play without explicitly using the language of class. The term 'single motherhood' is often used as a proxy for class, labelled with a stigmatized identity, whose members are blamed for raising a generation of disaffected young men. Combined with her previous thoughts about her difference in economic position compared to that of others (her circumstances clearly displayed in the form of her small, rented property), Lorraine's class anxieties bubbled up through a seemingly innocuous discussion about her local area. This also illustrated how closely class-structure positions are tied up with personal relationships – in Lorraine's case, her divorce was a catalyst for her downward social mobility and anxiety about her place in the world – and how class identities intersect with other ideas about gender and respectability.

Another way in which it was possible to detect the distinct presence of class identity was in scenarios when people described being thrust into social situations with people from very different class backgrounds. The existence of class often goes undetected in people's everyday lives because most people tend to spend most of their time with people who occupy similar class positions. In most situations, we tend to feel like a fish in water, with our sense of identity enacted instinctively, as if second nature. However, when we find ourselves in settings with different kinds of people, the very immediate sense of discomfort forces us to reflect on who precisely we are and to try to make sense of why we feel so uncomfortable. We found that it was through the self-reflection or charged emotion that accompanied such cross-class interaction that deep-seated aspects of people's class identity revealed itself. As we saw in Chapter 6, this was particularly acute for those who had experienced social mobility, though we found that instances of cross-class interaction were frequently reported throughout all our interviews. Two examples are telling here.

First, we return to Henry, our public-school-educated law student from Chapter 3. During most of Henry's interview he didn't mention class at all. Yet, significantly, when he described 'the mistake' of going into an Edinburgh pub and being subsequently made to feel 'distinctly uncomfortable' by the 'locals', his awareness of his own class identity emerged very clearly. 'I said one word and just instantly click, boxed,' he reflected. The guy behind the bar was like, 'You shouldn't be here, you must be friggin' royalty.' And of course I was there with a load of other kids from schools like mine who spoke like me and we were like [*accentuates his received-pronunciation (RP) accent*] – 'I'll have a gin and tonic, please.' It was just, you know, the end of the world, just from the second you've spoken. I sometimes think I wind people up the wrong way just for existing.

The profound impact of such class clashes was even more striking when we visited Benedict. His house was in the process of being extensively refurbished and there was a small army of builders scattered around it. He seemed to have a good relationship with them and began the interview by telling us that he enjoyed having them around, enjoyed talking to them about 'ordinary stuff'. Interestingly, though, at the end of the interview when Benedict became noticeably more comfortable and open, he confided that these interactions were not so straightforward after all, and that it was class that represented the pivotal barrier:

> *Benedict*: But sometimes I think I'm kind of talking at a level, at which I'm possibly just performing, and it's taking quite a lot of effort, you know? I'm having to kind of power down. And I don't really have the energy for that any more.
>
> *Questioner*: Is that about the subjects that you can connect on?
>
> *Benedict*: Yeah. The subjects, but also the way in which you talk about the subject, whether it's critical or not. Because my position is always, if you look at the whole thing, it just comes down to taking a critical position at all times and not snapping out of it. So that's the thing. Whatever the small talk, you just get to the critical position and that's where things get interesting. So I've found that the way I talk, what interests me, is ideas and that critical position. It's less about facts and stories and jokes. So that's the level at which I'm most comfortable and, paradoxically, it's more effort to be superficial.

Both Henry's and Benedict's recollections of cross-class interaction show how specific incidents initiated a heightened sense of self-awareness and class realization. Reflecting on the reactions of the Edinburgh pub's locals, Henry clearly gleaned a better awareness of the privileged class identity he exuded ('I suppose I must have looked like a walking stereotype'). With Benedict, the process was even more acute. The ability to take a 'critical position' in everyday conversation separated Benedict from his builders, who – in his mind, at least – were more interested in 'jokes', 'stories' and 'facts'. In this way, the boundaries of class identity, the sharpness of its edges and its capacity to mark difference, were most clearly brought into focus when people were thrust into interactions or relationships with people from different class backgrounds. These settings tended to produce heightened emotions that reminded people, suddenly fish *out* of water, and out of sync with their surroundings, very acutely of where they did and didn't belong.

What we see here is a very striking process, in which this reaction against class identity and the desire to proclaim 'normality' actually emphasize the symbolic focus upon those at the top and the bottom. People wanting to show they are 'ordinary' can do so by reacting against those at the bottom of the pile or/and against those at the top. And, in this way, the general reaction against the idea of class identity has the paradoxical effect of strengthening the symbolic boundaries at the extremes.

## Snobbery revisited

Contemporary class identities abound through differentiation from others. People rarely feel a sense of pride or loyalty in being working, middle or upper class. Rather, sensing uncertainties about where class boundaries actually lie, people feel inclined to *draw* boundaries, by being judgemental, even snobbish, towards others, often people they have quite a lot in common with. This snobbery is sophisticated, often not involving repudiation of specific kinds of people as such, as much as how 'certain people' behave in particular contexts. Nonetheless, this suppleness makes the snobbery itself more powerful. Implicit, class-based references are used by people in order to position themselves within the social structure.

Charlotte is a retired schoolteacher. She judged bad taste on the basis of what she saw as a lack of 'care', whether in terms of personal appearance, or looking after the garden. Charlotte could not understand people who let their grass grow to the point of being untidy and who left 'piles of rubbish' about, and she concluded that the less affluent neighbours she saw who acted in this way were not 'bothered' about the presentation of themselves and their homes to the outside world. This moral judgement was also clear in the way that she discussed her feelings about language and speech:

> And do they mind how they speak? Can they handle the English language? I mean, I find even now, I will deal with people . . . and they will say, 'How do you know that word? Have you swallowed a dictionary?' And they just don't know that language is so rich.

Language and accent were frequent implicit markers of class identity for many of our respondents. Being unable to converse in a way associated with having a 'good' education, for example, was often presented as a lack of 'standards', which were seen to somehow reflect the *personal* qualities of a person who just couldn't be 'bothered'. Fraser, for example, described swearing simply as 'an excuse for poor vocabulary'. Like many respondents, though, Fraser strongly rejected the idea that he was a snob. Fraser's neighbours were described as people like him who were from 'professional backgrounds', although he wanted us to know that he didn't mean this in 'a snobby, snooty sort of way, nothing against working class people, many of my friends are working class'. He took great pains to tell us about one friend of his who was from 'a real working class background', a 'toolmaker', but also he was 'very intelligent, the brightest working class person you will ever see' and 'a clever lad'. By not wanting to appear as a snob and also in order to highlight his diverse social network, Fraser marks his friend out as different from his usual social circle. But his implication is that 'working class' does not normally equal 'intellectual'. Thus, the irony here is that although some claim to shun snobbery and proclaim a distinct spirit of openness and egalitarianism, serious contradictions to this stance surface at the same time.

These moments of social judgement were not just made by those at the top 'looking down' on others positioned towards the lower end of the class structure. One of the most explicit boundaries drawn was between the working class and an 'underclass', which was generally defined as those who claim welfare benefits. Such views were popularized by the recent Channel 4 'real-life' documentary *Benefits Street*, which fuelled a renewed moral outrage over those with families who are out of work. Such people are, through the lens of this programme, seen as 'scroungers'. The programme attracted considerable criticism, but also reflected certain popularly held beliefs – that most people on benefits make fraudulent claims and live degenerate lifestyles which are funded by the taxes of 'hard-working families'. This is despite the fact that 20.8 per cent of all benefits paid in the UK go to people who are working but are on low incomes, with only 2.6 per cent going to the unemployed.[9] Nevertheless, some of our interviewees also frequently referred to a social group of 'benefit claimants' who were seen as not wanting to work, sharing in a culture of worklessness which had been passed down from generation to generation.[10] According to our interviewees, this underclass was outside normal society, its inhabitants lacking both education and a desire to work. This meant that working class participants were reluctant to identify themselves as such in case it meant they were 'tarred with the same brush'. For example, despite expressing concerns about being 'at the bottom', Lorraine was very wary of identifying herself as working class:

> If I put myself as working class I don't think I would want
> to be in the same class as somebody who takes what they
> can and has the attitude of 'Well, I'm better off not
> working', do you see what I mean? I don't think I'd want
> to, I think, 'cause, you know, I take pride in what I do, and
> I get up in the morning and, you know, I don't want to . . .
> I can't think of anything worse than being home all day
> doing nothing. You know, 'cause they're quite often fat,
> aren't they? And then they wonder why. Are you allowed
> to say things like that?

Lorraine's boundary-drawing here is based on a moral judgement about values: unlike those 'on benefits', she is hardworking (although she recognizes, of course, that she might not be 'allowed' to make such judgements). Other respondents spoke about a defective culture associated with the underclass based on 'laziness' and 'apathy'. Indeed, it seemed that the closer our respondents were to the real bottom of the class-structure order, the more explicit were the judgements they made about those whom they saw as beneath them – and the more emotional these judgements became. People's anxieties about their own proximity to the base of the social hierarchy were thus channelled not into drawing boundaries against those who were privileged, or into wider inequalities, but instead into resentment towards the 'underclass'. For example, Alison, a pensioner from Yorkshire, rejected the idea of a class society, but, nonetheless, was exceptionally angry about her having to scrimp and save to get by, when, in her eyes, people on benefits were much better off, making a 'career' out of receiving handouts, with 'no intention of going to work', while she struggled. Alison used very emotive language – the situation was 'disgusting' and it made her 'really cross'. Alison's anger was thus clearly driven by her own experience of inequality, but this was not expressed via a collective solidarity with others in the same position. Instead, Alison was more concerned with making it very clear what she was *not*. Widely held notions of ordinariness – that 'Everyone is as good as everyone else' – fed into a sense that everyone, including the least fortunate, should take individual responsibility for their position.

Of course it is difficult to know the impact that such veiled *and* naked snobbery has on wider British society. Among those with lower resources of capital we found some – albeit tentative – signs of felt snobbery, in those who were grappling with either the real or imagined threat of being looked down upon. One of our respondents, Sarah, was a nurse. She very explicitly wanted to distance herself from her working class background. She had married a middle class man from 'a really well-educated family' and spoke about hating her wedding because she was so embarrassed about her own relatives:

> my mother-in-law said to me, 'I felt at your wedding there was a social divide.' She says, 'Your family were all sat together drinking and smoking,' she says, 'Our family were all sat quietly chatting.' It was a nightmare, and I didn't like it, it was . . . it was awful, it was the worst day of my life, not the best.

Significantly, Sarah didn't reject the snobbish judgement of her mother-in-law, but accepted it – she too wanted to leave the stigma of her working class family background. 'I try to steer towards my husband's family, to be honest,' she told us. This anecdote very vividly highlights the potency of class markers and the pain of being judged; both the stigma associated with certain class identities and the injuries and emotional politics of class. In some ways, Sarah felt she had been able to leave her tarnished, working class identity behind, but she was also anxious that it was something she could never escape.

Imogen, a rebirthing practitioner from a working class background, described a similar feeling of being judged by her neighbours in south London. Imogen had lived in the area for twenty-five years, but described a creeping sense of inferiority, as the area had gentrified and become colonized by the wealthy. But it was not so much the economic differences that Imogen felt, but the more subtle cultural boundaries around language and discussion: 'Yeah, I think there's a snobbery, it's just somewhere in the background, you know, the odd comment, and I just find there's a certain way to be academic which can be a way of keeping away from other people, mental conversations which don't let others be part of a conversation.'

At one point in Katie Hopkins', chaotic *This Morning* appearance, during a brief moment of calm, she confided to the dismayed presenters: 'You know, parents often come up to me in the playground and say, "I read your article about class and children's names and . . . [*whispers*] I wouldn't say it, but that's what I do too."' Willoughby, Phillip Schofield, her fellow prosecutor and Mangan all shook their heads vigorously, clearly wanting to dismiss Hopkins's suggestion that today's Britain could possibly harbour such a critical mass of closet snobs.

Yet the uncomfortable truth is that the sneering of Hopkins (and those whispering parents she mentioned) may not be so anomalous. Hopkins was, in a sense, saying the unsayable, identifying class boundaries and voicing sentiments (which are the more powerful for normally being unsaid) about them. As this chapter illustrates, people regularly distance themselves from the idea of social class, and, particularly, class snobbery. As Table 11.1 on p. 368 shows, fewer than half of our survey respondents thought of themselves as belonging to a social class, and in interviews most registered strong objections to anti-meritocratic, judgemental views of class. Yet we have shown here that this was not the whole story. While most people in Britain might not directly identify with a particular class, the extent of inequality, and the way that it shapes people's life chances unequally, means that class is still deeply felt in people's identities. Most people continue to identify strong markers of class (through the identification of types of neighbourhood, family background and lifestyle, as well as through their interactions with those different to themselves). Our sense of class is often recognized, not through understandings of who we are, but rather who we aren't.

We live in a paradoxical world, then. The public disdain the idea of snobbery and class prejudice, but this is very different from its real eradication. Indeed, what people say about class on the one hand, and how they actually enact and perform class in their everyday lives on the other, are very different. When we chatted with our interviewees, many people drew distinct and aggressive class boundaries. While these judgements might not be as naked and self-conscious as that expressed by Katie Hopkins, they are nonetheless tremendously socially powerful. Class snobbery in twenty-first-century Britain is far from dead; it has simply gone underground.

# The Old New Politics of Class in the 21$^{st}$ Century

Numerous academics and politicians writing in the 1980s and 1990s proclaimed the 'death of class' and the rise of a post-modern social order based on 'individualization'. In this book, we have disputed such a benevolent view. We have argued that by focusing on the fundamental differentiation between the wealth-elite at the top and the precariat at the bottom – alongside the larger numbers of people located in the middle reaches of the class structure – we have opened the door to a more fertile (though also deeply worrying) way of recognizing the importance of class in the twenty-first century.

The idea of class has always, fundamentally, been wrapped up with the question of politics. Classes are not just abstract sociological classifications; but, if they matter, they do so because they shape history through the political contestation that they give rise to. How, then, does the alarming account we have developed in this book affect the charged political landscape today? In some respects the success of the Conservative Party in the 2015 British general election and the defeat of the Labour Party can indeed be read as a failure of older models of class, based on the distinction between middle and working class. However, we can also read the success of the Conservatives as testifying to the value of the approach we have developed here.

New mountains of inequality have opened up in Britain in recent decades, most notably in the economic domain. This has generated a widening class division between a small 'ordinary' wealth-elite at the top, who are the great beneficiaries, and a rather larger precariat at the bottom, who lack significant economic resources of any kind. Between these two extremes lie a number of groups in the middle ranges of the social hierarchy. The division between middle and working class, which has been strongly etched into British society and culture for centuries, has a much more muted importance in these conditions – though its cultural legacy persists. The boundaries between these classes are not closed, and social mobility is common, especially in the middle reaches. Yet it is also true that there is a cumulative process whereby those with advantages start from a much stronger competitive position which allows them much greater opportunities to enter the elite. This is underscored by geographical dynamics and the role of elite institutions, such as universities. Our generation is seeing the formation of an elite class different from that of the old aristocratic order, which was also highly distinctive in being markedly more advantaged than any other group.

This model of class poses major challenges for conventional class politics. If we firstly consider sociological perspectives – which have also been embedded in political mobilization over decades – we doubt that a focus on 'working class politics' has much purchase today. This stretches back to the old view – which we first discussed in Chapter 1 – that the axial division between middle and working class was, previously, central to political mobilization.

However, political parties are no longer closely affiliated to different occupational classes, and here there is a huge historical shift. Table C.1 indicates a clear class divide in the percentage of different (occupationally defined) social classes who allied themselves with the major political parties in 1983/4. Managers, owners and (to a slightly lesser extent) professionals were at least twice as likely to vote for the Conservative Party than the Labour Party. By contrast, those in the manual working class were twice as likely to ally themselves with the Labour Party. We see here the old politics of class clearly manifest in the party identifications of different occupational classes.

Further reflection reminds us why such powerful class divisions might have been in operation at this time. This was the period of the last major industrial conflict in Britain, the miners' strike, which dominated British politics for a whole year as the Conservative government faced up to a powerful mobilization by the National Union of Mineworkers to resist its pit-closure programme. Trade union membership had reached its all-time peak of thirteen million members in 1979 and was still in excess of twelve million in 1983. Nearly half of the workforce was unionized, and industrial conflict was much in the news. In the context of a major recession, unemployment had risen from one and a half million in the late 1970s to over three million by the mid-1980s, the highest level since the 1930s. The brunt of this fell on manual workers in industry. It is not surprising, then, that we might see

| | CONSERVATIVE | LABOUR | LIBERAL DEMOCRATIC ALLIANCE | OTHER |
|---|---|---|---|---|
| Managers | 61 | 23 | 11 | 2 |
| Owners and the self-employed | 69 | 17 | 11 | 2 |
| Professional and intermediate workers | 52 | 25 | 18 | 2 |
| Junior non-manual workers | 50 | 23 | 18 | 0 |
| Skilled manual workers | 29 | 52 | 11 | 1 |
| Semi- and unskilled manual workers | 25 | 54 | 12 | 3 |

## Table C.1

### Occupational Class and Party Identification 1983–4 (%)

Source: 'The Role of Class in Shaping Social Attitudes', Anthony Heath, Mike Savage and Nicki Senior, *British Social Attitudes*, 30, 2013, 173–99 ed. A. Park, C. Bryson, E. Clery, J. Curtice and M. Phillips

high levels of class polarization in support for the Labour and Conservative parties then.

Let us zoom forward in time and present exactly comparable figures from 2011–12. Thirty years have passed. Two long periods of rule by a Conservative government (during 1979–97 and 2010–14), and a New Labour government (1997–2010) have transformed the political landscape. Union membership has declined to seven million, little more than half what it had been, and is concentrated among public-sector professionals rather than among the iconic coal miners, railway workers, dock workers, steel workers and the like. A large programme of privatization in public amenities has radically reduced the size of the public sector and market principles have been introduced in many areas of welfare provision. The economy has become overwhelmingly reliant on the service sector and finance.

A very different set of political alignments are now to be found, and ones which have a much less clear association with occupational class. Table c.2 shows that managers, owners and junior non- manual workers no longer support the Conservative Party in droves. Indeed, they are hardly more likely to identify with the Conservatives than with the Labour Party. Professionals and the intermediate classes have actually become slightly more prone to identify with Labour than with the Tories, the first time this had ever happened. These trends are tribute to Tony Blair's determination to appeal to such groups as part of the rebranding of New Labour. And indeed, a largely uniform 'political class' of university-educated MPs have replaced previous generations of trade union activists, business people and professionals.

Table c.2 shows that even though manual workers remain markedly more likely to identify with the Labour Party than with the Conservatives, the proportion of Labour identifiers had fallen well below 50 per cent. Increasing numbers of working class voters also abstained and showed disenchantment with the political system as a whole.

On the face of it, these two tables indicate the end of old-fashioned class politics based on the fundamental cleavage between the working and middle classes which had dominated political mobilization during the twentieth century. However, as we have endeavoured to emphasize in this book, this does not mean that class itself is dead. We need to rethink the terms in which class and politics intersect. Occupational class politics – in which your current job defines your class and gives you a set of class interests which affect your political outlook – is now very limited. However, it seems that political parties' success depends on how far they can appeal to the future aspirations and values of different voters and – to use the terms of our argument – how they offer strategies for accumulating different sorts of capital. It is through this capacity to define plausible futures that the new politics of class operates.

What we are seeing now is an effective and powerful wealth-elite, who, broadly speaking, are highly engaged politically and know how to lobby, at one extreme, and a precariat, who are largely alienated from mainstream party politics, at the other. There is also a much larger group between these two extremes, who are more fluid and mobile in their orientation. We will return presently to consider this political

| | CONSERVATIVE | LABOUR | LIBERAL DEMOCRATIC ALLIANCE | OTHER |
|---|---|---|---|---|
| Managers | 40 | 32 | 6 | 6 |
| Owners and the self-employed | 33 | 30 | 4 | 16 |
| Professional and intermediate workers | 29 | 38 | 10 | 10 |
| Junior non-manual workers | 31 | 26 | 8 | 10 |
| Skilled manual workers | 24 | 40 | 3 | 12 |
| Semi- and unskilled manual workers | 17 | 41 | 4 | 8 |

### Table C.2

Occupational Class and Party Identification 2010–11 (%)

Source: 'The Role of Class in Shaping Social Attitudes', Anthony Heath, Mike Savage and Nicki Senior, British Social Attitudes, 30, 2013, 173–99 ed. A. Park, C. Bryson, E. Clery, J. Curtice and M. Phillips

landscape, but before we do this, we need to reflect on the problems for meritocratic class politics.

Over the past fifty years, meritocratic politics has been at the centre of political mobilization and lobbying. Having a strong base both in the Labour Party (its social-democratic but also its New Labour variants), as well as in the Conservative Party (in its 'one nation' thinking but also in its more Thatcherite form), its central plank is that inequalities are an inevitable feature of a competitive capitalist system, and indeed these inequalities are desirable insofar as they act to motivate people to work hard, be ambitious and strive to innovate. Given this belief, the political task was to make sure that there were no barriers preventing people getting to the top on the basis of their genuine merit and endeavour. Insofar as it was possible for anyone to succeed, inequality was not necessarily a problem in itself. Thus, Peter Mandelson, architect of New Labour, famously quipped that he was 'intensely relaxed about people getting filthy rich . . . as long as they pay their taxes'. But although his remark has been much reviled, he was only stating the political common sense of his time.

But it is worth remembering that this meritocratic ethos displaced a more egalitarian politics which insisted that equality itself was an issue which needed to be addressed. The current of this thinking was forcefully stated in Anthony Crosland's famous argument in *The Future of Socialism* in 1956:

> in Britain, equality of opportunity and social mobility [. . .] are not enough. They need [. . .] to be combined with measures [. . .] to equalise the distribution of rewards and

privileges so as to diminish the degree of class stratification, the injustice of large inequalities, and the collective discontents which come from too great a dispersion of rewards.[1]

Crosland's vision was a significant force within the Labour Party until the 1970s. It is striking that Britain then had among the most 'progressive' taxation system in the world, with income tax rates of up to 98 per cent and inheritance tax of 85 per cent until the 1980s[2]. We have, therefore, a fertile tradition, the relevance of which could surely be recovered in the context of accelerating inequalities. For there seems little doubt that the voices insisting that equality is a political issue which needs to be addressed directly are now very clearly back, to the extent that elements within the Labour Party are once more beginning to argue for redistribution (in the forms of arguments about a mansion tax, for instance). We have little doubt that these sorts of arguments will grow in future years, and we hope our book encourages this move.

Today, two fundamental problems confront proponents who think that meritocratic opportunities justify economic inequalities. First of all, there lies the challenge laid down by Piketty and other social scientists, and which is underscored in this book. Such has been the increase of inequality in the UK, as in other nations, it is hard to see that further accumulations of wealth on the lofty mountain tops will serve any additional meritocratic function. Indeed, by contrast, this accumulation has been shown to generate a series of social problems.[3] And this point becomes even more striking once the focus is upon wealth rather than income, when it becomes hard to attribute the soaring fortunes of the very wealthy to any kind of meritocratic process at work. Even though it might be possible to accept that some kind of meritocratic factors might operate in the middle ranges of the labour market, these cannot in any way explain what is happening at the top end, where the scope for *rentier* revenue is paramount. It is this which explains the mushrooming economic capital of the top layers of the economic distribution.

We have also insisted here on a second issue, following in the spirit of Michael Young. Meritocratic processes do not address inequalities in the prospects of different social groups, and in fact may even accentuate them. This is because when there is a highly competitive education system and labour market, it is those who can maximize every possible advantage and who start from the most advantaged positions who are best able to succeed within this meritocratic structure. We see this syndrome operating very actively in the search for 'talent' embarked upon by leading companies and organizations acting to 'hothouse' their star performers in 'Winner takes all' markets. Meritocracy is not a curb to escalating inequality; it is actually implicated within it.

In this respect, conventional images of George Osborne and David Cameron in their Bullingdon Club Oxford days, with the implication that the closed, old-fashioned elite world continues to look after its own, are misleading. Such images – for instance of an 'Establishment' – can be mobilized to suggest that if only we could have 'true' meritocracy and break down those remaining status barriers at the top, then we might be able to address the inequities of social class. But this harking back to a critique of an old aristocratic culture is unhelpful. Elite educational institutions succeed not because they are in the pocket of the former aristocratic elite (though, of course, old habits die hard and it is still possible to find traces of this), but because they are at the apex of highly competitive recruitment and training processes which lie at the heart of contemporary neo-liberal capitalism. Meritocracy goes hand-in-hand with the generation of the kind of intense inequalities we have identified in this book. It thus follows that calls for more 'education' as a means of encouraging social mobility and addressing class inequalities have considerable limitations in the face of the growing inequalities witnessed in recent decades.

## The new class politics of classification

We should once again take up a politics of equality. However, this does not mean we can simply recover an old-fashioned class politics or embrace a social-democratic legacy. Sociologically, we have shown that the nature of class divisions is such that to project them as clear categorical divides is far too simplistic. People cannot be neatly lined up and defined in unitary ways like this. Following Bourdieu's steering, we insist on a multidimensional approach to class which is better able to grasp the complexities of class dynamics today. And we also insist on the need to treat cultural and social processes – not just economic ones – as fundamental to the way that class operates in the present.

We therefore champion a new cultural politics of class which does not fixate on placing people into clear categories and judging them on the basis of their supposed membership of those. This may sound like a surprising salvo, given that this book might seem to contain many exercises of this kind, but we hope readers have seen that our endeavours have been placed within the context of a wider concern with a politics of classification and in relation to which we have drawn attention to the limits and absences that are generated by the definition and construction of groupings. The most striking finding here is the way that the precariat become invisible, if you rely on the GBCS web survey, whilst the elite become highly visible.

We have therefore challenged the characterization of those at the bottom – the precariat – and at the top – the 'ordinary' wealth-elite. We have insisted in this book on the way that modes of classification are inherently hierarchical and thus generate categories which are necessarily morally loaded. We have argued further that forms of emerging cultural capital have pushed this kind of classificatory politics even further, leading to proliferating modes of negative identification and reaction which have the effect of intensifying the already loaded stigmatization of those least well equipped to contest these definitions. This is only likely to make their situation even worse.

One response to this politics would be to refuse to classify, or to point to the limits of any kind of classification in general terms. Such a response, however, has two problems. Firstly, it harks back to an older aristocratic culture when it was seen to be 'vulgar' to classify. When in the 1950s Nancy Mitford talked about the different accents and social signifiers – the 'U' and 'non-U' – which distinguished the posh from the vulgar, she was reviled by her friends for making explicit what had always been an unwritten code. For these reasons, not engaging in the politics of classification is not an effective response. It leaves in place implicit privilege. Secondly it will not stop classification from happening, as it is so powerfully embedded in contemporary life. League tables, market profiling and categorization lie at the heart of today's 'knowing capitalism'.[4] By refusing to engage with this politics of classification, you dramatically limit how you can seek to influence these forces more positively. What we can more effectively do is to focus on these classifying processes as a political issue themselves and furthermore seek to align them more effectively so that they highlight those groups whose privileges may be called into question. This involves placing the classification process itself under the political spotlight. It involves the social sciences getting their hands dirty and seeking to wrest intellectual authority from market researchers, consultants, journalists and commentators.

And such an approach, we argue, allows us to better understand the meaning of class today. People don't like the idea of class precisely because its significance is so marked in daily life, as they see the proliferation of inequalities around them. On any high street the social-class coding of different kinds of shops proliferates: Waitrose, Aldi, corner shops, delicatessens – all carry with them a social as well as a practical meaning. Such classifications, however, point to the lack of clarity about the old division between middle and working class these days. Allied to the considerable social mobility which exists in the middle ranges of the social structure, there is a widespread sense of uncertainty about where class boundaries actually lie today. The response to this should not be to insist on the hard-and-fast nature of 'actual' class boundaries, but to see how these fluidities require a cultural politics of class.

We can suggest five points by way of conclusion. Firstly, a questioning of the stereotyping of those in the lowest rank of the social-class hierarchy. We have seen in this book how those at the bottom act as a lightning conductor for stigmatization and marginalization. This is linked to the instabilities and fragmentation of previous divisions between the middle and the working classes, as many people look below themselves to identify those whom they see as lower ranked than they are as disreputable and immoral groups. There is nothing new about this in some respects: but these currents operate with particular venom today. We have insisted that this kind of stigmatizing politics is deeply problematic in further damaging the already difficult lives of those eking out a living in on-the-breadline Britain. We can only endorse the arguments of numerous other researchers such as Imogen Tyler, Tracy Shildrick, Robert MacDonald and Beverley Skeggs, and social-policy experts such as John Hills, in insisting that in reality the lives of those at the bottom are not characterized by amoral scrounging on the *Benefits Street* model, but are in fact based on precariousness.[5] Challenging the stereotypes which abound involves presenting new and more challenging classifications, as we have done in our analysis of the Great British Class Survey.

Secondly, we need to bring those at the very top more directly into view. It is fundamental here to question the extent to which their mushrooming economic capital can be justified. Piketty's insistence that returns to capital generally exceed the rate of economic growth, and hence that there is a tendency for wealth to accumulate more rapidly than national economies, draws attention to the way that the highest levels of economic capital are self-generating in an increasingly intense way. To put this more directly, the more you have, the more you get. There has been an important campaign to raise visibility towards the excessive rewards accruing to the super-rich – such as by the Occupy movement – and we strongly support this concern. We would, however, argue that it is important not simply to concentrate on particular 'super-wealthy' individuals alone, or indeed even the 'one per cent', who are commonly singled out. There is a danger that this politics becomes both sensationalist and focused on particular individuals in a way which detracts from the wider socio-logical resonance of what we have called the 'ordinary' wealth-elite. We need to be clear here – the naming and sham-ing of particular 'robber barons', in specific sites such as Wall Street, is no doubt important, but we would also want to see a somewhat wider group being the subject of attention.

Thirdly, we seek to make the question of accumulation of different kinds of capital – economic, cultural and social – more central to our understanding of social divisions. Categorization classically operates on the basis of snapshots, and these obfuscate this fundamental temporal dimension. What we see in the top reaches of the class structure is mundane and ordinary accumulation – for example in the sphere of rapidly increasing house prices. Such forms of accumulation are increasingly becoming the object of political attention through a concern with wealth and mansion taxes and we see this as entirely appropriate. We do not think that an exclusive focus on the machinations of the super-wealthy is helpful, because it misses these more routine (but implicitly exclusive) processes of extreme accumulation.

Fourthly, we need to unravel more effectively the way that contemporary inequalities are associated with the interaction of different kinds of capital, and which lead to a range of vicious and virtuous circuits. Again, our challenge here is to resist simplistic and snapshot categorizations. We have thus emphasized the way that economic, cultural and social capital intersect and how these links are crystallized by specific institutions – elite universities – and by certain locations, and how these links are drawn via long-term processes of accumulation.

And fifthly, we finish this book by returning to our comments about the limits of meritocratic politics. We can extend this point by arguing that in order to fundamentally challenge the inequities we have revealed in this study, we need to question the competitive, capitalist, neo-liberal market system itself. The legitimacy of this system depends on its being seen as consistent with freedom and equality of opportunity. By questioning this association, we will be better placed to reflect on the power of other, more effective and inclusive models.

We therefore hope our book will open up debate about the meaning of class today and allow us to confront contemporary challenges by contributing to that increasing public debate, thereby putting pressure on politicians and policy-makers to challenge the unacceptable, gross inequalities that character-ize the opening decades of the twenty-first century.

# The Great British Class Survey

In this book we draw on data collected as part of the Great British Class Survey (GBCS). Anyone interested in learning more about the organization and conduct of the project should read Fiona Devine and Helene Snee, 'Doing the Great British Class Survey', *Sociological Review*, 63(2), 2015, 240–58).

There are three components of the data in the GBCS project which we use in this book.

1. The survey was hosted by the BBC Lab UK website, which was launched by the BBC on 26 January 2011. This survey took the form of a twenty-minute questionnaire. Details of the questionnaire are available from the UK Data Archive. The data was collected in two main batches. First were the 161,000 responses received by June 2011 which formed the data which we used in the initial analyses reported in Mike Savage et al., 'A New Model of Social Class? Findings from the BBC's GBCS Experiment'.[1] However, the survey remained live on the website until the end of June 2013, and especially in the light of the media publicity of the launch of the GBCS findings at the end of April 2013, a large number of new responses were submitted (there were

a further 164,000 responses in this second wave), making a total of 325,000 responses altogether. Most of the analyses in this book use the initial data set, since the latter wave had not been checked for errors by the time the analyses reported here were completed. Future research using the entire data-set may therefore qualify findings here, though our preliminary explorations do not suggest that this will lead to major revisions. In our analyses we have omitted respondents who were not UK residents. The complete data-set is archived in the UK data archive at the University of Essex, which also includes more information about the sample.[2]

2.  Secondly, when the sample skew of the GBCS came to light in the context of our initial investigations in April 2011, the BBC agreed to fund an additional, face-to-face survey to allow nationally representative patterns to be discovered. This particular survey was conducted by the market research firm GfK in April 2011, using quota sample methods (which are explained in Mike Savage, Fiona Devine, Niall Cunningham, Sam Friedman, Daniel Laurison, Andrew Miles, Helene Snee and Mark Taylor, 'On Social Class, Anno 2014', *Sociology* (forthcoming)), and had 1,026 respondents. This survey is also sometimes called the 'nationally representative survey' in this book. Additional information about this survey and its representative characteristics compared to other national surveys is included in the appendix to the essay by Savage et al., 'On Social Class, Anno 2014'. This data set is also

archived at the UK data archive which includes more information about the sample.

3. Thirdly, given the immense media and public interest in the GBCS, and the need to supplement survey findings with qualitative evidence, we followed up with fifty additional interviews in order to find out more about what people thought about class in their own words. We asked respondents similar questions to those which were on the GBCS, but also additional, qualitative questions about their life histories, attitudes and values. We directed these interviews across the social range, though with a particular focus on the two social classes we thought were of particular interest (given the GBCS findings), namely those at the top and the bottom of the social structure. This research was coordinated by Sam Friedman and Helene Snee, and all of the authors of this book were involved in the interviewing. The interviews were conducted in late spring 2014, transcribed and coded up for analysis (during which we systematically searched for key phrases and issues). Brief details of the interviewees are as follows:

| OCCUPATION | PSEUDONYM | LOCATION | SEX | AGE |
|---|---|---|---|---|
| Human resources manager | Hayley | Oxford | F | 50 |
| Retired teacher | Charlotte | Worcestershire | F | 77 |
| Accountant | Paul | Gloucestershire | M | 66 |
| Retired teacher | Monica | Somerset | F | 67 |
| Retired seamstress | Alison | Yorkshire | F | 69 |
| Drug rehabilitation officer | Yasmine | Lancashire | F | 49 |
| Nurse | Sarah | West Yorkshire | F | 51 |
| Nightclub bouncer | Craig | Leicester | M | 48 |
| Retired payroll administrator | Martin | Birmingham | M | 60–65 |
| Factory worker and carer | Tina | Essex | F | 51 |
| Forklift-truck operator | Lorraine | Northamptonshire | F | 44 |
| Retired headteacher | Fraser | County Durham | M | 66 |
| Antiques dealer | Pauline | Lincolnshire | F | 63 |
| Chemical engineer | Michael | Wolverhampton | M | 63 |
| Business owner | Indi | Wolverhampton | M | 71 |
| Retired/artist | Elizabeth | York | F | 60 |
| Retired railway signalman | Christopher | York | M | 75 |
| Academic/businessman | Nigel | York | M | 60 |
| Teacher | Roberta | Essex | F | (data missing) |
| Retired banker | Giles | Cheshire | M | 60 |
| University professor | Anthony | St Andrews | M | 57 |
| Retired shop assistant | Jane | London | F | 72 |
| IT manager | Fiona | London | F | 48 |
| Sales manager | Alan | Greater London | M | 34 |
| Author of fiction | Jennifer | South Lanarkshire | F | 52 |

| OCCUPATION | PSEUDONYM | LOCATION | SEX | AGE |
|---|---|---|---|---|
| Rebirthing specialist | Imogen | London | F | 54 |
| Lobbyist | George | London | M | 34 |
| Journalist | Pierce | Derby | M | 38 |
| Marketing executive | Jemima | Buckinghamshire | F | 32 |
| Further education lecturer | Roger | Greater Manchester | M | 59 |
| Law student | Henry | Edinburgh | M | 19 |
| Communications director manager | Georgia | London | F | 42 |
| IT manager | Benedict | Sussex | M | 51 |
| Marketing manager | Jeremy | Kent | M | 27 |
| Solicitor | Jarvis | Oxfordshire | M | 38 |
| Retired nurse | Stuart | Brighton | M | 60 |
| Retail consultant | Louise | London | F | 48 |
| Builder | Richard | Nottingham | M | 32 |
| Builder | Joe | London | M | 56 |
| Builder | Simon | London | M | 47 |
| Pipe fitter | Terry | London | M | 35 |
| Charity worker | Janice | Nottingham | F | 35 |
| Graphic designer | Gita | London | F | 44 |
| Lobbyist | Samantha | London | F | 29 |
| Sex worker | Lesley | Nottingham | F | 24 |
| Volunteer worker | Rosie | Nottingham | F | 52 |
| Nail technician | Laura | London | F | 34 |
| Cleaner | Barbara | London | F | 35 |
| Cleaner | Claire | London | F | 59 |

# Notes

## INTRODUCTION: THE GREAT BRITISH CLASS SURVEY AND THE RETURN OF CLASS TODAY

1. Danny Dorling, *Injustice* (Bristol: 2010), and Owen Jones, *The Establishment, and How They Get Away with It* (London: 2014).
2. Mike Savage, Fiona Devine, Niall Cunningham, Mark Taylor, Yaojun Li, Johannes Hjellbrekke, Brigitte Le Roux, Sam Friedman and Andrew Miles, 'A New Model of Social Class? Findings from the BBC's Great British Class Survey Experiment', *Sociology*, 47(2), 2013, 219–50.
3. This number had risen to nearly nine million by the end of 2014, with over ten thousand people continuing to click on the Class Calculator each week. See further, Fiona Devine and Helene Snee, 'Doing the Great British Class Survey', *Sociological Review*, 63(2), 2015, 240–58.
4. See http://xmedia.ex.ac.uk/wp/wordpress/a-class-act/.
5. Spatial units with fewer than a hundred GBCS respondents have been suppressed.
6. However, this was a particular problem for the analysis of ethnicity, since the numbers of ethnic minorities in the nationally representative sample gathered by the market-research company GfK (see also Appendix: The Great British Class Survey, section 2), were too few to allow inferences to be readily drawn. Readers should therefore be aware of this limitation and the implication that ethnicity cannot be satisfactorily analysed using either the data-set the GBCS provides or the nationally representative sample's data-set garnered by GfK.
7. See Colin Mills, 'The Great British Class Fiasco: A Comment on Savage et al.', *Sociology*, 48(3), 2014, 437–44, as well as the response by Mike Savage, Fiona Devine, Niall Cunningham, Sam Friedman, Daniel Laurison, Andrew Miles, Helene Snee and Mark Taylor, 'On Social Class, Anno 2014', *Sociology* (forthcoming).

8. See Tony Bennett, Mike Savage, Elizabeth Silva, Alan Warde, Modesto Gayo-Cal and David Wright, *Culture, Class, Distinction* (Abingdon: 2009).

---

## CHAPTER 1: CONTESTING CLASS BOUNDARIES: DIFFERENTIATING MIDDLE AND WORKING CLASS

1. See http://www.bbc.co.uk/labuk/articles/class/.
2. Mike Savage, Gaynor Bagnall and Brian Longhurst, 'Ordinary, Ambivalent and Defensive: Class Identities in the Northwest of England', *Sociology*, 34(5), 2001, 875–92.
3. Anthony Meath, Joan Martin and Gabriella Elgenius. 'Who Do We Think We Are? The Decline of Traditional Social Identities', in A. Park, J. Curtice, K. Thomson, M. Phillips and M. Johnson (editors), *British Social Attitudes: The 23rd Report – Perspectives on a Changing Society* (London: 2007), pp. 1–34.
4. It is telling that only a very small proportion of people think of themselves as upper class, whereas the majority of people are prepared to consider themselves working or middle class.
5. E.g. David Cannadine, *Class in Britain* (Harmondsworth: 1984), Ross McKibbin, *Classes and Cultures: England 1918–1951* (Oxford: 1998), Selina Todd, *The People: The Rise and Fall of the Working Class 1980–2010* (London: 2014).
6. The classic argument here is E. P. Thompson, *The Making of the English Working Class* (London: 1963).
7. William Wordsworth's famous poem 'Michael' is of course a famous elegy in the context of Lakeland Britain.
8. Keith Wrightson, *Earthly Necessities: Economic Lives in Early Modern Britain* (London: 2000).
9. Thompson, *The Making of the English Working Class*; Mike Savage and Andrew Miles, *The Remaking of the British Working Class, 1840–1940* (London: 1994).
10. Peter Cain and Anthony Hopkins, *British Imperialism, 1688–2000* (London: 1993).
11. See Carolyn Steedman, *Master and Servant: Love and Labour in the English Industrial Age* (Cambridge: 2007) and *Labours Lost: Domestic Service and the Making of Modern England* (Cambridge: 2009).
12. On the very limited social mobility into aristocratic rank, see Andrew Miles, *Social Mobility in Nineteenth-and Early Twentieth-century England* (Basingstoke: 1999).
13. Dror Wahrman, *Imagining the Middle Class: The Political Representation of Class in Britain, C. 1780–1840* (Cambridge: 1995).

14. Thus, the eminent sociologist T. H. Marshall argued that the only way to civilize the working class was to extend citizenship rights, notably through the building of a welfare state designed to allow workers full rights, which would extend their human decency and hence respectability. See T. H. Marshall, *Citizenship and Social Class, and Other Essays* (Cambridge: 1950). See also the arguments of David Lockwood about what he terms 'the problematic of the proletariat': David Lockwood, 'Marking Out the Middle Class(es)', in T. Butler and M. Savage (editors), *Social Change and the Middle Classes* (London: 1995).

15. This is the classic argument of Thompson in *The Making of the English Working Class.*

16. Maxine Berg, *Luxury and Pleasure in Eighteenth-century Britain* (Oxford: 2005); John Brewer, *The Pleasures of the Imagination: English Culture in the Eighteenth Century* (London: 1997).

17. See D. J. Taylor, *Orwell: The Life* (London: 2003).

18. For examples of these kinds of concerns, Mass Observation is an excellent source. See D. Kynaston, *Austerity Britain 1945–51* (London: 2007), as well as James Hinton, *Nine Wartime Lives* (Oxford: 2010). These concerns extended into the later twentieth century, as explored by Beverley Skeggs in *Formations of Class and Gender* (London: 1997).

19. Gareth Stedman Jones, *Outcast London* (Harmondsworth, 1971).

20. For further details, including a chance to look at Charles Booth's detailed social map of any part of London, consult the online resource http://booth.lse.ac.uk/.

21. Donald A. MacKenzie, *Statistics in Britain, 1865–1930: The Social Construction of Scientific Knowledge* (Edinburgh: 1981), Siman Szreter, *Fertility, Class and Gender in Britain, 1860–1940* (Cambridge: 2002).

22. One might argue that the strange British obsession with finding an additional means of dividing within the middle layers is also found within university degree classifications, which differentiate between 'upper' and 'lower' second-class degrees.

23. T. H. C. Stevenson, 'The Vital Statistics of Wealth and Poverty', *Journal of the Royal Statistical Society*, 91(2), 1928, 207–30. For a more general review, see Szreter, *Fertility, Class and Gender.*

24. In the British case, extensive studies examining this issue in the post-war years concluded that in fact it was hard to differentiate people's actual views of the prestige of jobs from their awareness of the public repute in which such jobs were held. See A. Coxon and C. Jones, *The Images of Occupational Prestige* (London: 1978) and T. Coxon, 'The Misconstruction of Occupational Judgment', *British Journal of Sociology*, 34(4), 1983, 483–90.

25. See more generally here, Mike Savage, *Identities and Social Change in Britain since 1940: The Politics of Method* (Oxford: 2010).

26. See Ross McKibbin, *Classes and Cultures: England 1918–1951* (Oxford: 1998) and Savage, *Identities and Social Change in Britain since 1940*.

27. See Rosemary Crompton and Gareth Jones, *White-collar Proletariat: Deskilling and Gender in Clerical Work* (Basingstoke: 1984).

28. Annie Phizacklea and Robert Miles, *Labour and Racism* (London: 1980) and from the Centre for Contemporary Cultural Studies, *The Empire Strikes Back: Race and Racism in 70s Britain* (London: 1982).

29. See the online resource http://www.ons.gov.uk/ons/guide-method/ classifications/current-standard-classifications/soc2010/soc2010-volume-3-ns-sec--rebased-on-soc2010--user-manual/index.html#skiptotop.

30. The key discussion and demonstration of this argument is in Gordon Marshall, Howard Newby, David Rose and Carolyn Vogler, *Social Class in Modern Britain* (London: 1988). More generally, see David Rose and David Pevalin (editors), *A Researcher's Guide to the National Statistics Socio-economic Classification* (London: 2003)

31. See notably David Lockwood, *The Black-coated Worker* (London: 1958), and Susan Halford, Mike Savage and Anne Witz, *Gender, Careers and Organisations* (Basingstoke: 1997).

32. See, for instance, the demonstration by Anthony Heath and his associates that it predicted voting behaviour during the 1980s much more accurately, in Anthony Heath, Roger Jowell and John Curtice, *How Britain Votes* (Oxford: 1985), or the work of Patrick McGovern, Stephen Hill, Colin Mills and Michael White, who claim it was associated with employment divisions, in *Market, Class and Employment* (Oxford: 2007).

33. See Mike Savage and Karel Williams (editors), *Remembering Elites* (Oxford: 2008).

34. On social mobility, see, for instance, Robert Erikson and John Goldthorpe, *The Constant Flux* (Oxford: 1992).

35. The key contributions here are Tony Bennett, Mike Savage, Elizabeth Silva, Alan Warde, Modesto Gayo-Cal and David Wright, *Class, Culture, Distinction* (Abingdon: 2009), and, more specifically, Brigitte Le Roux, Henry Rouanet, Mike Savage and Alan Warde, 'Class and Cultural Division in the UK', *Sociology*, 42(6), 2008, pp. 1049–71.

36. See Mike Savage, Alan Warde and Fiona Devine, 'Capitals, Assets and Resources', *British Journal of Sociology*, 56(1), 2005, 31–47.

37. Pierre Bourdieu, 'The Forms of Capital', in Imre Szeman and Timothy Kaposy (editors), *Cultural Theory: An Anthology* (Oxford: 2010), p. 81.

38. See I. F. Silber, 'Bourdieu's Gift to Gift Theory: An Unacknowledged Trajectory', *Sociological Theory*, 27(2), 2009, 173–90.

39. http://www.aqa.org.uk/subjects/english/as-and-a-level/english-literature-a-2740/subject-content.

40. Mike Savage, Gaynor Bagnall and Brian Longhurst, *Globalization and Belonging* (London: 2005).

## CHAPTER 2: ACCUMULATING ECONOMIC CAPITAL

1. John Hills, *Good Times, Bad Times: The Welfare Myth of Them and Us* (Bristol: 2015), p. 37.

2. The Gini coefficient measures household income within a nation and reports a score between 0 (perfect equality) and 100 (complete inequality). For precise definition, see http://www.ons.gov.uk/ons/guide-method/method-quality/specific/social-and-welfare-methodology/the-gini-coefficient/index.html.

3. For overviews, see Peter Nolan, 'Shaping the Future: The Political Economy of Work and Employment', *Industrial Relations Journal*, 35(5), 2004, 378–87, and 'The Changing World of Work', *Journal of Health Services Research and Policy*, 9(suppl. 1), 2004, 3–9.

4. See, more generally, Mark Williams, 'Occupations and British Wage Inequality, 1970s–2000s', *European Sociological Review*, 29(4), 2013, 841–57.

5. These findings also conform with those of Mark Williams, who shows that although much of the increasing variation in income levels can be mapped on to the NS-SEC classes, it is the gap between those in class 1 (professionals and managers) and the rest which explains most of this variance.

6. There is one important caveat to note, however, and this is that the GBCS only has information on household income, so the figures for Table 2.3 will be affected by whether there are two or more income-earners in the household. Subsequent analysis by Sam Friedman, David Laurison and Andrew Miles in 'Breaking the "Class" Ceiling? Social Mobility into Elite Occupations', *Sociological Review*, 63(2), 2015, 259–89 (which compares the GBCS findings with those from the Labour Force Survey on individual incomes), suggests that similar patterns can be found in both sources.

7. See Thomas Piketty, *Capital in the Twenty-first Century* (Cambridge, MA: 2014), p. 116, Figure 3.1.

8. Markus Jäntti, Eva Sierminska and Philippe Van Kerm, 'The Joint Distribution of Income and Wealth', in Janet C. Gornick and Markus Jäntti (editors), *Income Inequality: Economic Disparities and the Middle Class in Affluent Countries* (Redwood City, CA: 2013), pp. 312–33.

9. Eva Sierminska, Timothy M. Smeeding and Serge Allegrezza, 'The Distribution of Assets and Debt', in Gornick and Jäntti (editors), *Income Inequality: Economic Disparities and the Middle Class*, pp. 285–311, at p. 294. Note that these figures do not include debts.

10. J. Hills, F. Bastagli, F. Cowell, H. Glennerster, E. Karagiannaki and A. McKnight, *Wealth in the UK* (Oxford: 2013), p. 20, Figure 2.3. The figures quoted are for marketable wealth at 2005 prices.

11. Hills et al., *Wealth in the UK*, p. 21, Figure 2.4.

12. See also Mike Savage, 'Piketty's Challenge for Sociology', *British Journal of Sociology*, 65(4), 2014, 591–606.

13. Hills et al., *Wealth in the UK*, p. 21, Figure 2.4.

14. Hills et al., *Wealth in the UK*, p. 113, Figure 5.9. This financial support is often for education.

15. Hills et al., *Wealth in the UK*, p. 108, Figure 5.6. Figures are in 2005 prices, and for those households with household heads aged twenty-five or over in 1995.

16. Hills et al., *Wealth in the UK*, p. 145.

17. Peter Saunders, *A Nation of Homeowners* (London: 1990).

18. Owen Jones, *Chavs: The Demonization of the Working Class* (London: 2011); Danny Dorling, *All That Is Solid: The Great Housing Disaster* (London: 2014), pp. 288–9.

19. Tim Butler and Paul Watt, *Understanding Social Inequality* (London: 2007), pp. 82–91; S. Sassen, *The Global City: New York, London, Tokyo* (Redwood City, CA: 1991), p. 267.

20. UK population census, 2011.

21. 'Almost Two Million Young Working Adults Still Living with Mum and Dad', press release, Shelter, 2014: see http://england.shelter.org.uk/news/july_2014/almost_two_million_young_working_adults_still_living_with_mum_and_dad. (Accessed 22 May 2015.)

22. Dorling, *All That Is Solid*, pp. 147–54.

23. See http://www.localgovernmentexecutive.co.uk/news/59-bedroom-tax-tenants-arrears-official-review-finds.

24. Dorling, *All That Is Solid*, pp. 175–6.

25. This point is developed in detail in Mike Savage, 'The Politics of Elective Belonging', *Housing, Theory and Society*, 27(2), 2010, 115–61.

26. Hilary Osborne, 'Poor Doors: The Segregation of London's Inner-city Flat Dwellers', *Guardian*, 25 July 2014. See http://www.theguardian.com/society/2014/jul/25/poor-doors-segregation-london-flats.

27. Roger Burrows, 'Life in the Alpha Territory: Investigating London's "Super-Rich" Neighbourhoods', LSE Blogs – British Politics and Policy, 2013. See http://blogs.lse.ac.uk/politicsandpolicy/life-in-the-alpha-territory-londons-super-rich-neighbourhoods/. Also Roger Burrows, 'The New Gilded Ghettoes: The Geodemographics of the Super-Rich', *Discover Society*, (3), December 2013. See http://www.discoversociety.org/2013/12/03/the-new-gilded-ghettos-the-geodemographics-of-the-super-rich/.

28. John Hills, *An Anatomy of Economic Equality in the UK: Report of the National Equality Panel* (London: 2010), p. 386.

29. This process by which social differences are identified as 'natural' is seen by Bourdieu as a fundamental way in which the meaning of social inequalities are obscured.

30. Katharina Hecht, forthcoming PhD thesis, 'A Sociological Analysis of Economic Inequality at the Top End of the Income Distribution', London School of Economics, and see http://www.discoversociety.org/2014/12/01/why-sociologists-should-research-the-increase-in-top-income-and-wealth-inequality/.

## CHAPTER 3: HIGHBROW AND EMERGING CULTURAL CAPITAL

1. Georg Simmel's crispest elaboration of this approach comes in his accessible essay 'Fashion', which has been reprinted in the *American Journal of Sociology*, 62(6), 1957, 541–58.

2. The key work of his here is *Distinction* (London: 1984). However, this is a difficult text to digest at one sitting, and a more accessible account can be found in David Swartz, *Culture and Power* (Chicago: 1997).

3. See Yujia Liu and David B. Grusky, 'The Payoff to Skill in the Third Industrial Revolution', *American Journal of Sociology*, 118(5), 2013, 1330–74.

4. It is telling that Bourdieu's ideas have informed the thinking of market researchers who seek to 'segment' lifestyles in order to allow firms to target their products more effectively.

5. Shamus Rahman Khan, *Privilege: The Making of an Adolescent Elite at St. Paul's School* (Princeton, NJ: 2010).

6. The discussion here is necessarily brief. Readers wanting fuller discussion should look at Tony Bennett, Mike Savage, Elizabeth Silva, Alan Warde, Modesto Gayo-Cal and David Wright *Culture, Class, Distinction* (Abingdon: 2009), and Dave O'Brien, *Cultural Policy: Management, Value and Modernity in the Creative Industries* (London: 2014).

7. See Sam Friedman, *Comedy and Distinction: The Cultural Currency of a 'Good' Sense of Humour* (London: 2014).

8. See Les Back, *New Ethnicities and Urban Culture: Racisms and Multiculture in Young Lives* (London: 1996), and Mike Savage, David Wright and Modesto Gayo-Cal, 'Cosmopolitan Nationalism and the Cultural Reach of the White British', *Nations and Nationalism*, 16(4), 2010, 598–615.

9. Notably, Bennett et al., *Culture, Class, Distinction*. Similar findings can be found for many other nations. See Annick Prieur and Mike Savage, 'Updating Cultural Capital Theory: A Discussion Based on Studies in Denmark and in Britain', *Poetics*, 39(6), 2011, and Philippe Coulangeon and Julien Duval (editors), *The Routledge Companion to Bourdieu's Distinction* (London: 2015).

10. Strictly speaking, we are using multiple correspondence analysis, a tool used by Bourdieu in *Distinction*. We are using the nationally representative GfK data set here. Brief analysis can be found in Savage et al., 'A New Model of Social Class?', and a comprehensive account in Mike Savage, Brigitte Le Roux, Johannes Hjellbrekke and Daniel Laurison, 'Espace culturel britannique et classes sociales', in Frédéric Lebaron and Brigitte Le Roux (editors), *La méthodologie de Pierre Bourdieu en action: espace culturel, espace social, et analyse des données* (Paris: 2015).

11. Notably, Bennett et al., *Culture, Class, Distinction*.

12. This argument is made at length in Bennett et al., *Culture, Class, Distinction*, Chapter 4.

13. We do not have scope to summarize the extensive literature on the 'cultural omnivore' debate, but interested readers might look at a number of contributions in Laurie Hanquinet and Mike Savage (editors), *Routledge International Handbook of the Sociology of Art and Culture* (London: 2015), where this debate is fully rehearsed.

14. And here, of course, we can begin to see why the GBCS itself would appeal to – and also appal – people such as this. Our own research was caught up in this dynamic of 'emerging cultural capital'.

15. Bjørn Schiermer, 'Late-modern Hipsters: New Tendencies in Popular Culture', *Acta Sociologica*, 57(2), 2014, 167–81.

## CHAPTER 4: SOCIAL CAPITAL: NETWORKS AND PERSONAL TIES

1. Robert Putnam, *Bowling Alone* (New York: 2000).
2. David Halpern, *Social Capital* (Cambridge: 2004); Richard G. Wilkinson, *Unhealthy Societies: The Afflictions of Inequality* (London: 1996).
3. Mark Granovetter, 'The Strength of Weak Ties', *American Journal of Sociology*, 78(6), 1973. This is one of the most cited sociological articles of all time.
4. Ronald Burt, 'The Network Structure of Social Capital', in B. Staw and R. Sutton (editors), *Research in Organizational Behaviour*, vol. 22 (Greenwich, CT: 2000), pp. 345–423; S. Ball, *Class Strategies and the Education Market: The Middle Classes and Social Advantage* (London: 2003).
5. Bonnie Erikson, 'Culture, Class and Connections', *American Journal of Sociology*, 102(1), 1996, 217–51.
6. See, most recently, Owen Jones, *The Establishment, and How They Get Away with It* (London: 2014).
7. Nan Lin, Yang-chih Fu and Ray-May Hsung, 'The Position Generator: Measurement Techniques for Investigations of Social Capital', in Nan Lin, Karen Cook and Ronald S. Burt (editors), *Social Capital: Theory and Research* (New York: 2001), pp. 57–81.
8. Of course, care needs to be taken in analysing the findings. Some of the social ties might be family members who work in specific occupations. It might also be the case that people might claim to know someone in a relatively public-facing occupation such as a nurse, solicitor or teacher because they have more chance of coming into contact with them.
9. We used multiple correspondence analysis for these purposes.
10. CAMSIS is sometimes called the Cambridge score and was developed by researchers at Cambridge University to assess the status of every occupation in Britain according to what kinds of people these occupational members selected as close friends or as marriage partners. The logic is similar to that of our inquiry here and we would expect to see similar patterns in their ranking and in ours.
11. For details of this analysis, see Daniel Laurison, 'The Right to Speak: Differences in Political Engagement among the British Elite', *Sociological Review*, 63(2), 2015, 349–72.
12. Nan Lin, 'Social Networks and Status Attainment', *Annual Review of Sociology*, 25, 1999, 467–87; Ted Mouw, 'Social Capital and Finding a Job: Do Contacts Matter?', *American Sociological Review*, 68 (6), 2003, 868–98.
13. See Laurison, 'The Right to Speak: Differences in Political Engagement'.

## CHAPTER 5: THE NEW LANDSCAPE OF CLASS: THE INTERPLAY OF ECONOMIC, CULTURAL AND SOCIAL CAPITAL

1.  For technical details of our analysis, see Savage, Fiona Devine, Niall Cunningham, Mark Taylor, Yoojun Li, Johannes Hjellbrekke, Brigitte Le Roux, Andrew Miles and Sam Friedman, 'A New Model of Social Class? Findings from the BBC's Great British Class Survey Experiment', *Sociology*, 47(2), 2013, and Mike Savage, Fiona Devine, Niall Cunningham, Sam Friedman, Daniel Laurison, Andrew Miles, Helene Snee and Mark Taylor, 'On Social Class, Anno 2014', *Sociology* (forthcoming). We do not dwell here on the considerable debate about our data and the analytical methods used, though the critical comments of Colin Mills in 'The Great British Class Fiasco: A Comment on Savage et al.', *Sociology*, 48(3), 2014, 437–44, are important. However, Mills largely reiterates issues which we ourselves are alive to. As we made clear, the 'seven class' model is dependent on the measures used to construct it and the quality of the data set, and should not be seen to have been 'proven' on the basis of our analysis of the GfK survey and the GBCS alone. It has been quite correctly pointed out by Mills that a larger nationally representative data-set, with a different approach to representative sampling than that used by the market-research company GfK, might have identified somewhat different latent classes. However, this objection does not affect the substantive point we make here, as it is likely that slightly different classifications would tend to produce a reclassification of the classes in the middle of the social structure, which we argue are relatively much more blurred than those at the top and bottom. Indeed, further research on the GBCS by the leading French mathematician Professor Brigitte Le Roux, using a different technique – multiple correspondence analysis – and somewhat different measures of social and cultural capital – also demonstrates that the most distinctive cluster continues to be at the top and that in the middle reaches of the social structure there is much more fuzziness. See Mike Savage, Brigitte Le Roux, Johannes Hjellbrekke and Daniel Laurison, 'Espace culturel britannique et classes sociales', in Frédérie Lebaron and Brigitte Le Roux (editors), *La méthodologie de Pierre Bourdieu en action: espace culturel, espace social, et analyse des données (paris. 2015)*.

2.  Danny Dorling, *Inequality and the 1%* (London: 2014), Thomas Piketty, *Capital in the Twenty-first Century* (Cambridge, MA: 2014).

3.  The same general point also applies to gender: but because we asked about household income, gender differences are not well defined when using the GfK sample (since some badly paid women might be living with well-paid men, and vice versa).

4. We repeat our earlier comments about the problems of using the GBCS and the GfK survey to analyse ethnicity in detail. There is, however, considerable supporting evidence on this point: see S. Longhi, C. Nicoletti and L. Platt, 'Explained and Unexplained Wage Gaps Across the Main Ethno-religious Groups in Great Britain', *Oxford Economic Papers*, 65 (2), 2013, 471–93.

5. Louis Chauvel, 'The Long-term Destabilization of Youth, Scarring Effects, and the Future of the Welfare Regime in Post-*Trente Glorieuses* France', *French Politics, Culture and Society*, 28(3), 2010, 74–96.

6. See Longhi et al., 'Explained and Unexplained Wage Gaps'.

7. The argument here is a condensed version of that which is made in much more detail in Tony Bennett, Mike Savage, Elizabeth Silva, Alan Warde, Modesto Goyo-Cal and David Wright, *Culture, Class, Distinction* (Abingdon: 2009).

8. For a much fuller elaboration of this argument, see Mike Savage, *Identities and Social Change since 1940: The politics of method* (Oxford: 2010) as well as Annick Prieur and Mike Savage, 'Emerging Forms of Cultural Capital', *European Societies*, 15(2), 2013, 246–67.

## CHAPTER 6: CLIMBING MOUNTAINS: THE SOCIAL MOBILITY EXPEDITION

1. Michael Young, *The Rise of the Meritocracy 1870–2033: An Essay on Education and Equality* (London: 1958).

2. Young, *The Rise of Meritocracy*, pp. 11–12.

3. Young, *The Rise of Meritocracy*, p. 12.

4. Robert Erikson and John Goldthorpe, 'Has Social Mobility in Britain Decreased? Reconciling Divergent Findings on Income and Class Mobility', *British Journal of Sociology*, 61(2), 2010, 211–30.

5. See, most recently, Erzsébet Bukodi, John Goldthorpe, Lorraine Waller and Jouni Kuha, 'The Mobility Problem in Britain: New Findings from the Analysis of Birth Cohort Data', *British Journal of Sociology*, 66(1), 2015, 93–117.

6. See also Mike Savage, 'Introduction to elites: From the "problematic of the proletariats" to a class analysis of "wealth elites" *The Sociological Review* 63.2 (2015): 223–39.

7. Jo Blanden, Alissa Goodman, Paul Gregg and Stephen Machin, 'Changes in Intergenerational Mobility in Britain', in M. Corak (editor), *Generational Income Mobility in North America and Europe* (Cambridge: 2004), pp. 122–46.

8. This is not to deny that Blanden et al.'s measures have a number of shortcomings (acknowledged by the authors of the work). That the younger of two generations twelve years apart seems to be experiencing lower social mobility than the older doesn't mean that there's a more general decline in social mobility across generations; what's more, the questions that were asked about household income aren't directly comparable. See Erikson and Goldthorpe, 'Has Social Mobility in Britain Decreased?'.

9. The analysis on which this chapter draws is in Sam Friedman, Daniel Laurison and Andrew Miles, 'Breaking the "Class" Ceiling? Social Mobility into Elite Occupations', *Sociological Review*, 63(2), 2015, 259–89, where all the technical challenges in using the GBCS data to examine social mobility are discussed, and interested readers should consult these. The GBCS findings need to be carefully interpreted given issues of sample skew and respondents' self-selection, and there is also the added drawback that we do not have measures for a person's origin within the new GBCS class scheme.

10. See http://www.lancaster.ac.uk/alumni/alumni-profiles/alan-milburn/.

11. See http://webarchive.nationalarchives.gov.uk/+/http:/www.cabinetoffice. gov.uk/media/227102/fair-access.pdf.

12. These are all occupations which are classified as being in the highest ranks of the National Statistics Socio-Economic Classification, that is to say, NS-SEC 1.

13. Mike Savage, James Barlow, Peter Dickens and Tony Fielding, *Property, Bureaucracy and Culture: Middle-class Formation in Contemporary Britain* (London: 1992), and see more generally, Tim Butler and Mike Savage, (editors), *Social Change and the Middle Classes* (London: 1995).

14. See, on the experience of social mobility more generally, Sam Friedman, 'The Price of the Ticket: Rethinking the Experience of Social Mobility', *Sociology*, 48(2), 2014, 352–68.

15. John Goldthorpe (in collaboration with Catriona Llewellyn and Clive Payne), *Social Mobility and the Class Structure in Modern Britain* (Oxford: 1980).

16. Friedman, 'The Price of the Ticket'.

17. For more discussion of this issue, see Chapter 10 in Bennett et al., *Culture, Class, Distinction*. The relationship between ethnicity, immigration and class is vital but one which, for reasons explained in the Introduction, the GBCS is poorly equipped to analyse.

## CHAPTER 7: A TALE OF TWO CAMPUSES: UNIVERSITIES AND MERITOCRACY

1. Michael Young, *The Rise of the Meritocracy 1870–2033: An Essay on Education and Equality* (London: 1958). More detailed analyses of the findings referred to in this paragraph can be found in Paul Wakeling and Mike Savage, 'Entry to Elite Positions and the Stratification of Higher Education in Britain', *Sociological Review*, 63(2), 2015, 290–320, and in P. Wakeling and M. Savage, 'Elite Universities, Elite Schooling and Reproduction in Britain', in A. van Zanten and S. Ball, with B. Darchy-Koechlin (editors), *Elites, Privilege and Excellence: The National and Global Redefinition of Educational Advantage*, World Yearbook of Education 2015 (Abingdon: 2015).

2. The two non-graduates were Iain Duncan Smith and Cheryl Gillan. The nine Oxford graduates included the Prime Minister and the holders of the other 'great offices of state', Foreign Secretary William Hague, Home Secretary Theresa May and Chancellor of the Exchequer George Osborne. The Cambridge graduates included the Deputy Prime Minister Nick Clegg.

3. Former English Rugby Union captain Will Carling didn't manage even that, graduating with a pass.

4. See http://oxford.tab.co.uk/2013/08/20/new-top-norrington-table/.

5. See http://www.bristol.ac.uk/spais/research/paired-peers/quotes. UWE is the University of the West of England, Bristol, formerly Bristol Polytechnic.

6. This could mean that successful graduates from lower-status universities were more likely to complete the GBCS, in which case our statistics may under-represent the differences in outcomes for graduates of older and newer universities. However, we must also be careful to point out that small differences, like those in the number of members in the elite group between the University of Sheffield and Oxford Brookes University, might not be confirmed with a larger survey.

7. We need to remind ourselves that the sample skew of the GBCS means that the elite are over-represented in it to the tune of about 3.5 times. Therefore, the proportions in Table 7.1 need to be divided by roughly this amount to give an estimate of the probable number of actual graduates from these universities entering the elite.

8. We need to be careful to recognize here that the new universities cannot simply be compared with the older ones. In general, they have lower response rates in the GBCS, and given the known skew of the GBCS this may mean that it was their relatively more elite graduates who replied compared to the somewhat more representative responses from those

universities with higher response rates. This fact may also explain why City University, where the response rate was much lower than Oxford, appears to come so high in Table 7.1.

9. Once again, the sample skew of the GBCS should be borne in mind here: these figures would need to be divided by about 3.5 to provide an estimate of the actual number of such people who would be in the elite group – but this would still be sizeable at nearly 20 per cent.

10. According to the Office for National Statistics, in 2011 the median annual salary for graduates aged from twenty-two to sixty-six was £29,900. Within the GBCS, we have a measure for household, not individual income, with a median of £47,500 for graduates. Median household income in the UK for 2011/12 was £23,200 (and so lower than the median graduate salary). Still, the sample skew of the GBCS means that higher-earning households may be over-represented. Here, though, we are interested in the relative differences in earnings between graduates from different universities.

11. Full details can be found in Wakeling and Savage, 'Entry to Elite Positions'.

12. See Wakeling and Savage, 'Entry to Elite Positions'.

---

## CHAPTER 8: CLASS AND SPATIAL INEQUALITY IN THE UK

1. Peter Bramham and John Spink, 'Leeds – Becoming the Postmodern City', in Peter Bramham and Stephen Wagg (editors), *Sport, Leisure and Culture in the Postmodern City* (Farnham: 2009), pp. 9–32; Paul Dutton, 'Leeds Calling: The Influence of London on the Gentrification of Regional Cities', *Urban Studies*, 40(12), 2003, 2557–72.

2. The power of the Hackney imaginary is explored by Hannah Jones, *Negotiating Cohesion, Inequality and Change: Uncomfortable Positions in Local Government* (Bristol: 2013). On J. G. Ballard, see his novel *Concrete Island* (London: 1974), allegedly set under the Westway, near White City in London.

3. British chains of booksellers in every part of the UK now contain large sections devoted to London, often exceeding the shelf space given to books about the local area.

4. Owen Jones, *Chavs: The Demonization of the Working Class* (London: 2011); James Delingpole, 'A Conspiracy against Chavs? Count Me In', *The Times*, 13 April 2006; Imogen Tyler, 'Chav Mum Chav Scum: Class Disgust in Contemporary Britain', *Feminist Media Studies*, 8(1), 2008, 17–34.

5. Roger Burrows and Nicholas Gane, 'Geodemographics, Software and Class',

*Sociology* 40(5), 2006, 793–812; Mike Savage, Gaynor Bagnall and Brian Longhurst, *Globalization and Belonging* (London: 2005).

6. See Savage, Bagnall and Longhurst, *Globalization and Belonging*.

7. Evan Davis, 'The Case for Making Hebden Bridge the UK's Second City', BBC News website, 10 March 2014. Available online at: http://www.bbc.co.uk/news/business-26472423 (accessed 15 July 2014). George Osborne, 'We Need a Northern Powerhouse' [speech transcript, 23 June 2014]. Museum of Science and Industry, Manchester. Available online at: https://www.gov.uk/government/speeches/chancellor-we-need-a-northern-powerhouse (accessed 15 July 2014).

8. 'The Great Divide', *The Economist*, 15 September 2012.

9. This is aggregated in a Geographical Information System to 2 kilometres.

10. Chris Hamnett, *Unequal City: London in the Global Arena* (London: 2003), p. 132.

11. Garry Robson and Tim Butler, 'Coming to Terms with London: Middle-class Communities in a Global City', *International Journal of Urban and Regional Research*, 25(1), 2001, 70–86.

12. For further information on these complex geographies, see Niall Cunningham and Ian Gregory, 'Hard to Miss, Easy to Blame? Peacelines, Interfaces and Political Deaths in Belfast during the Troubles', *Political Geography*, 40, 2014, 64–78.

13. Gary Bridge, 'The Space for Class? On Class Analysis in the Study of Gentrification', *Transactions of the Institute of British Geographers*, New Series, 20(2), 1995, 236–47; Tim Butler, 'People Like Us: Gentrification and the Service Class in Hackney in the 1980s', unpublished PhD thesis, Open University (1991); Jon May, 'Globalization and the Politics of Place: Place and Identity in an Inner London Neighbourhood', *Transactions of the Institute of British Geographers*, New Series, 21(1), 1996, 194–215.

14. Mike Savage, 'The Politics of Elective Belonging', *Housing, Theory and Society*, 27(2), 2010, 115–61.

15. Savage, Bagnall and Longhurst, *Globalization and Belonging*.

16. Mark Crinson and Paul Tyrer, 'Clocking Off in Ancoats: Time and Remembrance in the Post-industrial City', in Mark Crinson (editor), *Urban Memory: History and Amnesia in the Modern City* (London: 2005), pp. 49–74; Justine O'Connor and Derek Wynne, 'Left Loafing: City Cultures and Post-modern Lifestyles', in Justin O'Connor and Derek Wynne (editors), *From the Margins to the Centre: Cultural Production and Consumption in the Post-industrial City* (Aldershot: 1996), pp. 49–90.

17. Kevin Dowling, 'Life's Really Not So Bad, You Soft Southerners', *Sunday Times*, 6 July 2014, p. 7, and see also the list of towns in http://www.craptownsreturns.co.uk/2013/06/14/easington/.

18. Bruce M. S. Campbell, 'North–South Dichotomies, 1066–1550', in Alan R. H. Baker and Mark Billinge (editors), *Geographies of England: The North–South Divide, Imagined and Material* (Cambridge: 2004), pp. 145–74.

19. Ronald L. Martin, 'The Contemporary Debate over the North–South Divide: Images and Realities of Inequality in Late-twentieth-century Britain', in Baker and Billinge (editors), *Geographies of England: The North–South Divide*, pp. 15–43, at p. 36.

20. Jeremy Paxman, *The English* (London: 1998), p. 157.

21. Doreen Massey, 'Geography and Class', in David Coates, Gordon Johnston and Ray Bush (editors), *A Socialist Anatomy of Britain* (Cambridge: 1985), pp. 76–96, at p. 91.

22. Martin, 'The Contemporary Debate over the North–South Divide', p. 35.

23. LISA works by detecting statistically significant clusters of places that have similar characteristics for one or more indicators. See Luc Anselin, 'Local Indicators of Spatial Association – LISA', *Geographical Analysis*, 27(2), 1995, 93–115.

24. Thomas Piketty, *Capital in the Twenty-first Century* (Cambridge, MA: 2014).

## CHAPTER 9: THE VIEW AT THE TOP: BRITAIN'S NEW 'ORDINARY' ELITE

1. David Cannadine, *The Aristocracy* (London: 1992).

2. The *Sunday Times* Rich List offers an excellent gauge of these shifts.

3. John Scott, *The Upper Class* (Basingstoke: 1982).

4. Peter York, 'The Fall of the Sloane Rangers', *Prospect Magazine*, 19 February 2015 or online at http://www.prospectmagazine.co.uk/sound-and-vision/the-fall-of-the-sloane-rangers-made-in-chelsea.

5. 'Review of Mitford', *Encounter*, 5(5), 1955; also to be found in Mike Savage, *Identities and Social Change in Britain since 1940: The Politics of Method* (Oxford: 2010), Chapter 4.

6. York, 'The Fall of the Sloane Rangers'.

7. Owen Jones, *The Establishment and How They Get Away with It* (London: 2014). A useful recent exploration of the 'Establishment' concept is Peter Hennessy, *Establishment and Meritocracy* (London: 2014).

8. See Dominic Sandbrook, *Never Had It So Good* (London: 2005), pp. 526f.

9. See Pierre Bourdieu, *The State Nobility* (Cambridge: 1996).

10. See Paul Wakeling and Mike Savage, 'Entry to Elite Positions and the Stratification of Higher Education in Britain', *Sociological Review*, 63(2),

2015, 290–320, and Niall Cunningham and Mike Savage, 'The Secret Garden? Elite Metropolitan Geographies in the Contemporary UK', *Sociological Review*, 63(2), 2015, 321–48.

11. See Mike Savage and Karel Williams (editors), *Remembering Elites* (Oxford: 2008).

12. Though admittedly the GBCS *was* completed by a 'Master of the Universe', as well as 'God'.

13. Notably a documentary fronted by Andrew Neil, *Posh and Posher: Why Public School Boys Rule Britain*, which appeared a week after the launch of the GBCS and which encouraged viewers to do the GBCS.

14. These tweets were harvested by Farida Vis in the aftermath of the BBC media campaign, many of which were a response to being placed in the elite class by the Class Calculator. The Twitter reaction to the GBCS is currently the subject of a specific research project undertaken by sociologists Farida Vis (University of Sheffield), Susan Halford and Ramine Tinati (University of Southampton), in collaboration with Andrew Miles, Mike Savage and Helene Snee.

15. See Wakeling and Savage, 'Entry to Elite Positions'.

---

## CHAPTER 10: THE PRECARIOUS PRECARIAT: THE VISIBLE INVISIBLE PEOPLE

1. See, more broadly, Mike Savage, *Identities and Social Change in Britain since 1940: The Politics of Method* (Oxford: 2010).

2. See Lisa Mckenzie, *Getting By: Estates, Class and Culture in Austerity Britain* (Bristol: 2015).

3. Les Back, *New Ethnicities and Urban Culture: Racisms and Multiculture in Young Lives* (London: 1996), p. 40; Steph Lawler, *Identity: Sociological Perspectives* (Cambridge: 2008), p. 133.

4. Diane Reay, '"Mostly Roughs and Toughs": Social Class, Race and Representation in Inner City Schooling', *Sociology*, 38(4), 2004, 1005–23; Beverley Skeggs, *Formations of Class and Gender* (London: 1997); Beverley Skeggs, *Class, Self, Culture* (London: 2004); Beverley Skeggs, 'The Re-branding of Class: Propertising Culture', in F. Devine, M. Savage, J. Scott, and R. Crompton (editors), *Rethinking Class: Culture, Identities and Lifestyles* (Basingstoke: 2005).

5. See Lawler, *Identity: Sociological Perspectives*, p. 133.

6. See Skeggs, *Class, Self, Culture*, p. 37.

7. The pictures were in fact supplied to the BBC by the Experian market-research agency.

8. P. Willis, *Learning to Labour* (London: [1977] 2000).

9. More generally on this difference, see Tony Bennett, Mike Savage, Elizabeth Silva, Alan Warde, Modesto Gayo-Cal and David Wright, *Culture, Class, Distinction* (Abingdon: 2009), Chapter 4.

10. Guy Standing, *The Precariat: The New Dangerous Class* (London: 2011).

11. William J. Wilson, *The Truly Disadvantaged: The Inner City, the Underclass and Public Policy* (Chicago: 1987).

12. See J. Welshman, *Underclass: A History of the Excluded 1880–2000* (London: 2006).

13. Tracey Jensen, 'Welfare Commonsense, Poverty Porn and Doxosophy' *Sociological Research Online*, 19(3), 3.

14. Tracy Shildrick, Rob MacDonald, Colin Webster and Kayleigh Garthwaite, *Poverty and Insecurity: Life in Low-pay, No-pay Britain* (Bristol: 2012).

15. Oscar Lewis, *The Children of Sánchez: Autobiography of a Mexican Family* (Harmondsworth: 1961).

16. See, notably, Beverley Skeggs, *Class, Self, Culture*, and Mike Savage, *Class Analysis and Social Transformation* (Milton Keynes: 2000).

CHAPTER 11: CLASS CONSCIOUSNESS AND THE NEW SNOBBERY

1. Simon Cable and Deni Kirkova, 'Femail' column, *Mail on Sunday*, 5 July 2013 (and see http://www.dailymail.co.uk/femail/article-2356736/This-Morning-row-Holly-Willoughby-Katie-Hopkins-baby-bust-gets-million-YouTube-hits-days.html).

2. E. P. Thompson, *The Making of the English Working Class* (London: 1963). Other historical accounts which, broadly, chart the forging of collective class identities in Britain include Ross McKibbin, *Classes and Cultures: England 1918–1951* (Oxford: 1998). Selina Todd in *The People: The Rise and Fall of the Working Class 1910–2010* (London: 2014) offers a more nuanced account, which links collective identities more closely to individual ones. For further sociological reflections, see Mike Savage, *Class Analysis and Social Transformation* (Milton Keynes: 2000).

3. Beverley Skeggs, *Formations of Class and Gender* (London: 1997).

4. Mike Savage, Gaynor Bagnall, Brian Longhurst, 'Ordinary, Ambivalent and Defensive: Class Identities in the Northwest of England', *Sociology*, 35(4), 2001, 875–92.

5. Richard Sennett and Jonathan Cobb, *The Hidden Injuries of Class* (New York, 1972).

6. Savage, Bagnall and Longhurst, 'Ordinary, Ambivalent and Defensive: Class Identities in the Northwest of England'.

7. On these themes, see also Savage, Bagnall and Longhurst, 'Ordinary, Ambivalent and Defensive', and Mike Savage, 'Working-class Identities in the 1960s: Revisiting the Affluent Worker Study', *Sociology*, 39(5), 2005, 929–46.

8. Annette Kuhn, *Family Secrets: Acts of Memory and Imagination* (London: 1995), p. 98.

9. J. Browne and A. Hood, 'A Survey of the UK Benefit System' (IFS Briefing Note BN13), Institute for Fiscal Studies, 2012 (http://www.ifs.org.uk/bns/bn13.pdf). See also T. Shildrick and R. MacDonald, 'Poverty Talk: How People Experiencing Poverty Deny their Poverty and Why They Blame "the Poor"', *Sociological Review*, 61(2), 2013, 285–303.

10. T. Shildrick, R. MacDonald, C. Webster and K. Garthwaite, *Poverty and Insecurity: Life in Low-pay No-pay, Britain* (Bristol: 2012).

## CONCLUSION: THE OLD NEW POLITICS OF CLASS IN THE TWENTY-FIRST CENTURY

1. Anthony Crosland, *The Future of Socialism* (London: 1956), p. 237.

2. Thomas Piketty, *Capital in the Twenty-first Century* (Cambridge, MA: 2014), Chapter 14.

3. See, notably, Richard Wilkinson and Kate Pickett, *The Spirit Level: Why More Equal Societies Almost Always Do Better* (London: 2009).

4. See Nigel Thrift, *Knowing Capitalism* (London: 2005).

5. See Imogen Tyler, *Revolting Subjects* (London: 2013); T. Shildrick, R. MacDonald, C. Webster and K. Garthwaite, *Poverty and Insecurity: Life in Low-pay, No-pay Britain* (Bristol: 2012); Beverley Skeggs, *Class, Self, Culture* (London: 2004); and John Hills, *Good Times, Bad Times: The Welfare Myth of Them and Us* (Bristol: 2015).

## APPENDIX

1.  Mike Savage, Fiona Devine, Niall Cunningham, Mark Taylor, Yaojun Li, Johannes Hjellbrekke, Brigitte Le Roux, Andrew Miles and Sam Friedman, 'A New Model of Social Class? Findings from the BBC's Great British Class Survey Experiment', *Sociology*, 47(2), 2013, 219–50.
2.  The data-set is at: https://discover.ukdataservice.ac.uk/catalogue/?sn=7616.

# Index

# Classical
# Literature
## Richard Jenkyns

**What makes Greek and Roman literature great?**

**How has classical literature influenced Western culture?**

**What did Greek and Roman authors learn from each other?**

Richard Jenkyns is emeritus Professor of the Classical Tradition and the Public Orator at the University of Oxford. His books include *Virgil's Experience* and *The Victorians and Ancient Greece*, acclaimed as 'masterly' by *History Today*.

A PELICAN
INTRODUCTION

# Economics:
# The User's Guide
## Ha-Joon Chang

**What is economics?**

**What can – and can't – it explain about the world?**

**Why does it matter?**

Ha-Joon Chang teaches economics at Cambridge University and writes a column for the *Guardian*. The *Observer* called his book *23 Things They Don't Tell You About Capitalism*, which was a no.1 best-seller, 'a witty and timely debunking of some of the biggest myths surrounding the global economy'. He won the Wassily Leontief Prize for advancing the frontiers of economic thought and is a vocal critic of the failures of our current economic system.

A PELICAN
INTRODUCTION

# Greek and Roman Political Ideas

## Melissa Lane

**Where do our ideas about politics come from?**

**What can we learn from the Greeks and Romans?**

**How should we exercise power?**

Melissa Lane teaches politics at Princeton University, and previously taught for fifteen years at Cambridge University, where she also studied as a Marshall and Truman scholar. The historian Richard Tuck called her book *Eco-Republic* 'a virtuoso performance by one of our best scholars of ancient philosophy'.

A PELICAN
INTRODUCTION

# How to See the World
## Nicholas Mirzoeff

**What is visual culture?**

**How should we explore the huge quantity of visual images available to us today?**

**How can visual media help us change the world?**

Nicholas Mirzoeff is Professor of Media, Culture and Communication at New York University. His book *Watching Babylon*, about the Iraq war as seen on TV and in film, was described by art historian Terry Smith as 'a tour de force by perhaps the most inventive – certainly the most wide-ranging – practitioner of visual culture analysis in the world today.'

A PELICAN
INTRODUCTION

# Human Evolution
## Robin Dunbar

**What makes us human?**

**How did we develop language, thought and culture?**

**Why did we survive, and other human species fail?**

Robin Dunbar is an evolutionary anthropologist and Director of the Institute of Cognitive and Evolutionary Anthropology at Oxford University. His acclaimed books include *How Many Friends Does One Person Need?* and *Grooming, Gossip and the Evolution of Language*, described by Malcolm Gladwell as 'a marvellous work of popular science'.

A PELICAN
INTRODUCTION

# Revolutionary Russia, 1891–1991
## Orlando Figes

**What caused the Russian Revolution?**

**Did it succeed or fail?**

**Do we still live with its consequences?**

Orlando Figes teaches history at Birkbeck, University of London and is the author of many acclaimed books on Russian history, including *A People's Tragedy*, which *The Times Literary Supplement* named as one of the '100 most influential books since the war', *Natasha's Dance*, *The Whisperers*, *Crimea* and *Just Send Me Word*. The *Financial Times* called him 'the greatest storyteller of modern Russian historians'.

A PELICAN
INTRODUCTION

# The Domesticated Brain

## Bruce Hood

**Why do we care what others think?**

**What keeps us bound together?**

**How does the brain shape our behaviour?**

Bruce Hood is an award-winning psychologist who has taught and researched at Cambridge and Harvard universities and is currently Director of the Cognitive Development Centre at the University of Bristol. He delivered the Royal Institution's Christmas Lectures in 2011 and is the author of *The Self Illusion* and *Supersense*, described by *New Scientist* as 'important, crystal clear and utterly engaging'.

**A PELICAN INTRODUCTION**

# The Meaning of Science
## Tim Lewens

**What is science?**

**Where are its limits?**

**Can it tell us everything that is worth knowing?**

Tim Lewens is a Professor of Philosophy of Science at Cambridge University, and a fellow of Clare College. He has written for the *London Review of Books* and *The Times Literary Supplement*, and has won prizes for both his teaching and his publications.

A PELICAN
INTRODUCTION

# Who Governs Britain?

## Anthony King

**Where does power lie in Britain today?**

**Why has British politics changed so dramatically in recent decades?**

**Is our system of government still fit for purpose?**

Anthony King is Millennium Professor of British Government at the University of Essex. A Canadian by birth, he broadcasts frequently on politics and government and is the author of many books on American as well as British politics. He is co-author of the bestselling *The Blunders of Our Governments*, which David Dimbleby described as 'enthralling' and Andrew Marr called 'an astonishing achievement'.

A PELICAN
INTRODUCTION